KEY WORKSKI

KEY WORKSKILLS

Rosie Bingham
and
Sue Drew

Gower

© Rosie Bingham and Sue Drew 1999

Published by
Gower Publishing Limited
Gower House
Croft Road
Aldershot
Hampshire GU11 3HR
England

Gower
Old Post Road
Brookfield
Vermont 05036
USA

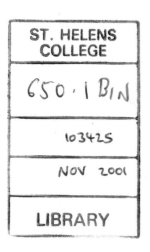
Rosie Bingham and Sue Drew have asserted their right under the Copyright, Designs and Patents Act 1988 to be identified as the authors of this work.

British Library Cataloguing in Publication Data
Bingham, Rosie
Key WorkSkills
1.Career development 2.Success in business
I.Title II.Drew, Sue
650.1

ISBN 0 566 08183 0

Library of Congress Cataloging-in-Publication Data
Bingham, Rosie.
    Key WorkSkills / Rosie Bingham and Sue Drew.
        p. cm.
    ISBN 0-566-08208-X (loose leaf). -- ISBN 0-566-08183-0 (pbk.)
    1.Vocational qualifications. 2. Career development.
    3. Performance. 4. Professional employees. I. Drew, Sue.
    II.Title. III.Title: Key work skills.
    HF5381.6.B56   1999
    650.1--dc21   98-53695
                                                                        CIP

Printed in the United Kingdom at the University Press, Cambridge

CONTENTS

★Sections of these chapters are based on Drew, S. and Bingham, R. (1997), *The Student Skills Guide*, Gower.

FOREWORD

I am delighted that Stockport and High Peak Training & Enterprise Council Limited has worked in close collaboration with Rosie Bingham and Sue Drew to produce this *Key WorkSkills* book, the use of which will enable graduates and undergraduates to develop and maintain their employability skills.

One of our objectives is to strengthen the workforce of Stockport and the High Peak, and for two years we have been working on a National Higher Education Business Partnership (HEBP) project to support local economic growth. Informed by independent market research, commissioned by Stockport and High Peak Training & Enterprise Council Ltd, *Key WorkSkills* is a practical response to the challenge of assisting higher education to prepare students for work, especially in small and medium enterprises (SMEs), which are likely to provide a higher proportion of employment opportunities in the future.

Key WorkSkills is a demonstration of the value of working partnerships between the TEC and higher education. Its use will contribute to personal fulfilment and lifelong learning throughout every community.

Trevor Jones, Chief Executive
Stockport and High Peak Training & Enterprise Council Ltd

ACKNOWLEDGEMENTS

We wish to acknowledge the help of:

Rick Bingham, for feedback and encouragement.
Chris Bingham and Mark Pettigrew, for computing support.
Bryony and Kate Milner, for literary searches.
Bryony Milner, for proofreading and formatting.

The production of these materials has been commissioned by Stockport and High Peak Training & Enterprise Council Ltd (TEC). This was part of a national Department for Education and Employment (DfEE) funded Higher Education Business Partnership Graduate Employment Project, which involved extensive research with small and medium-sized enterprises (SMEs).

The views expressed are those of the authors and do not necessarily reflect those of the Department for Education and Employment (DfEE) or any other government department.

Contents

HOW TO USE THIS BOOK

1 WHO SHOULD USE THIS BOOK?

This book is mainly intended for use by

- those with HND, degree, postgraduate or professional qualifications in the first years of their professional employment
- people in junior management roles who have worked their way there via routes other than higher education – perhaps via NVQs
- those in middle management roles, as a reminder of skills, or to help them think about new skills they might need
- students on sandwich placements who are operating at a professional level
- trainers or staff developers, who may wish to use it with trainees or other staff
- people wishing to obtain Key Skill qualifications (see section 5 below).

In the first years of professional life you need to develop and use a wide range of skills and to learn to do so very quickly. Your organisation may have high expectations of you, even though you may not have worked in such a situation before. Using your skills effectively will help you achieve more in your work. The consequences of not carrying out a skill well may be immediate and not only affect you but also your colleagues and the organisation for which you work.

Whether or not you are new to professional life, it is very likely that you will have done some work before. New graduates or diplomates may have worked in vacations, or part time while studying. You may have been a mature student with many years' experience behind you when you began your studies. You may have studied part time while working full time. You may need this book because you now find yourself in a new situation, perhaps in a new job, or working at a new level.

You will, however, be building on your existing skills. Through work or your education you will have developed a whole range of skills, *e.g. you will have used information, written, worked with others, agreed things with others*. This book builds on such experience.

2 YOUR ORGANISATION AND ITS NEEDS

Increasingly, companies see it as more effective for people to learn 'on the job'. There is a trend towards Continual Professional Development (CPD), where individuals take more responsibility for their own development. You can use this book to develop your skills at work while you are engaged on work tasks.

You may be working for:

- a small or medium-sized enterprise (SME). Many SMEs need their employees to 'hit the ground running'.
- yourself. You may have your own business, alone or with one or two others. Days spent away training are days when you cannot earn.
- a larger organisation. Even if your organisation has a training department and facilities, it may still have its main focus on learning on the job. There is a move away from formal training schemes and towards job-centred learning.

Regardless of size and type, most organisations are changing the structure of employment. There is a move towards shorter lines of management and for people at all levels to have more responsibility and to be accountable for their work. There is an increase in 'multi-skilling' – for individuals to be able to do a whole range of tasks. There is also an increasing tendency for people to work in teams, whose composition often changes as needs change. This means working with and being able to communicate with professionals from other functional areas.

These trends have arisen in part because such structures are more able to cope with the rapidly changing nature of work and because organisations have to adapt flexibly to the new requirements. Recent publications have talked about the need for 'transformative' employees – people who can create change. All of this puts a greater demand on employees to be highly skilled.

3 HOW TO USE THIS BOOK
··············

This book is based on the principles that effective performance in any work area is about:

◆ being able to identify what is appropriate for a situation, during the situation/event
◆ being able to draw on a range of skills or aptitudes or behaviours in order to meet the needs of the situation.

In other words, there are rarely 'right' ways to behave. There are good and less effective ways for you to behave in a particular situation.

Each chapter in this book focuses on skills you need at work and suggests that you use the chapter in relation to a current task. This will help you to complete the task and to learn the skill, not out of context, but while you are working.

The book is based on materials which were developed and trialled with over 2000 students at Sheffield Hallam University. The trial showed that the materials were most likely to be used if they were seen as highly relevant by students to their immediate concerns and if they were used in relation to specific tasks.

This book follows the same principle – that the chapters will be most useful if they relate to real tasks you have to do at work and if you use them at the time when these tasks are needed.

The book aims to:

◆ take you through the processes involved in performing effectively
◆ help you think about what works for you and what does not
◆ give you suggestions to try
◆ encourage you to think, after the event, about what worked and what didn't and how to improve it for the future.

You can use this book wherever and whenever convenient, in relation to the sort of situations the book covers.

The book is designed for you to write in and to use as your own working document. It may form part of a Continuing Professional Development scheme, it may help you seek membership of professional bodies, it may help in your staff appraisals. Above all, it will help you improve your day-to-day work, and increase your effectiveness.

4 THE STRUCTURE OF THE BOOK
··················

It is not intended that you read this book starting at the beginning and working through to the end, but rather that you use the chapters when they are relevant to you, as the need arises.

Most of the chapters suggest that you use them:

◆ when you are faced by a specific situation
◆ generally to help you improve that skill. Here something may spark off your need to look at a particular chapter – *e.g. an experience at work, a comment by somebody, a feeling that you did not do something very well.*

The book is divided into chapters which cover common types of activity at work. These activities are interconnected and not separate at all. For the purposes of this book, we have divided them into 'chunks' which seem to make sense and which might relate to all sorts of situations. It is hard, for example, to think of many work tasks where you will not have meetings of some description (Chapter 13). If you have to carry out a project (Chapter 9) you are likely to be working in a team (Chapter 12), you will need to communicate with others (Chapters 3, 4, 5), planning time will be very important

(Chapter 2), as will agreeing things with other people (Chapter 14).

Where do you start? There are a number of possible routes through the book:

◆ if you have no immediate need then a starting point might be Chapter 16, Reviewing Your Effectiveness, and Chapter 17, Identifying Strengths and Improving Skills. This will help you identify areas for improvement.
◆ you could start by looking at the contents list of each chapter. This tells you in more detail what it covers.
◆ you could start with a chapter which meets an immediate need. For example, you may be about to embark on a project and Chapter 9, Project Work, may therefore be appropriate. That chapter will then refer you to others you might need.

5 KEY SKILLS
....

Key Skills are those skills which are relevant in any work situation.

The Qualifications and Curriculum Authority (QCA), which is responsible for developing National Vocational Qualifications (NVQs) and General National Vocational Qualifications (GNVQs), has developed specifications for Key Skills at five levels (NCVQ 1996). The QCA Key Skills are:

◆ communication
◆ application of number
◆ information technology (IT)
◆ working with others
◆ improving own learning and performance
◆ problem solving (not yet formally approved by QCA).

Examining bodies such as Education for Excellence (EDEXEL, formerly BTEC), City and Guilds of London Institute (C&G, now part of AQA, Assessment and Qualifications Alliance) and the Royal Society of Arts (RSA, now part of OCR, Oxford, Cambridge and RSA) all validate Key Skill units, where you submit evidence for a skill at one of the QCA skill levels (normally through a college which runs courses validated by those bodies). Those who have done GNVQs will know that the first three Key Skills are mandatory in any GNVQ.

This book covers all the Key Skills apart from IT. Each chapter is based on a set of learning outcomes which are given at the start of the chapter and which are themselves based on, although not identical to, the Key Skill specifications at Level 5. This is the highest level, for those operating professionally. The exception is Chapter 8, Using and Presenting Numerical Data, which is based on Level 3. **This means that if you wish to provide evidence for your Key Skills in order to obtain a Key Skills unit or qualification, this book might help you work towards this.**

QCA was formerly known as NCVQ and Key Skills were formerly known as Core Skills (see the NCVQ reference at the end of this chapter – this publication gives the Key Skills Specifications at Level 5). If you wish to gain a Key Skills qualification you can contact the examining bodies for further information (see appendix).

The main relationship between the chapters and the Key Skills are shown on the next page, although there are many areas of overlap. The links are made clear in the chapters.

6 SUMMARY
....

This book should help you in a very practical way, not only to improve your performance in work tasks, but also to develop your skills in managing those tasks. It will therefore support you in your current job and in your ongoing professional development.

Key Skill	Chapter	Title
Communication	3	Communicating at Work
	4	Report Writing
	5	Making Presentations
	6	Gathering and Using Information
	7	Keeping Notes, Records and Minutes
	14	Putting Your Case: Negotiating and Assertiveness
Working with numbers	8	Using and Presenting Numerical Data
Working with others	12	Working in Teams
	13	Meetings
Improving own learning and performance	2	Planning and Managing Your Workload
	10	Ethics at Work
	15	Dealing with Pressure
	16	Reviewing Your Effectiveness
	17	Identifying Strengths and Improving Skills
	18	Mentoring, Appraisal and Interviews
	19	Professional Development
	20	Professional Exams
Problem solving*	9	Project Work
	11	Solving Problems and Making Decisions

*Not yet formally approved by QCA.

7 REFERENCES AND BIBLIOGRAPHY
....

Drew, S. and Bingham, R. (1997), *Student Skills Guide*, Gower.

NCVQ (1996), *Core Skills (with Guidance on How to Use the Units in Educational/Vocational Contexts)*. Obtainable from QCA, 29 Bolton Street, London W1Y 7PD. Tel. 0171 509 5555.

Contents

2

PLANNING AND MANAGING YOUR WORKLOAD

WHY IS THIS SKILL IMPORTANT?

Being well organised and using time efficiently will help you to make the most of opportunities. Time is a resource and you have to use it effectively to achieve more. Your organisation needs employees to prioritise and meet deadlines, and your performance at work is likely to be much better if you are well organised.

Being busy does not necessarily mean you are using your time well. It is what you are doing and achieving which is important, and which indicates how well you are using time. When you are not using time effectively, productivity and efficiency will be reduced, with costs to both you and your organisation.

If you plan ahead to manage your workload, you are more likely to be able to cope with pressure and less likely to succumb to stress.

We suggest you use this chapter:

◆ to help you plan and organise your actual work
◆ particularly at the beginning of a busy period, to help you plan and monitor your actions.

By the end of this chapter you should be able to:

1 identify your current practices in planning and managing your workload and the strengths and weaknesses of those practices, based on appropriate evidence
2 identify and agree aims and targets based on relevant information
3 identify and explore strategies and resources in order to maximise effectiveness in planning and managing your own workload
4 select, plan and use strategies, building on strengths and addressing weaknesses, to maximise opportunities to meet aims and targets
5 regularly review and revise aims and targets
6 monitor and report on progress
7 identify and use feedback to improve effectiveness
8 effectively seek and use support from others
9 meet targets
10 evaluate your own effectiveness in planning and managing workloads, identify areas for improvement and take action.

See Chapter 1 for the relationship between these learning outcomes and the Key Skills qualifications.

1 HOW YOU CURRENTLY SPEND YOUR TIME

. . . .

A starting point is to find out where your time goes. You can then work out how to manage it and your workload more effectively.

Keeping a daily log of your activities for a week helps you appreciate how you spend your time. You could use either the following diary or the pie chart below it to help you.

This log is in one-hour blocks but you could select a four or five hour period in one day to record activities in more detail in 15-minute blocks.

DAILY LOG

TIME	MON	TUES	WED	THURS	FRI	SAT	SUN
6–7am							
7–8am							
8–9am							
9–10am							
10–11am							
11–12am							
12–1pm							
1–2pm							
2–3pm							
3–4pm							
4–5pm							
5–6pm							
6–7pm							
7–8pm							
8–9pm							
9–10pm							
10–11pm							
11–12pm							

PIE CHART

You might prefer the following as a way of recording your time.

Identify and list eight major activities over a week, *e.g. meeting clients, routine tasks, etc.*

What proportion of time is spent on each? Transfer the information to the pie chart opposite.

PIE CHART

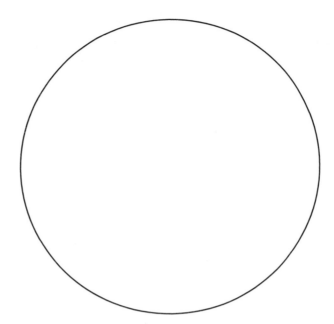

You can now consider:

Why did I spend my time in that way?

Is the way I spend my time helping me to work efficiently? What is good about how I use time?

Am I surprised by anything?

Do I need to change anything? What?

Is there anything I really can't change? What?

You might find it useful to discuss your log or pie chart and responses to these questions with others. Their feedback may be very helpful.

2 GOALS AND PRIORITIES

. . . .

Good planning means not only dealing with immediate targets, but also identifying overall aims and directions. You can then see how your short-term and day-to-day actions match what you want. Are you putting effort into the right areas?

2.1 Long-term goals

What are your long-term goals? What do you want to have achieved at work in a year's time, *e.g. promotion, further qualifications, success in your field, gaining an important client?* You might also want to consider areas other than work, *e.g. relationships, social, family.* Once you have identified these goals, you could prioritise them as high, medium or low.

In prioritising for the long term it can help to identify:

◆ what would definitely determine your future
◆ what might influence your future to some extent
◆ what would have little effect on your future
◆ what would have no effect on your future at all.

What do I want to achieve in the next year?	Priority (high, medium or low)

It is also important to identify your organisation's or section's long-term plans, *e.g. move to new premises, expand abroad.* If you are unsure, it is worth finding out.

What does my organisation want to achieve in the next year?	Priority (high, medium or low)

It will be useful to compare your own long-term goals with those of your organisation, so that you can work out how to bring them together and allocate your efforts.

Goals which correspond	Goals which clash	If different, how will I reconcile the two?

2.2 Short-term goals

What are your short-term goals? What do you need to do now or in the near future? Again, could you prioritise them as high, medium, or low? By when do you need to complete them?

Short-term goal/task	Priority (high, medium or low)	Deadlines

2.3 The relationship between long-term and short-term goals and priorities

You could now consider the following questions.

Will my short-term goals/tasks support my long-term goals? Which will support them most?

Which short-term goals/tasks are irrelevant to my long-term goals?

Do I want to reconsider or reprioritise my short-term goals? How?

3 PLANNING YOUR WORKLOAD

....

You need to work out systematically how you can plan your tasks so that they lead to effective action. It is worth spending time on planning ahead rather than merely dealing with what arises day to day. This can lead to feeling out of control. Failing to plan ahead can mean not making new opportunities – *e.g. salespeople need to allow time to obtain new clients as well as to maintain current ones.*

Realistic planning is a balance between the available time and what can be achieved within it. This will involve setting priorities and monitoring your progress to adjust plans accordingly.

3.1 Priorities

What tasks do you have to do? How long will each take? Can each task be broken down into more realistic subtasks? How long will each subtask take? Priorities need to be set against each, based on their:

◆ importance
◆ urgency
◆ contribution to long- and short-term goals
◆ how long it will take, in relation to the benefits
◆ how one task relates to another
◆ any 'political' considerations (*e.g. will it affect your position in the organisation, will it please/offend important people?*)
◆ resources requirements and their availability.

Nobody can do everything which comes their way. Effectiveness is improved by deciding what should be done now, what later, and what can be left.

In prioritising it can help to identify what is:

1   **urgent and important** – *do it.*
2   **urgent and not important** – *do it if you can.*
3   **important but not urgent** – *start it before it becomes urgent.*
4   **not important and not urgent** – *don't do it.*

Task	Priority (high, medium or low)	Subtasks	Time needed	Deadline

3.2 Working styles

Everyone has different ways of working which suit them and it will help to assess your preferred working style before planning daily tasks.

What time of day do I work best? Each person has a natural cycle to the day, with peaks and troughs, *e.g. dips after lunch.* Use your peak times for important activities.

How long can I concentrate before I need a break?

Where do I work best? Does your organisation allow/encourage homeworking for tasks needing long periods of concentration?

What circumstances help me work? *E.g. quiet environment, access to refreshments.*

3.3 Daily plans

What is the first thing you do when you get to work? *E.g. routine tasks to clear your desk? Do the most difficult task while you are feeling fresh? Do the most unpleasant to get it over?* Have you planned your daily activities?

You could list all the tasks for the day (refer back to section 3.1) and when you will do them. (When calculating the time needed for each, it is helpful to add on half again – most of us seriously underestimate the time required.)

Are your tasks achievable given the time and resources available?

◆ Set realistic small goals and record when you have met them. Unrealistic, large tasks can cause panic. Break them into smaller chunks.
◆ You can only do one thing at a time. Has your planning allowed for this?
◆ Do you have to do it? Could someone else do it? (See section 4.3)
◆ What would happen if you did not do it?
◆ Anticipate problems which might cause delay.
◆ Build in extra time.

Tasks	Time needed	Resources needed	When I will do it	Completed

Many people have a particular system for being organised, *e.g. a diary, a personal organiser*. These can be useful for planning and managing your work, but make sure you always know where they are if they contain much valuable information.

3.4 Monitoring and review

Monitoring and reviewing your progress with goals and achievements is important for reviewing your efficiency and productivity. You may have to submit staged interim reports on your work, and it will help to keep a record of your activities with dates and reviews. When will you do this and how often? Daily, weekly? You may need to re-prioritise in the light of your review.

Suppose you have prioritised but still have too much to do in too short a time. Possibilities are:

◆ make a list of what you must do. If it adds up to more time than you have, reprioritise.
◆ make a list of what is to be done in order of priority. If after three days items are still on the list, put them at the top or discard them.
◆ discuss the situation with colleagues, your manager or mentor (see Chapter 19, Professional Development).

Tasks	Achieved by deadline?	If not, what prevented achievement?	Action to be taken

4 THE WORKING ENVIRONMENT

4.1 How do you currently organise your workspace?

Efficient management of your working area will enable you to spend more time carrying out your plans and less time trying to get organised before you start.

	Yes	No
Office space/work area Is your desk facing away from distractions, *e.g. people, windows?*		
Is your filing cabinet within reach?		
Do you have a wallboard, *e.g. to remind you of important information, things to do?*		
Desk/work station Can you find equipment quickly, *e.g. pens, calculator, files, paperclips?*		
Are frequently used files within easy reach?		
If you use a computer is it in a suitable position, *e.g. avoiding glare from sunlight, at an appropriate height?*		
Is your desk tidy? (*You may leave papers on your desk to remind you about work to be done, but these may pile up.*)		
Filing systems Do you have an efficient system for filing information? *E.g. could you quickly find information for a piece of work you did two months ago?*		
Do others know how it works? Do you know how theirs works (in case you need information during their absence)?		
Do you have a bin and do you use it? (*Discard any papers you do not need again. What would be the consequences of throwing something away?*)		

Open-plan offices may mean that teams are able to work together and communicate throughout the day. However, there may be times when you need to concentrate and not be interrupted. You cannot close a door, so you will need to devise other strategies for ensuring your privacy, *e.g. visible notices, redirecting your phone, telling others when you will be available, using an empty office and closing the door.*

What improvements could I make in my working area?

4.2 Using resources and systems

You can save hours of wasted time by using resources and setting up systems which suit you (avoid elaborate systems you won't stick to). What could make things easier and reduce effort? Possibilities include:

◆ find out what resources exist – an hour spent doing this could avoid future time wasting. Who would know? *E.g. videoconferencing facilities can save time on travel to meetings, email means you don't waste time on phone calls.*

◆ find out what office systems are in place, *e.g. central filing, templates for memos, faxes, procedures for getting secretarial support.* Could you instigate any systems which would help everyone?

◆ use computers to wordprocess (it is easier to correct work once you can use a keyboard).

◆ use computers to organise your documents, *e.g. file management structures* (see Chapter 7, Keeping Notes, Records and Minutes).

◆ use computers to create databases so that you can find things more easily.

◆ find ways of reducing time spent on routine tasks. Develop systems to suit you. Suggestions include:

 – handle each piece of paper only once, *e.g. put on a file reference straight away so it can be filed quickly and easily.*

 – deal with mail as it comes in, *e.g. have trays for 'deal with today', 'deal with within a week', 'pass to others'.*

 – set aside a regular time each week for routine tasks, *e.g. sort out papers, files, do planning.*

 – use trays for categorising papers, *e.g. urgent, action later, for information.*

4.3 Working with others as a resource

Your role and responsibilities may include having access to others' skills in your organisation, *e.g. secretaries, colleagues, technicians.* These are a valuable resource which can be used to help you manage your own workload and organise your time efficiently, *e.g. if your computer breaks down, do you try to fix it yourself or is a better use of your time to seek help from others with the necessary skill?* Secretaries may screen your mail and prioritise it for you. Colleagues may have ideas and contacts you could use.

Who could I ask?	What could they do?	Why might they agree? E.g. is it their job? Can I do something in return?

DELEGATION

There may be times when asking others to do something for you and delegating tasks are difficult. Reasons could be that you:

◆ do not have authority
◆ fear you may lose control over the activity
◆ are unsure that others can do it
◆ may not get the credit
◆ fear others may do it better.

You could ask yourself the following questions:

◆ How critical is the delegated task to my goals?
◆ Will this lessen my workload and allow me to use my skills in a more productive way?
◆ How sensitive or confidential is the task?
◆ How urgent is the task?
◆ Who could do this better than I can?

When you ask someone to do something, you need to be sensitive to the person and their situation. You need not only to delegate the responsibility for a task, you also need to allocate the credit for doing it. This requires effective communication and specified deadlines and you will need to monitor and evaluate progress.

Chapter 14, Putting Your Case: Negotiating and Assertiveness, will help you in this area.

5 IDENTIFYING AND MANAGING TIME WASTERS

If you look at what prevents you from effectively managing your own workload, you could probably make quite a long list in a short time. Some of these will be caused by yourself and/or others.

5.1 Interruptions

If you don't plan and allocate time, others may influence how you spend it. You might find it helpful to record interruptions to your flow of work, who makes them and the effect they have. Of those made by others, some will be negative, *e.g. losing concentration which may be difficult to regain*, some may be more positive, *e.g. getting valuable information, making useful contacts*. You may find that you interrupt yourself, *e.g. thinking about and making a phone call*. If you do this over a week, you may see patterns of times and events emerging. This will help you plan to minimise the effect of negative interruptions.

Time of interruption	What the interruption is	Who interrupts	Why?	The effect on my work

What action can I take?

5.2 Using time effectively

What is the cost of wasting time to both you and your organisation? The following is a list of possible time wasters. You may wish to eliminate some altogether. Others may be enjoyable but detract from your working time and you may, reluctantly, need to limit them. You could add your own items to the list.

Item	Possible ways of limiting	Can eliminate	Can limit
Unwanted phone calls	◆ Ask people to call at specific times ◆ Answer the phone but say you'll call back ◆ Keep calls short and to the point ◆ Redirect calls to someone else (with their agreement) ◆ End all calls tactfully but firmly ◆ Arrange to answer a colleague's phone for an hour, then swap over ◆ Get an answering machine		
Unexpected or unwanted visitors	◆ Use an appointment book and keep up to date, block out time for important tasks ◆ Specify a time when you will be available ◆ Lock the door, if possible ◆ Ask a secretary to screen visitors ◆ Have an appointment system		
Junk mail	◆ Remove your name from mailing lists ◆ Use your bin		
Not able to contact people	◆ Leave phone messages with times you will be in ◆ Write notes/send emails or faxes rather than making repeated calls ◆ Say where you can be contacted		
Unexpected or long meetings	◆ See Chapter 13, Meetings ◆ Keep to the point ◆ State the time you have available ◆ Use videoconferencing, email		
Locating information	◆ Ask others ◆ Know others' filing systems ◆ Maintain a good filing/recording system (see Chapter 7, Keeping Notes, Records and Minutes) ◆ See Chapter 6, Gathering and Using Information		
Using resources	◆ Find out what you need and where it is ◆ Attend appropriate training courses, e.g. using computers, videoconferencing ◆ Use systems for reporting faults		
Poor communication systems	◆ See Chapter 3, Communicating at Work ◆ Discuss options with your manager and colleagues		
Routine tasks	◆ Use proformas and templates for letters and faxes ◆ Delegate (see section 4.3)		

Item	Possible ways of limiting	Can eliminate	Can limit
Routine tasks	◆ Read summaries of reports, use quick reading strategies, e.g. skimming		
Checking your understanding of a task	◆ Listen well first time round ◆ Make notes at the time ◆ Make a list of areas for clarification and identify the appropriate people to ask		
Puttings things off	◆ See section 5.3		
Demands of others	◆ Ask yourself: 'Have I got time to do this?' ◆ Also ask: 'Do I want to do this?' ◆ Learn to say 'no' (see Chapter 14, Putting Your Case: Negotiating and Assertiveness) ◆ Clarify your role and responsibilities		
Operating by trial and error	◆ Plan ahead (see this chapter and Chapter 9, Project Work) ◆ Ask for advice from others		
Difficult decisions	◆ See Chapter 11, Solving Problems and Making Decisions ◆ Assess its importance and urgency ◆ Discuss it with others		
So much to do you don't know where to start – so you don't	◆ List all your tasks, then number them according to priority (see section 3.1) ◆ Address the procrastination (see section 5.3) ◆ Talk it through with colleagues, manager, mentor (see Chapter 18, Mentoring, Appraisal and Interviews)		
Own items			

Other areas which might affect you are:

◆ **no clear objective or deadlines**. You may waste time working out what your organisation wants from you. You need to discuss this with your manager or mentor. Your colleagues may also give information.
◆ **lack of feedback on what you are doing**. This may mean you are constantly checking for approval that you are doing it right. How can you manage this? (See Chapter 17, Identifying Strengths and Improving Skills, for how to seek feedback.)
◆ **office socialising**. In a work environment, this can be important for developing working relationships, knowing what others are doing and how your work fits in with theirs. However, there may be times when too much means reduced productivity. You need to work out how to keep a balance.
◆ **travelling**. You can use the time productively, *e.g. reading reports, using a dictaphone/laptop computer/mobile phone (if you have them), planning your day*. If you travel on business frequently, make an overall packing list to use each time.
◆ **unexpected visitors**. If you choose to meet them because they are important to your work, some strategies you could use to reduce the time are:

- meet them and deal with the purpose outside your office/workspace
- if people sit down, they are likely to stay longer
- tell them what time you have available at the beginning; keep to that time and arrange further meetings if necessary
- keep to the business in hand
- avoid social chat
- ask someone to remind you of a meeting after a given time.

5.3 Dealing with procrastination

Even if you develop very good plans and systems to help you work more effectively, you may find yourself putting off doing certain tasks. You may choose to do something else, usually a less important task, *e.g. tidying your desk*. This may be because:

- ◆ you dislike the activity
- ◆ you know you are not good at it
- ◆ you think it's a waste of time, *e.g. it may not be your priority, but someone else's*
- ◆ it may be mentally or physically difficult
- ◆ it could be emotionally unpleasant, *e.g. lead to conflict*
- ◆ you don't know how to tackle it
- ◆ the task seems too big.

The overall effect of procrastination is that it prevents you from achieving your goals and adds pressure and stress because you will be anxious about incomplete tasks. It could lead to loss of self-respect and may affect your relationship with colleagues and clients.

You may find it helpful to identify those tasks not done, inadequately done or put off and the reason for this. Looking at the consequences, both positive and negative, of not doing the task will help you decide what action to take. This might include:

- ◆ breaking the task down into more manageable chunks, listing steps
- ◆ putting the activity at the top of your priority list
- ◆ telling others you are going to do it
- ◆ setting deadlines
- ◆ rewarding yourself for getting it done
- ◆ seeking further information and help.

Task	Reason for procrastination	Effects of not doing it	Benefits of doing it	Action I could take

6 DEALING WITH THE UNEXPECTED

What about the sudden crisis, the additional piece of work, the breakdown of equipment? What do you normally do when faced by the unexpected?

Possible strategies are as follows:

◆ build in time for the unexpected. *E.g. going for an interview? Allow for the train to be late. Need to use a computer? Assume there will be a queue.*
◆ when estimating how long a task will take, always add half on again.
◆ consider delegating work to somebody else (see section 4.3).
◆ share a task with other colleagues, *e.g. researching information.*

When the unexpected happens, ask yourself:

◆ how urgent is it?
◆ what would happen if I didn't deal with it?
◆ have I got time to deal with this?
◆ do I want to do this?
◆ could someone else deal with it better?

7 IMPROVING THE BALANCE

At work. You may find it difficult to concentrate for long periods of time. It helps to plan activities with short breaks or a change of pace. Any 'lost' time will be made up by increasing effectiveness. It can help to build in treats when a task is done.

You may find it helps to do some relaxation exercises during the day.

If you are tired or under pressure you are more likely to make mistakes and perform less effectively. See Chapter 15, Dealing with Pressure.

Outside work. Exercise is important to your mental and physical health and it affects your performance. If you are fit you will be more alert. Regular exercise will help, *e.g. walking to work.*

If you find you are taking work home most evenings, you may need to reprioritise your work.

Planning time is not just about managing your workload. It also involves managing the other areas of your life, *e.g. relationships, family, social.*

What if you have conflicting demands – *e.g. you need to do different things at the same time; your family wants you to go on holiday with them?* In this case, you may need to prioritise or to identify other ways of meeting one of the demands. Could anybody else do it? Could it be done on a different day? Could it be done in any less time? Could it be done in advance? Do you need to make a decision about what is important to you?

8 CURRENT AND FUTURE PRESSURES

....

If you plan and manage your workload you will hopefully rarely feel under too much pressure and will be more able to cope with the demands on your time. What do you need to do to improve your self-management? Other chapters in this book may help you:

- ◆ Chapter 3, Communicating at Work
- ◆ Chapter 6, Gathering and Using Information
- ◆ Chapter 7, Keeping Notes, Records and Minutes
- ◆ Chapter 9, Project Work
- ◆ Chapter 11, Solving Problems and Making Decisions
- ◆ Chapter 13, Meetings
- ◆ Chapter 15, Dealing with Pressure.

Where do you need to improve planning and managing your workload? You may find it helpful to set dates by actions and keep notes on how well you are progressing.

Area needing improvement	Actions	By when?	Notes on progress

What will you do with the time you save?

9 REFERENCES AND BIBLIOGRAPHY

....

Buzan, T. (1973), *Using Your Head*, BBC Publications.

Hopson, B. and Scally, M. (1989), *Time Management: Conquer the Clock*, Lifeskills.

Northedge, A. (1990), *The Good Study Guide*, Open University Press.

Scott, M. (1992), *Time Management*, Century Business.

Williams, G. (1988), *Getting Results with Time Management*, Pavic Publications, Sheffield Hallam University.

3

COMMUNICATING AT WORK

Contents

WHY IS THIS SKILL IMPORTANT?

All jobs involve communication, using media such as letters, memos, faxes, emails and phones. This chapter focuses on these, rather than face-to-face communication. Other chapters in this book consider different forms of communication, e.g. Chapter 4, Report Writing, Chapter 5, Making Presentations, and Chapter 12, Working in Teams.

We suggest you use this chapter:

◆ to improve the way you communicate generally at work
◆ to help you with a particular communication issue.

By the end of this chapter you should be able to:

1 identify the most appropriate means of communicating a message
2 identify the purpose of the communication, identify and clarify the needs and likely reactions of others
3 make contributions relevant to others
4 use practices, formats and conventions relevant for the workplace which are appropriate for the others involved, the context and the purpose and which emphasise the meaning
5 check others' understanding of your communications, seeking appropriate feedback
6 use clear and concise language, which is appropriate for the caller/recipient/reader, content and purpose and which emphasises meaning
7 apply rules of etiquette/netiquette appropriate for others, the content and the purpose
8 use accurate information which is relevant to others, the content and the purpose
9 apply legal requirements as appropriate
10 clarify and carry out follow up actions
11 evaluate effectiveness of your own communications, identify areas of improvement and implement action.

See Chapter 1 for the relationship between these learning outcomes and the Key Skills qualifications.

1 WHAT FORM OF COMMUNICATION WOULD BE BEST?

....

The different forms of communication at work have both advantages and disadvantages and each is best used for different purposes.

What are your communication needs? How do you normally communicate at work? Do you feel equally confident and competent in using all these means? Have you received feedback from the recipients about how well you communicate (see Chapter 17, Identifying Strengths and Improving Skills)? Which ones do you need to improve? You could make notes on these issues in the table below.

Medium	Uses/advantages	Issues/disadvantages	Notes – my needs
Letter/mail	◆ Mainly for external communication ◆ Virtually anyone/anywhere can be reached by mail ◆ Can take time over composition ◆ Can enclose bulky papers or objects ◆ Gives a record of communication	◆ Takes time to arrive ◆ Cannot be retracted once sent ◆ Junk mail	
Memo	◆ Mainly for communication internally ◆ Similar to letter/mail above	◆ Internal post may take time to reach people ◆ Similar to letter/mail above	
Fax	◆ Used externally and internally between sites ◆ Arrives immediately ◆ Quick response ◆ Gives a record of communication	◆ Not everybody has a fax ◆ Can take time to feed in copy or await redial if number is engaged ◆ Copy may be poor quality	
Email (electronic mail – via networked computer)	◆ Quick communication overseas ◆ Not dependent on time differences or a person's availability at a particular time (as with the phone) ◆ Can contact several people at once ◆ Can send attachments ◆ Gives record of two-way communication	◆ Increases volume of communication ◆ Junk emails ◆ Systems can crash ◆ May not encourage thoughtful composition (too easy to type quickly and send) ◆ Not everybody has access	
Computer conferencing (usually based on email systems)	◆ As email ◆ Members of the conference do not need to communicate simultaneously ◆ More than two people can communicate together with access to each other's communications ◆ Gives a record of communication between several people	◆ Don't see person so don't pick up on non-verbal clues ◆ Can be hard to work out who is responding to whom	

Medium	Uses/advantages	Issues/disadvantages	Notes – my needs
Video-conferencing	◆ Transmits pictures and sound between two or more sites simultaneously ◆ Can see people/observe reactions ◆ Two-way conversation or more ◆ High impact – e.g. plenary or question/answer sessions in conferences/workshops	◆ Need access to hardware/software ◆ System may crash ◆ People may be nervous of cameras or be too casual ◆ There may be language difficulties/image and voice may not be synchronised/responses may be delayed	
Telephone	◆ Immediate ◆ Allows for discussion between two or more people ◆ Can be informal/personal	◆ Hard to connect with busy people ◆ No record of the communication ◆ Hard to judge reactions ◆ Need to think on feet ◆ Mobile phones can disrupt other people ◆ There may be language difficulties	
Answerphone (machine plugged into telephone) or voicemail (networked into a central server)	◆ Records message over phone, not dependent on person's availability at that moment ◆ Best for short/clear messages ◆ Voicemail accessed by telephone keys/code numbers ◆ Messages on voicemail and some answerphones can be accessed by phone from other sites	◆ Some people dislike/feel nervous of them ◆ May go wrong ◆ Busy people may ignore messages ◆ Frustrating to callers who cannot reach a 'real' person ◆ Others may listen to messages and not pass them on	
Dictaphone	◆ Records information tape for self to use later or for another person (e.g. secretary) to type from ◆ Small, portable	◆ Increasing use of desktop computers can mean people type own work/have no secretarial support ◆ Can be hard to hear what is said ◆ Hard to relocate specific sections	
Others (please list)			

2 MEETING NEEDS

....

Before you make any communication you need to consider the needs of those involved: your organisation; yourself; the person with whom you are communicating. You may do this automatically when communicating in a way you find familiar and comfortable. However, you may need to explicitly think about it when using an unfamiliar medium or facing an unusual situation, or you may generally not be communicating very effectively because you have never considered it.

The following gives possible scenarios in which you might have to communicate using any of the methods listed in section 1 above.

You may find that needs are conflicting.

Example: You telephoned another organisation to chase up a service which was overdue. The person you spoke to was rude to you. You may feel the need to let off steam or even retaliate. Your organisation may need to keep on good terms with the other organisation. The 'rude' individual may have been frustrated by others' incompetence and may now be embarrassed.

In the above example you might need to put aside your own feelings and deal with the person in a way which would be helpful for your organisation. Whose needs are paramount may depend on the situation and your overall aims. In order to further your organisation's long-term interests, it may be that in the short term your own needs may be paramount (*e.g. if you need something to complete a job*) or those of the other person (*e.g. if you need to generate goodwill*).

You could use the following table:

◆ in relation to similar situations you have experienced. Did you think through the various needs in the situation or react spontaneously and perhaps in a way you regret?
◆ in relation to situations you currently face or may face.
◆ either as the instigator or the recipient (you could use the table as if you are requesting information or as if others are requesting information from you).

Scenario	Your needs	Your organisation's needs	Their needs	In this instance whose needs are paramount?
Requesting or giving information				
Buying or selling something				
Requesting cooperation				
Requesting payment				
Making or dealing with a complaint				
Making or dealing with an apology				

Scenario	Your needs	Your organisation's needs	Their needs	In this instance whose needs are paramount?
Dealing with lies/distortions/excuses				
Formal warning of poor work performance				
Giving a reference				
Others (please list)				

You could ask for feedback from others about whether you have correctly anticipated their needs (*e.g. 'Is this the information you needed?', 'Can I be of any further help?', 'What is our organisation looking for here?'*).

3 ACCEPTED PRACTICES, FORMATS AND CONVENTIONS

In all workplaces there are generally accepted practices and conventions in relation to the media mentioned in section 1 above.

There may also be practices and conventions used in your particular organisation, *e.g. a 'house style' for written communications, which may include the 'font' (i.e. the size and style of the typeface), when to underline and when to use bold and punctuation.* Your organisation may have ways of answering the phone (*e.g. 'Bloggs and company', 'Good morning, I'm John, how may I help you', 'Hello, Jane Brown'*).

If your organisation has conventions you should use them. Who will know what they are? You could ask secretaries, receptionists, administrators, the training department, your boss or mentor, or you could observe others' practice (ask if you can see copies of memos or letters or listen to how others answer the phone).

If your organisation does not have particular practices or conventions, you need to follow those which are generally accepted. Be careful in your use of books on letter writing. Older books may be out of date in their advice, as wordprocessing has led to changes in the conventions (*e.g. paragraphs are no longer indented and punctuation is not used in addresses*).

In the appendix at the end of this chapter are examples which you could use or adapt for:

◆ letter headings and endings
◆ memo headings
◆ invitations
◆ fax cover sheet
◆ email headings
◆ answering the phone and answerphone/voicemail messages.

Most written communication today is wordprocessed. Wordprocessing packages have standard formats or templates you can use, *e.g. for letters or for emails.*

4 LANGUAGE

············

In using language you need to return to section 2 to consider the needs of the other person. Whatever your purpose you need to communicate it clearly. You also need to consider the impression you are creating about yourself and your organisation.

4.1 The other person's needs

Who is the other person? Is English their first language? Is it a fellow professional who will understand professional language? If it is a member of the public, are they likely to be familiar with your area of work? Will they understand the terms you use in your work?

What is the context? Your language needs to be appropriate for the situation (*e.g. you would not use the same language to a colleague who had just been bereaved as to one who had just failed to obtain promotion*). How formal is the situation? Is the communication legally binding?

What is the purpose? Are you persuading somebody about something, or explaining something or requesting something?

It will help you to get into this way of thinking about your communications. You could complete the table below in relation to some communications you need to make shortly.

Who is the other person? What language would be appropriate for them?	What is the context? What language would be appropriate for it?	What is my purpose? What language would be appropriate for it?

Some points to consider:

◆ unless you are certain that the other person is a fellow professional who will understand jargon, it is safest to avoid it. Even professionals in other areas may not understand it.

◆ avoid using abbreviations or acronyms, *e.g. TQM (total quality management)*, as the other person may not be familiar with them.

◆ it is even more important to avoid jargon, abbreviations and acronyms on the phone. If the communication is in writing the other person can use a dictionary, but on the phone they may lose the thread of what you are saying or be embarrassed to ask what you mean.

◆ if you are speaking on the phone to somebody for whom English is not their first language, you need to speak slowly, or ask them to speak slowly if you are trying to follow another language. Unless you speak a language really well it may be best to use English or to ask somebody who does speak the language to write for you (have you ever been amused by translations into English of instructions about how to use products – might this be how others see your attempts at their language?).

◆ do you have any speech mannerisms which others might find irritating on the phone (*yeah, yeah, uhuh, right, OK, sure!*)?

4.2 Your image

A first written or spoken communication is like meeting somebody for the first time. We are all influenced by first impressions.

Many people have prejudices and biases about language. If you unwittingly use one of their 'pet hates', it could colour their view of you and your competence in a way which is out of all proportion to your 'error'. It is best to err on the side of caution by trying to make your use of language as correct as possible. For example, when writing:

◆ avoid any contractions such as 'I've' or 'don't'
◆ spell check *everything* and use a dictionary
◆ use conventional grammar and punctuation. If you are unsure, get a book or ask somebody to proofread your written work.

(See Chapter 4, Report Writing, for further suggestions.)
    In writing and speaking:

◆ avoid clichés (*e.g. 'this is the offer of the year'*)
◆ only use official language if the reader is likely to understand it.

In speaking:

◆ regional accents are attractive, but beware of using dialect words which others may not understand or may misunderstand (*e.g. in the North East 'bonnie' means 'pretty', in Derbyshire it means 'plump'*).

5 ETIQUETTE/ NETIQUETTE
················

'Netiquette' refers to the use of etiquette in relation to computer applications, such as email. Etiquette is about working practices which are polite and non-offensive to others. All groups have their own forms of etiquette and these may differ from those of other groups, *e.g. in your organisation, is everyone on first-name terms, or does it depend on your status?* You need to find out what is etiquette in your context.
    The following may spark off your ideas about what might be considered etiquette. They cover aspects of etiquette which are applicable to most contexts in the UK.

Area, suggestions	Issues, examples	What do I normally do in this area?
Try to avoid patronising others. Assume that everybody is doing as important a job as you, no matter what their level, and that they deserve as much respect as you do.	You can be patronising in the way you address people (*e.g. calling women 'dear', referring to 'girls' or 'lads'*) or in the things you say (*'Well done!'*) or in your tone of voice.	
Be aware of gender stereotyping. It is good practice to use language which is not gender specific (*i.e. 'their', 'her/his'*).	If you work in a male-dominated area, you may be used to 'his' to refer to other professionals. If you do so where this is not the norm, it may be seen as offensive.	
Address people as they wish to be addressed. Find out beforehand how somebody wants to be addressed (ring the switchboard, ask a receptionist/secretary, ask the person themselves).	People's titles reflect their status. A title may be the result of great effort (*e.g. Dr*) or an honour (*e.g. Sir*) and a person may be offended if you do not use it. Find out if a woman wishes to be addressed as Ms, Mrs or Miss.	
Avoid using humour unless you know the other person very well and are sure they will appreciate it.	Something that sounds funny verbally can look quite different in writing. We do not all share the same sense of humour. You may offend someone or they may misunderstand you.	

Area, suggestions	Issues, examples	What do I normally do in this area?
Avoid swearing or losing your temper.	Even if you feel justified, swearing or losing your temper puts you in the wrong. Keeping cool means that any fault can stay where it belongs.	
Acknowledge receipt of a communication and say thank you.	The sender may be uncertain that you have received it.	

6 THE CONTENT OF YOUR COMMUNICATION

6.1 The information to include

What information should you include in your communication? You could use the following for a communication you have to make shortly.

Suggestions	What my communication should include
Identify what the other person needs to know.	
Identify what is relevant for the context, situation or purpose and omit everything else.	
Avoid irrelevancies or too much detail, which may confuse the other person.	
Ensure that they will not need to come back for further information (e.g. phone with reference details to hand, ensure that meeting dates/times/ locations are given with instructions for how to get there).	
Be explicit about follow-up action needed (e.g. ask them to confirm attendance, or to reply within a given time).	
Say explicitly what you are enclosing or attaching.	
Include in your letter/fax/memo/email etc. a list of all those receiving copies.	
Others (please list)	

6.2 *Organising your information*

You need to connect ideas logically, particularly on the phone (the other person will not have anything in writing from you to check their understanding subsequently).

Whatever your type of communication you need to:

◆ use any available standard formats – they have been devised because they give all the relevant information needed (*e.g. an email heading tells you who has sent it, when, and what the topic is*)

◆ make the purpose of the communication clear at the start (*e.g. if you chat for a long time on the phone to a busy person before getting to the point they may become frustrated*)

◆ organise your information into clear and meaningful sections (*e.g. in a letter the introduction can give background information, the middle can develop this further, and the end can indicate what should happen next*)

◆ provide 'signposting', *i.e. direct the person's attention to where you want them to give attention.*

You may need to use Chapter 14, Putting Your Case: Negotiating and Assertiveness. For example, you could use assertiveness techniques like 'going up the scale' in a situation where somebody owes you money (*your first letter could enclose the bill, your second could repeat the request for payment and give a date by which it must be paid before you take further action, the third could say you will put the matter in the hands of a solicitor*).

7 THE LAW
....

There are legal issues relating to work communications. If in doubt check with somebody who knows. For example:

◆ the company secretary (the term here does not mean a typist or wordprocessing operator but refers to a senior role responsible for legal matters – not all organisations have them)

◆ the buying, procurement or contracts department

◆ your organisation's solicitor

◆ the Citizens' Advice Bureau

◆ your union or professional body

◆ personnel or human resources department.

Beware of advice from well-meaning colleagues who may be wrong. There are many myths about legal matters. It is best to get advice in writing.

Some areas to be aware of include:

◆ copyright

◆ libel/slander

◆ 'privileged' information

◆ negligence

◆ confidentiality

◆ liability.

8 EDITING
....

You can use the checklist overleaf for written communications to reread and check whatever is written before sending (this is especially important with email where it is so easy to dash it off and send it), or for phone calls to check in advance what you will say.

Is all my information accurate (*e.g. meetings – do I have the right date and day of the week, are the figures correct, are names spelt correctly*)?

Have I been as brief as possible (everybody is busy)?

Have I been clear (*e.g. no unnecessary information to confuse, logical order*)?

Will I and the other person both know exactly what the situation is/what is required?

Will my communication save time, not waste time?

Have I used accepted practices, formats or conventions?

Have I used language which is appropriate for the other person and the context?

Have I observed etiquette/netiquette?

Have I checked on any legal aspects of my communication?

9 WHERE DO YOU NEED TO IMPROVE? ACTION PLANNING

Which communication media do I feel confident with? What are my particular strengths in using the various types of communication media?

How can I build on these strengths?

What are the main areas where I need to improve?

What actions can I take to improve (this may include seeking advice, training etc.)? When will I take these actions?

What progress have I made with regard to the actions I identified above?

10 REFERENCES AND BIBLIOGRAPHY
....

Doherty, M., Knapp, L. and Swift, S. (1987), *Write for Business*, Longman.

Gordon, I. (1973), *Basic Business Letters*, Heinemann Educational Books.

Mitchell, E. (1977), *The Businessman's Guide to Letter Writing and to the Law on Letters*, Business Books.

APPENDIX
....

1 Letter headings and endings

```
                                            (Your address and today's date)
                                            White and Co
                                            3 Green Lane
                                            Redland
                                            Leicestershire
                                            RE3 9ER
                                            3 March 1999

(The address of the person you are writing to)
Black and Co
4 Brown Street
Bluetown
Northumbria
BL4 8LB

CC: (A list of people receiving copies of your letter)
Mrs A Orange
Mr B Violet
(NB this could go at the bottom of the letter)

(Greeting)
Dear Ms Purple (or Dear Sir or Dear Madam if you do not know the name)

(Topic of the letter)
MEETING ON 10 MARCH 1999

(Text of the letter)
I wish to confirm that the meeting between ourselves, Mrs Orange and
Mr Violet will take place at 10 am on the above date in my office.
I look forward to seeing you then.

(Closure)
Yours sincerely (or 'Yours truly' – both can be used if you use the person's name in the greeting. If
you address the letter to Dear Sir or Dear Madam, you end it 'Yours faithfully')

(Your signature – if you are unable to sign it, another person can do so if they place 'pp' before their signature)


A White


(Your name typed beneath the signature – it should be your name even if another person has signed the
letter)
Miss A White
```

2 Memo headings

```
To:
Copies:
From:
Date:
Subject:
```

3 The invitation

> White and Co cordially request the company of Ms Purple at the launch of their new range of cookware at 6.30 pm on Thursday 18 April 1999 at the Crown Hotel, Redland.
>
> White and Co
> 3 Green Lane
> Redland
> Leicestershire
> RE3 9ER
> RSVP *(this means you wish the person to reply)*

The reply

> Ms Purple thanks White and Co for their kind invitation to the launch of their new range of cookware on Thursday 18 April 1999 at the Crown Hotel, Redland and is pleased to accept (or but must unfortunately decline).
>
> Black and Co
> 4 Brown Street
> Bluetown
> Northumbria
> BL4 8LB

4 Fax cover sheet

```
To  (name of recipient):
Department/organisation:
Fax number:

From  (name of sender):
Department/organisation:
Fax number:

Date:
Number of pages including cover sheet:
Subject:
Message:
```

5 Email headings

```
From:       John Jones <jjones@bloggs.co.uk>
Sent:       24 July 1999 08:31
To:         Jack Thomas <jthomas@bloggs.co.uk>; John Smith
            <jsmith@white.com>
Subject:    FW: Handbooks - Have you got your copy?
```

6 Answering the phone and answerphone/voicemail messages

ANSWERING THE PHONE

Good morning, White and Company.
Good morning, Ann White.
Hello, Ann White.

ANSWERPHONE/ VOICEMAIL MESSAGES

Hello, this is White and Company (*or* this is Ann White). We are (*or* I am) unable to take your call at the moment. Please leave your name, number and the date and time you called after the long tone (*or* please leave a message after the long tone).

Contents

4
REPORT WRITING

WHY IS THIS SKILL IMPORTANT?

Reports are the most common way of presenting information and advice related to a specific purpose. They are used by industry, business, commerce, professional bodies, charities and government as a basis for decisions and policies.

People who need reports are busy. A good report is one you don't need to reread to understand the point. It should be concise and have an orderly structure, using headings and subheadings.

Reports may be written by individuals or groups and their purposes may be varied. However, they follow similar patterns of organisation. Examples might be:

- annual reports
- progress reports
- briefing documents
- sales reports
- investigation/research reports
- site visits
- laboratory reports
- press releases
- minutes of meetings (see Chapter 7, Keeping Notes, Records and Minutes)
- test/technical reports
- feasibility studies
- reports for a public inquiry

Some reports may have standard forms to fill in, e.g. legal reports, staff appraisals and accident reports.

The ability to produce good reports is valuable. Authors of reports will be judged on the quality of their written work. This chapter aims to help you turn an adequate report into a good one and produce more in-depth, professional reports.

We suggest you use this chapter:

- to help you write a particular report
- before you begin any work on it
- while you are gathering your information and writing your report.

By the end of this chapter, you should be able to:

1 identify the purpose of the report and the needs and characteristics of the audience
2 include accurate information appropriate to the purpose and audience
3 produce a report in a format appropriate to the subject area, purpose and audience, and present it legibly, with a clear layout
4 use images to support or clarify main points
5 use language which is appropriate for the subject area, purpose and audience and use grammar, punctuation and spelling which follow standard conventions.

See Chapter 1 for the relationship between these learning outcomes and the Key Skills qualifications.

1 INITIAL QUESTIONS – WHO, WHAT AND WHY?

·········

For your report consider the following questions.

What is the purpose of the report – *to inform, persuade, predict or recommend? Will it lead to decisions or policies?*

Will the information be used for any other purpose?

What might be the implications/effects of the report? *For me, for others, for my organisation?*

How confidential is it to be?

What information and how much should go in the report? *E.g. a detailed analysis, essential facts only, mainly recommendations?*

What is the deadline?

What is the budget for the production of the report?

What resources are available? *E.g. administrative/technical support?*

Who is my report for? Being sure of this is crucial to the success of your report. The remainder of this section focuses on your readership.

1.1 Getting inside your reader's head

Good reports meet the readers' needs. What will your readers want and why? The answer will determine the structure and tone of the report.

◆ Who will be the principal reader(s)? What do they already know about the subject? Are they decision makers or influencers? What is their role or purpose?
◆ Others are likely to read your report too. Who are the secondary readers? What do they already know about the subject? Their purpose and characteristics may differ from those of the principal readers.

It may be helpful to imagine you are the reader in answering the following questions.

	Principal readers	Secondary readers
Why do I (the reader) want the report?		
What do I (the reader) already know?		
What do I (the reader) need to know?		
What are my (the reader's) characteristics? *E.g. decision maker, technically knowledgeable, cultural considerations*		
Why have I (the reader) asked you to write the report?		

Your answers to the above questions will help you identify the implications for your report and work out what you need to keep in mind while you are writing it.

Implications for the report – what I need to keep in mind

2 GETTING STARTED
....

Initial ideas should be flexible, to be adapted as you progress. The following questions may help:

◆ what are the main issues/ideas to cover?
◆ what will the main points be?
◆ what other information might be useful?

Different strategies work for different people. Any of the following could be a starting point.

2.1 Make a list/brainstorm

Write down all your ideas. This will show how many ideas you already have and if you need to read, talk or listen to generate more.

2.2 Draw a spider diagram/mind map

These can help structure your ideas. Start with the main words in the central box. Other key words radiate from there and can be linked with lines. See the example below:

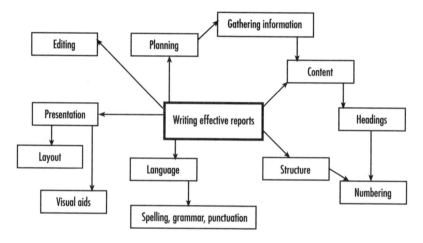

2.3 Talk to others

Talking to others (*e.g. mentor, colleagues*) helps to clarify ideas and test them out. See Chapter 18, Mentoring, Appraisal and Interviews.

3 PLANNING – TIME AND RESOURCES
....

To meet your deadline, you will need to plan for time, resources available, including other people, and the likely costs involved. The tasks you need to plan for include:

◆ **Gathering information**, *e.g. documents, primary data (your own investigations), second-ary data (others' work)*. You may need to break this down into subtasks later, and amend your plan accordingly (see section 4 and Chapter 6, Gathering and Using Information).
◆ **Structuring, drafting and editing**. On average, drafting, editing and presenting the report will take as long as gathering the information – it is common to under-estimate this.
◆ **Administration time**, *e.g. typing, printing, photocopying, binding and distributing.*

You might find Chapter 2, Planning and Managing Your Workload, helpful.

Tasks	Who will do it?	Time needed/ deadline	Resources	Cost

4 GATHERING
INFORMATION
··················

This chapter focuses on writing the report rather than on gathering information for it. Chapter 6, Gathering and Using Information, will help you in that.

It helps to list the information needed for your report and where you might find it (see Chapter 6). This may change as your ideas develop.

Information needed	Where might I find this?	Who could I ask for help?

The following points are particularly important:

- **identifying your purpose** will help you see what information you need. Keep this in mind throughout.
- **the reader should be able to trace your information**. This means that you will need a good recording system with all the necessary details for when you actually produce the report (see Chapter 6, Gathering and Using Information).
- **you may need to criticise and evaluate the information** (see Chapter 6, Gathering and Using Information).
- **you may need to refer to evidence for any arguments, views or conclusions**. If you have collected the evidence yourself (*e.g. from an experiment or a survey*) you need to include how you gathered it, as well as what the evidence is. Again, this means having a good recording system.
- **information must be accurate**.
- **check the copyright**. You may need permission to use the material (*e.g. from an author, employer or other source of the information*). You might get advice from your legal department (if your organisation has one), or from a library.
- **information must be relevant**. What should you include or omit? The following checklist may help.

Is the information	
Relevant to my purpose?	
Relevant to my readers?	
Necessary as evidence/as part of an explanation?	
Up to date?	
Accurate?	

5 CRITICISING AND EVALUATING THE INFORMATION

A good report gives accurate and objective information. It should also criticise and evaluate the information. Being critical and evaluating means not accepting information at face value but asking why it is as it is.

This is covered in more depth in Chapter 6, Gathering and Using Information, but the essential points are:

- check your own assumptions
- check others' assumptions
- check for distorted information.

For the purposes of your report, it may help to ask yourself the following questions:

Do I have an existing stance before I start my investigations?
Are any values or political issues involved? Vested interests?

Are there any hidden agendas?
Would I like the reader to come to any particular conclusions?

5.1 Presenting your criticisms and evaluation

Good reports make any criticisms clear for the reader. It helps to:

◆ back up criticisms and evaluation with evidence
◆ be concise – long-winded explanations are tedious
◆ be relevant – make sure your criticisms and evaluation are relevant to your purpose and that you are not going off at a tangent
◆ be meaningful to the reader – what might seem crucial to one reader may seem trivial to another. Check back with your readers' characteristics (p 35).

Information	Criticism of this information	Evidence for my criticism

6 THE STRUCTURE OF THE REPORT

....

6.1 Format

As there is no one correct format for a report, it helps to clarify what your primary reader expects. Your organisation may have a standard format, or examples to look at.

An effective report is designed so that readers can easily identify the sections they want. General rules which are applicable in most situations are:

◆ tell them what you are going to tell them
◆ tell them
◆ tell them what you have told them.

The following gives examples of possible formats. Example 1 may be more appropriate for formal, large reports (*e.g. government reports*) rather than for a short report to colleagues.

Example 1	Example 2	Example 3	Example 4
(The preliminaries) Title page Acknowledgements Contents list Terms of reference List of tables/figures Foreword Abstracts/synopsis *(The main part)* Introduction Findings Conclusions Minority report *(Supplementary)* References/bibliography Appendices Glossary Index Distribution list	Title page Aims/objectives Methodology *(for gathering information)* Findings Conclusions Recommendations References/bibliography Appendices Distribution list	Title page Aims Methods Results Conclusions Distribution list	Title page Summary Contents Introduction Findings/conclusions Appendices Distribution list

The following clarifies the terms given in the above examples. However, note that not all the following elements are needed in all reports – *e.g. an index is only needed for long reports where readers need to locate items; not all reports have terms of reference.*

◆ **Abstract/synopsis.** A short paragraph at the beginning of a report which says what is in it and which allows readers to see if it is relevant to them.
◆ **Acknowledgements.** Business-like thanks to people or organisations who have helped. Include details of their qualifications or professional body status.
◆ **Aims.** The overall purpose of the report (*e.g. to investigate chemical pollution in Yorkshire rivers*).
◆ **Appendices.** Detailed information which is important but which may distract from the flow of the report can be included.
◆ **Conclusions.** Draws together your findings.
◆ **Contents list.** This lists all the headings in your report in order with page numbers, and the appendices with their number and title.
◆ **Distribution list.** Those to whom the report will be sent. If this is long, it should go at the end of the report.
◆ **Findings/results.** Statement of what you found out (*e.g. results of an experiment or a survey or a project*) with the interpretation and analysis.
◆ **Foreword.** Sets the scene (*e.g. why the report is needed, why it is important*). It could be written by another person who feels they should be represented.

- **Glossary**. A list of abbreviations/terminology, if readers are likely to be unfamiliar with them.
- **Index**. Alphabetical list of topics covered, with page or section numbers where they can be found.
- **Introduction**. Outlines what the report is about. May include background to the report, aims, objectives.
- **List of tables/figures**. All tables and figures should be numbered. You can list them in number order.
- **Method/methodology**. How you gathered information, where from and how much (*e.g. if you used a survey, who was surveyed, how did you decide on the target group, how many were surveyed, how were they surveyed – by interviews or questionnaire?*)
- **Minority report**. If the report is produced by a group, there may be members who disagree with the majority. Their report should be included if they choose. It should not contain any criticism of individuals but offers an alternative opinion. It needs to be written tactfully.
- **Objectives**. More specifically what you want to achieve (*e.g. to identify the causes of chemical pollution, to identify solutions*).
- **Recommendations**. What you think should happen based on your conclusions. Include timescales if appropriate.
- **References/bibliography**. References are items referred to in the report. A bibliography is of additional material not specifically referred to, but which readers may want to follow up.
- **Summary**. Gives the key points. It can be used at the start, so that those readers with no time to read the report can grasp the main points, or at the end, to draw things together. It should only contain information covered in the main part and it should be a page or less in length.
- **Terms of reference**. Specification of what they want by those commissioning a report. Indicates the scope of the report (*e.g. if the report is to consider chemical pollution in Yorkshire rivers, it would be outside its terms of reference to consider air pollution, or pollution in Devon*).
- **Title page**. Succinct title, then your name, organisation, address and contact number. Include date, file reference and, if it is not the final version, 'draft'. If the report is confidential, give security classification and number of the copy. Distribution list, if small (six or fewer).

NB Avoid footnotes as they can distract the reader. Page numbers are important.

6.2 Structuring the content

MAIN POINTS

A starting point is to be clear about the crucial points you must convey to the reader. List these below.

Crucial points

Then ask yourself:

◆ what will interest readers?
◆ what angle is most likely to capture their interest?
◆ what do I want them to be most interested in?

The answers to these questions can influence how you order your material. There is little point in having a fascinating conclusion if the reader stopped reading long ago. Use your introduction to gain interest.

The content of the report should be ordered logically to fit the purpose. Possibilities are by chronology (i.e. what happened first goes first), by themes, or by following a line of argument – *e.g. if you want to persuade it may be an idea to start with a punchy key point.* Refer back to the purpose which you identified in section 1.

Outline the order of your content in the box below.

Order for the content

6.3 Signposting

Signposting means helping the reader find their way through your report. **A reader should very quickly be able to scan the report and extract the relevant information.** Some strategies for signposting are given below:

USING STRUCTURE

◆ a **contents page**
◆ an **introduction** which explains what is to follow, or an initial **summary** or **synopsis** of the main points
◆ a **logical order**

USING LANGUAGE (SEE SECTION 8)

◆ being **concise** – removing padding, repetition and too much detail
◆ **summarising** – telling the reader what s/he has just read (*'to summarise …'*)
◆ **leading** – telling the reader what is coming next (*'as the following section indicates …'*).

USING PRESENTATION   The overall impact is important and reports should be typed or wordprocessed. Your organisation may have a 'house style':

◆ a clear **layout** – *e.g. short blocks of text*. Lists or key points should be consistent in style, either a dash (–) or a bullet (•).
◆ use of **images/visuals** at appropriate points (see section 7).
◆ use of **spacing**. Margins and indents – ensure words are not lost in binding.
◆ **headings**. Headings should be clearly identified by using different fonts, upper and lower case and sizes, italics and highlighting. If you look at this chapter you will see there are three styles of headings – one for main sections, one for subsections and one for further subsections.
◆ **numbering**. Numbering your sections makes the report easier to follow. The decimal system is the most common, e.g.:

1	Primary heading
1.1	Secondary heading
1.1.1	Subheading
1.1.2	Subheading

Try to avoid going to four or more points, *e.g. 1.1.2.1*. Appendices are often numbered using Roman numerals (*e.g. Appendix III*). Each paragraph may be numbered.

The following example gives possible headings and section numbers for a report on public transport.

1	INTRODUCTION	
	1.1	Background
	1.2	Aims
	1.3	Objectives
2	METHODS	
	2.1	The questionnaire
	2.2	The sample group
3	FINDINGS	
	3.1	Response rate
	3.2	Findings
		3.2.1 Who are the transport users?
		3.2.2 Transport routes
		3.2.3 Users' opinions of transport provision
4	CONCLUSIONS	
5	RECOMMENDATIONS	
	5.1	Public transport
	5.2	Private transport
6	REFERENCES	
7	APPENDICES	
	I	The questionnaire
	II	Summary tables

7 USE OF IMAGES/VISUALS

....

Images/visuals should be used to make something clearer, rather than for mere decoration. Use them when something is difficult to describe in words; to aid comprehension; to reinforce a verbal message; to make it easy to pick out information; to help the reader see relationships. They must be relevant, helpful and appropriate for the reader.

For example:

◆ to display statistics – *tables or graphs*
◆ to show the appearance of something – *photographs, plans, maps, line drawings*
◆ to show how something works – *diagrams, flowcharts or algorithms.*

For example, in car driving:

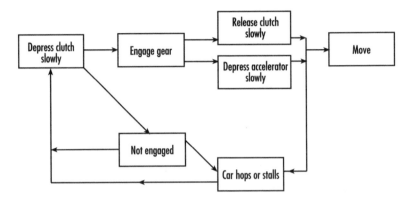

Some general tips:

◆ will readers be familiar with your images? For example, accountants may use '+' on a balance sheet for outgoings and '−' for income (for most of us the reverse seems more logical).
◆ are your visuals misleading? A short book, referred to in section 12, by Huff (1973), indicates how statistics can 'lie', *e.g. Are graphs to scale? Are they accurate?*
◆ visuals should appear in the text for the convenience of the reader. They should not interrupt the flow of information.
◆ each visual should be titled and numbered.
◆ any abbreviations should conform to conventions of either your organisation or British Standards (*e.g. m for metre*).
◆ check copyright permission (see section 4).
◆ ensure visuals are of high quality, especially if photocopying.
◆ are visuals pleasing to the eye?
◆ is there too much information crammed in?

Note down below the visuals/images you wish to include.

Images to be included

8 APPROPRIATE LANGUAGE

....

Using language effectively gives clarity to your report and avoids confusion in meaning. **Your style of writing leaves an impression on the reader** and you need to give careful consideration to your use of language.

The language should reflect the purpose of the report and the reader's needs. It may help to answer the following as if you were the reader.

> What sort of language would I (the reader) understand?
>
>
> What sort of language would impress me (the reader)?

The level of formality will depend on the type of report, the readers, or the conventions of your organisation. A very formal style of writing can seem pompous (or look like a desire to impress), *e.g. using 'remunerate' instead of 'pay'.*

It is **not** necessary for formal writing to be in the third person (i.e. 'the writer'). The use of the first person (i.e. 'I') makes for more comfortable reading and can still be objective.

General tips for using language include:

◆ be precise (*e.g. 'The victims may have been hit with a blunt instrument' – were they or weren't they?*).
◆ reports need to be concise and should be free of unnecessary padding and repetition. Can you tighten up your writing?
  e.g.   *'Salaries which are paid to teachers make up 65% of the school budget.'*
        'Teachers' salaries make up 65% of the school budget.'
  e.g.   *'The committee took into consideration the adoption of the proposal.'*
        'The committee considered adopting the proposal.'
◆ you may need to be diplomatic, *e.g. 'Efforts should be made to…', 'Priority should be given to…'.*
◆ chatty language should rarely be used, *e.g. 'can't', 'won't'.* Clichés are also inappropriate, *e.g. 'as fast as lightning'.*
◆ beware of using superfluous words, *e.g. 'absolutely fatal', 'completely empty', 'the reason … because'.*
◆ double negatives give a positive meaning, *e.g. 'not never' means 'always'.*
◆ check for non-sequiturs, i.e. a conclusion which does not follow from what has previously been stated.
◆ keep to one main idea per paragraph.
◆ abbreviations should be written in full at first mention, with the abbreviation in brackets; after this the abbreviation alone can be used – *e.g. 'Continuing Professional Development (CPD)' and thereafter simply 'CPD'.*

Look at examples of reports in your organisation. What sort of language do they use?

8.1 Choosing words

A thesaurus or Gower's *The Complete Plain Words* (1986) can help in selecting words to use. Choose your words carefully. They give an impression of your competence.

◆ Some words have different meanings in different contexts, *e.g. 'variance' means one thing to an accountant and another to a statistician.*
◆ Avoid jargon and 'in-vogue' words
◆ 'Pseudo-words' (i.e. words which are made up) are not appropriate, *e.g. constructionability.*

Examples of inappropriate words:

◆ 'ridiculous' and 'illogical' are judgmental and emotive
◆ 'fairly' and 'quite' imply vagueness
◆ 'basic' means 'fundamental', not 'simple'
◆ 'essential' means 'indispensable', more than just 'important'.

Improvements needed in my use of words

8.2 Spelling

Poor spelling can detract from the content of your report and give a negative impression. If you are unsure, use a dictionary. A spellchecker on a computer can be useful but will only find incorrectly spelled words, not those out of context, *e.g. principle/principal, license/licence, affect/effect*. It may also give American spellings rather than English ones.

If you need to use specialist terminology or people's names, make sure you have the correct spelling.

8.3 Grammar

Examples of common grammatical mistakes (corrections are in italics):

◆ writing as you might speak, e.g. 'I could of (*have*) been more thorough.'
◆ incomplete sentences, e.g. 'Further investigation (*is recommended*) such as researching the possibility of corrosion.'
◆ pronouns that do not match, e.g. 'The workforce has a responsibility to their (*its*) employer.'
◆ tenses that do not match, e.g. 'Employees must collect an identity pass before they could (*can*) enter the building.'

APOSTROPHE
BEFORE S

This can cause problems but the rules are:

◆ **it indicates the possessive (belonging to).** There is an apostrophe before the *s* in singular possession and after the *s* in plural possession, *e.g. 'The employee's (one employee) report was good. The employees' (more than one employee) reports were good.'* However, an exception is 'its' (of it), which does not have an apostrophe (but see bullet point below).
◆ **it indicates where letters are missing**, *e.g. can't (cannot), she's (she has), it's (it is).*

8.4 Punctuation

Punctuation helps the reader make sense of the sentence, where s/he would pause for a breath. If you are unsure, only use commas and full stops. Colons and semi-colons are mainly used to punctuate lists, *e.g. 'There are many dwellings: houses; flats; bungalows; caravans'.*

Some guidelines are:

◆ check that quotations have **quotation marks** around them.
◆ check that all questions have a **question mark** instead of a full stop.
◆ avoid **exclamation marks** (they are usually used in a more conversational style).
◆ read your sentences out loud. Use punctuation to break up long sentences. Keep them between 15 and 20 words and vary the length to avoid monotony. If sentences are too long, they may be difficult to understand; if they are too short, the ideas may seem fragmented. If English is not your first language or you find writing difficult, short sentences may help you avoid grammatical mistakes.
◆ Acronyms are not normally punctuated, *e.g. BBC, GB.*

What do I need to improve in spelling, grammar and punctuation?

9 REFERENCING

You may quote from or refer to someone else's work in your text. You should list all references (i.e. the details of the publications you used) at the end of your report. It is helpful to record the works you use while you are gathering information.

Your organisation may have a convention for referencing. If not, the Harvard system could be used (see Chapter 6, Gathering and Using Information).

Reports are based on evidence and you may need to refer to other information, *e.g. a publication, internal reports, original survey material, notes or data.* You will need to acknowledge and reference the source of your information so that others can find it if they need to (see Chapter 6, Gathering and Using Information).

10 EDITING

It can be useful to put your draft report aside for a few days before rereading it. In this way, you will be more distanced from it and be able to spot errors more easily. The following checklist should help you edit your report.

Editing checklist	
The purpose Have I clarified the purpose? Have I identified my readers' needs/characteristics? Have I kept the purpose in mind throughout?	
Information Have I included the main points? Are points supported by evidence? Have I criticised and evaluated the content of my report? Is the information relevant to the purpose and to the readers? Have I obtained the necessary copyright permissions?	
Accuracy Are there any spelling mistakes? Do any numbers add up? Are the references correct, in the text and at the end? Are all sources of information listed in the References section? Are abbreviations consistent?	

Images/visuals Are images clear and understandable? Are they all titled and numbered?	
Format Is the report easy to follow and well signposted? Is it easy to find information in the report? Are section headings and numbering clear? Are the arguments followed through logically?	
Language Is it clear, direct and easy to read? Will the readers understand it? Will its tone help me achieve the purpose? Have any unnecessary words/phrases been deleted? Is the grammar/punctuation correct? Is there any repetition? Is there consistency, e.g. in tenses and pronouns?	
Presentation Is the layout appealing? Does it highlight important points? Are the pages numbered?	

11 IMPROVING THE EFFECTIVENESS OF YOUR REPORTS

How effective is your report and what do you need to improve in the future? When completing the box below, it will help to look at your report as the reader would. It will be even more useful if you can get feedback from your readers.

	Notes on improvement needed	Actions to be taken
Identifying purposes		
Identifying readers' needs		
Planning time needed to produce it		
Format of the report		

	Notes on improvement needed	Actions to be taken
Information gathering for the report		
Criticising/evaluating the contents		
Presentation		
Images/visuals		
Signposting		

FINALLY

- ◆ Keep a copy of your report and background notes, just in case the reader loses it, you need to revise it, you need to produce a further report, or somebody wants to check your data.
- ◆ Confidentiality. Your organisation may have a system for maintaining security of information. If not, number the copies and keep a record of who has them.
- ◆ Legal considerations, *e.g. libel, copyright, Trade Descriptions Act (1968), Sex Discrimination Acts (1975 and 1986)*. If you are in doubt, seek expert legal advice.

12 REFERENCES AND BIBLIOGRAPHY

....

Bell, J. (1987), *Doing your Research Project: A Guide for First-time Researchers in Education and Social Science*, Open University Press.

Cooper, B. M. (1964), *Writing Technical Reports*, Penguin.

Gowers, E. (1986), *The Complete Plain Words*, HMSO.

Huff, D. (1973), *How to Lie with Statistics*, Penguin.

Macdonald, J. (1992), *Management Skill Guide: Report Writing*, Croner Publications.

Peel, M. (1990), *Improving Your Communication Skills*, Kogan Page.

Stanton, N. (1990), *Communication*, Macmillan Education.

Sussams, J. E. (1993) (2nd edn), *How to Write Effective Reports*, Gower.

Wainwright, G. (1984), *Report Writing: A New Practical Guide to Effective Report Writing Presented in Report Form*, Management Update.

Contents

5

MAKING PRESENTATIONS

WHY IS THIS SKILL IMPORTANT?

In your professional practice you are likely to have to make a presentation to other people, e.g.:

◆ your colleagues, managers
◆ actual clients (local, national or international)
◆ potential clients (local, national or international)
◆ the media
◆ members of the public

The presentations could cover a wide range of areas, e.g.:

◆ sales
◆ sales conferences
◆ tenders for work
◆ business launches
◆ public inquiries
◆ fund raising
◆ videoconferencing

Whatever the occasion, and whatever the size of the audience, you need to make the best of your case and yourself.

We suggest you use this chapter:

◆ to help you prepare for an actual presentation
◆ to refer to before you begin any preparatory work.

By the end of this chapter you should be able to:

1 select material which is appropriate for the purpose, audience and context
2 structure material for the purpose, audience and context
3 prepare relevant visual aids effectively and at appropriate junctures
4 use language, tone and manner (including non-verbal behaviour) suited to the purpose, audience and context, and which draw on the presenter's personal style
5 encourage audience participation (e.g. questions) and respond effectively
6 actively check audience understanding, observe audience reaction and make appropriate responses
7 for group presentations, allocate tasks which make best use of individual abilities and expertise
8 evaluate your own effectiveness in giving presentations and apply strategies for improvement.

See Chapter 1 for the relationship between these learning outcomes and the Key Skills qualifications.

1 INTRODUCTION

···················

1.1 Your existing skills

If you have given a presentation before, you may find it helpful to review your existing presentation skills in order to identify where you need to improve.

These are listed below and you can rate yourself against each item, where 1 = 'very good' and 4 = 'in need of considerable attention'.

Existing skills	1	2	3	4
Before the presentation				
Identifying the purpose of the presentation				
Identifying audience characteristics and needs				
Identifying the time available				
Checking out the room/location, its facilities and seating				
Selecting material to use				
Structuring material				
Having useful speaker's notes				
Preparing and using visual aids				
During the presentation				
Dressing appropriately				
Being organised				
Time keeping				
Your voice and manner				
Handouts				
Combating nerves				
Using group members in group presentations				
Working with your audience:				
◆ relating to your audience				
◆ responding to audience reactions				
◆ dealing with interruptions/hecklers				
◆ summarising the discussion.				

1.2 What makes a presentation good?

If you can do all the above your presentation should be satisfactory, but you could make it better. What makes a presentation really good?

It may help to think of individuals you know (*a teacher, colleague, salesperson, politician*) and identify what makes them good or bad presenters. Does the situation in which the presentation takes place influence what is appropriate?

Presenter	What they do

Could you now turn your notes under 'what they do' into criteria against which to judge your own presentations?

2 THE CONTEXT

2.1 Purpose

Is the presentation to inform, train, persuade, entertain, sell, demonstrate? Being clear about its purpose helps you decide what to include or omit, and what approach to use. For example:

- if the presentation is to **inform** or **explain** it helps to have a logical order and to use examples and analogies (*e.g. 'It's a bit like … '*).
- if the presentation is to **persuade** it helps to be convincing, use evidence and show enthusiasm.

You also need to identify your objectives. What do you want to achieve by the end of the presentation? Your objectives may be much more specific than your overall purpose.

Purpose	Objectives

2.2 The audience

◆ Who will your audience be?
◆ What will they expect or need?
◆ How many will there be?
◆ What will their interests and level of knowledge be?

To pitch a presentation correctly you must consider the audience, *e.g. in terms of their level of knowledge, the degree of formality and the type of language used.*

Audience characteristics	What I need to do in my presentation to allow for these characteristics

2.3 Time

How long will your presentation be? Audience attention tends to diminish after the first 10 minutes, to reach a low point after 30 minutes and then increase in the last 10 minutes.

Twenty minutes is probably the maximum time for an effective presentation. More than that can be tedious for the audience. If you have longer than 20 minutes to fill, you could try to break up your presentation up with different types of activities (see later sections for suggestions).

You need to work out the timing carefully. If you go over time, the audience may be unhappy (they may have other activities to go to, other pressures). Will you allow time for questions? If it is a group presentation, how will you divide the time between the presenters?

2.4 The room

The location and seating arrangement can influence what you do. It helps to look at the room in advance. Avoid having too large a gap between you and the audience. The greater the gap, the more difficult interaction between you and the audience will be.

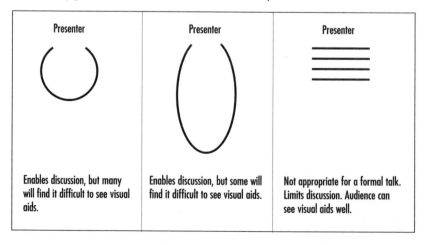

3 PREPARING MATERIAL

....

Preparing your material in good time reduces anxiety and knowing your topic well increases confidence. If preparing for a group presentation, you need to come to a clear agreement on who is preparing what material. Putting it in writing can avoid confusion.

3.1 Selecting material

Chapter 6, Gathering and Using Information, will help you assemble your information. You should then consider how to select your material bearing in mind your aims, the audience, the time allowed and the room. The following questions may help.

What material is relevant to my aims and audience?

What key messages do I want to put across?

How long will it take to deliver the material (a rehearsal, possibly in front of someone else, may help you to find out)?

What are the absolute essentials (audiences tend to be able to take in less than you think)?

What could I omit if I run out of time?

What could be added if I have time to spare?

3.2 Structuring the material

How could the material be ordered? You could write it up, get an overview and decide on an order, or write the main points on cards and shuffle them until the best order emerges.

General rules are as follows:

◆ tell them what you are going to tell them (the beginning).
◆ tell them (the middle).
◆ tell them what you have told them (the end).

TELL THEM WHAT YOU ARE GOING TO TELL THEM (THE BEGINNING)

Making the format clear to the audience at the start tells them what to expect (*e.g. 'We will leave questions until the end'; 'Please ask questions as we go through'*). Outline the content you will cover (*e.g. 'I am going to describe the project and its outcomes'*).

You need to set the tone and grab attention. Do something you feel comfortable with. Beginnings can include:

◆ a question
◆ a true story
◆ a provocative statement
◆ a quotation
◆ a visual aid
◆ a joke (but take care – if it is not funny, it can embarrass)
◆ a surprise (*e.g. a surprising statistic*).

TELL THEM (THE MIDDLE)

Ordering the material into 'chunks' rather than flitting from one point to another helps the audience to follow you. You need to decide on the best order for your 'chunks' (*e.g. if you are describing a project you could 'chunk' by background, purpose, process, outcomes*). The following questions may help:

◆ are you explaining something where one step follows from another?
◆ is date or time order important?
◆ do you need to give one side of an argument, then the next?
◆ what will the audience want to hear first (*e.g. they may be less interested in the process of your project than in the outcomes – perhaps they should be first*). What seems the most logical order is not always the best one.

Without structure audiences can become confused or bored. The following are ways of creating structure:

◆ **verbal clues** (*e.g. 'We've looked at the background to the project; now we'll look at what we actually did'*).
◆ **visual aids** (*e.g. a new overhead projector (OHP) slide can signal a change of topic or new point*).
◆ **varied activities** (*e.g. asking for questions, asking if the audience have understood before moving on*).
◆ for group presentations, using **different presenters** (*e.g. 'Now Jane will look at…'*).

TELL THEM WHAT YOU HAVE TOLD THEM (THE END)

Possible ways of ending the presentation include the following:

◆ briefly repeat the main points and draw them together.
◆ refer to your objectives for the presentation.
◆ emphasise the main point or 'angle'.
◆ some of the 'beginnings' can be useful here too – *e.g. a visual aid or an anecdote*.
◆ if discussion was involved, review the main points or future implications (*e.g. 'It looks like we need to focus on … in the future'*).
◆ thank the audience.

3.3 Speaker's notes

Speaker's notes are important, especially if you are nervous, but listening to a speaker reading a script can be boring for the audience. There are various ways of making notes, and you should choose the one which works for you:

◆ **cards**. Put each main point with notes on a card and number the cards.
◆ **OHP slides**. Use them to remind you of the main points.
◆ **notes under bold headings** on sheets of paper. Margins can be used to indicate how long each section should take (and, in group presentations, who is covering it).
◆ **fully written-out text**. Use this method for difficult sections, but rehearse, and use the notes to reassure, not to read from. Highlighting key words/phrases may help you. If you are nervous it is very tempting to read fully written-out text and this can be boring for the audience. If you think you may do this, use another method for your notes.
◆ **mind maps**. See example opposite.

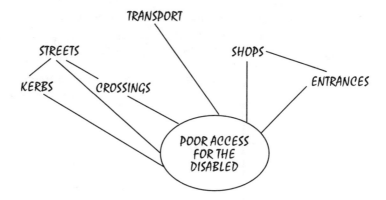

4 PREPARING AND USING VISUAL AIDS

....

> Visual aids grab attention, help the audience understand, make the presentation look professional, and help you if you are nervous (the audience will look at the visual aid – not at you).

4.1 Preparation

They should be clear, usable, visible, so make them big and bold, avoid pastel colours and keep words to a minimum if using an OHP. What would have more impact as an OHP slide – using the above paragraph or the format below?

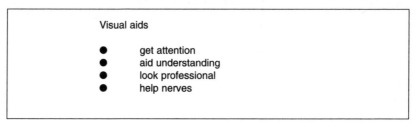

Visual aids

- get attention
- aid understanding
- look professional
- help nerves

Aim to keep visuals simple – making them complex can cause problems.

4.2 Usage

Visual aids should support what you are saying. They add emphasis and variety to your presentation and must serve a clear purpose.

◆ Use enough visual aids, *e.g. change your visual aid whenever you move to a new section or major point*. If you use OHP aids or a computer presentation, you need five or six for a 10-minute presentation (inexperienced presenters tend not to use enough visual aids).
◆ But ... an audience cannot focus on too many things at once, so try not to use too many visual aids (think of watching friends' holiday slides!).
◆ The more nervous you are, the more you should use visual aids. If you don't the audience will focus on you. If you do they will focus on the visual aids.
◆ Remember to refer to the visual aids as the audience will be confused if you don't.
◆ When using visual aids always look at the audience, not at the aids.
◆ Point to the OHP slide on the projector and not at the image on the screen.
◆ Circle any figures in a table to which you intend to refer.
◆ It may be helpful to provide copies of visual aids for the audience.
◆ Be careful about using a presentation to try out something new.
◆ Practise using visual aids in advance.

Different visual aids suit different purposes:

	Visual aid	Good for...	Cautions
Simple/cheap ↑	Black/whiteboard	Spontaneous use, simple messages permanent background information	Have spare pen, dry wipe for whiteboards, chalk, duster, rubber Use quickly Can interrupt the flow of your talk
	Flipchart	Background information, revealing successive bits of 'story' Can record ideas from discussions and keep for future reference Can be prepared in advance	Cumbersome to use Needs to be bold Leaving it up can distract
	Overhead projector (OHP)	Prepared slides or acetates which can be written on during presentation Can have complex 'overlays' of slides	Turn off when not using Cover words not referring to as can distract Get slides in right order (paper between each one helps) Check the slides are the right way up and that all the slide appears on the screen Learn to focus in advance Remove when finished
	Slide projector	Real photos Makes an impact	Use preloaded magazine Check slides are the right way up Learn to focus in advance Can leave slides on too long/short a time Can inhibit discussion
	Video	Real/live input Entertaining	Load, rewind, check sound/picture in advance Be selective for quality and quantity
	Computer based, e.g. *Powerpoint*	Can project via computer Can use special effects, *e.g. fade in/out* Can move easily between slides	Needs equipment (*computer, screen* etc.) Check carefully in advance (can crash) Practise using
	Film	Real/live input Entertaining	Have a projectionist Preview the material Have a contingency plan in case the film breaks
Expensive/complex ↓	Objects (models, experiments, products)	Demonstrations Makes an impact Explains a process Makes a dry subject interesting	Model/experiment – ensure it will work and is big enough to see Allow time to pass items round the audience Can distract them from listening

5 THE DELIVERY

····················

5.1 Clothes

Dress appropriately and in a way which makes you feel comfortable. Here you need to return to section 2.2, the audience. What will they expect? What impression will your clothes have on them? What are their conventions?

How you dress can:

◆ build or reduce your confidence
◆ tell the audience how seriously you regard them
◆ set the tone (formal, informal)
◆ give messages about you (your lifestyle, your interests, your tastes)
◆ indicate your level of professionalism
◆ relate to ethical practice (see Chapter 10, Ethics at Work, *e.g. women having bare arms and short skirts for a Moslem audience*)
◆ make you look at ease or nervous (*e.g. if you wear a watch or earrings, will you fiddle with them?*).

Ask advice from colleagues or from those organising the event.

5.2 Organisation

Being well organised helps. Try, within the room's limits, to organise seating in advance or just before the presentation starts. Arriving at the last minute means you can be thrown off balance if all is not as expected. Check all the technical equipment in advance.

Have your notes and visual aids handy and ordered – being unable to find something can fluster you.

5.3 Time keeping

Put your watch where you can see it easily or, for group presentations, give each other warnings (*e.g. 'You've got two minutes left'*). Do not overrun! This leaves other speakers less time, can ruin the organisation of the event and can bore the audience.

Be tough on timing. Allow a specific time for each section and move on (*e.g. 'I'm afraid we need to move on if we are going to cover everything', 'Can we stop at that point and move on?'*).

How much audience participation do you want? Allowing 10 minutes for questions or discussion at the end is easy to plan for. Have extra material available in case the audience keeps quiet.

5.4 Voice and manner

Identify any possible problems with your voice. Tips include:

◆ speak slowly – consciously slow yourself down. It is very hard to hear if somebody 'gabbles'.
◆ if you are a woman, speaking slowly is particularly important – a mixture of a high-pitched voice and speaking too fast may make it very hard to hear what you say.
◆ speak to an imaginary person at the back of the room (i.e. project your voice).
◆ avoid potentially irritating, frequently repeated speech mannerisms (*e.g. 'yeah', 'uhuh', 'OK', 'fine', 'good'*).
◆ if you suspect that your voice sounds monotonous break your speech up: use visual aids; ask questions of the audience; change pace; use pauses.

Turning your back on the audience or looking at the screen on the wall may prevent them from hearing you and break 'rapport'. Use a pointer (such as a pen).

In group presentations the behaviour of those not currently speaking can distract – *e.g. chatting, passing notes, looking uninterested.*

You also need to avoid physical mannerisms such as fidgeting or swaying.

5.5 Using your personal style

It is important to know and play to your strengths and to identify your weaknesses and allow for them. If you are a terrible joke teller, it is better to avoid jokes; if you are very good at visuals, you could emphasise visual aids. Once you have identified your strengths and weaknesses, you must decide what to do about them.

For example:

Strengths	Weaknesses
Funny	Nervous
Strong voice	Fidgeting
Open manner	Too quiet
Good sense of timing	Rambling/over wordy
Concise/pithy	Unfocused
Relaxed	Aggressive
Provocative	Defensive

What are yours?

Strengths	Weaknesses

How could you maximise your strengths? For example:

◆ **humour**. Devise a way of fitting your particular brand of humour into the presentation.
◆ **good sense of timing**. Consider incorporating different types of short inputs.
◆ **provocative**. Give the audience a chance to react to your statements and space to challenge or argue.

How can you allow for weaknesses? If you find it difficult to think of solutions to your particular problems, you could ask colleagues for ideas. You may find a training course helpful. For example:

◆ your **mannerisms**, *e.g. swaying, playing with your hair, covering your mouth, fidgeting*. Identify any irritating mannerisms by asking others for feedback or videoing your presentation. Then decide what practical things you do about them (*e.g. give your hands something to do such as hold prompt cards*).
◆ **quiet voice**. Practise projecting your voice. Use lots of visual aids, rearrange the seating, use a microphone if you have a large audience.

Actions I can take

5.6 Handouts

Use handouts to emphasise or remind the audience of points in your presentation. When will you give them out?

◆ If you give them out at the start, the audience may read them rather than listening to you.
◆ If you give them out at the end, the audience may be irritated if they have made notes unnecessarily (you could tell them at the start that they do not need to make notes).
◆ Will they need to look at the handout while you are talking to them?

6 NERVES

....

Being prepared and organised can be the biggest help in combating nerves, as can:

◆ rehearsing in advance
◆ using visual aids to direct attention away from you and on to the visuals
◆ wearing something to give you confidence, appropriate dress for the audience
◆ sitting/standing in a comfortable position
◆ reminding yourself that everybody feels nervous; audiences often don't notice nerves and, if they do, will make allowances
◆ asking what is the worst thing that could happen and preparing for it (*e.g. drying up? Have good speaker's notes to prevent drying up. Awkward questions? Prepare answers in advance to any potential awkward questions*)
◆ trying to relax; relaxation techniques include deep breathing, tensing and then relaxing muscles, visualising a pleasant scene – leaving everything to the last minute will also increase tension
◆ having a glass of water at hand.

What do you usually do when you are nervous? What could you do about it? Identifying the symptoms may make the solution obvious, *e.g. if you fidget with your hair hold cue cards to give your hands something to do, if you sway sit down or stand against something, but avoid leaning.* Who or what might help? You may find Chapter 15, Dealing with Pressure, helpful.

My symptoms of nerves are ...	Actions I could take are ...

7 USING GROUP MEMBERS IN GROUP PRESENTATIONS

If you are giving a group presentation, it may help to refer to Chapter 12, Working in Teams. How can you use all the group members in the presentation, and how can you exploit their particular skills and minimise their weaknesses?

When allocating roles, consider the following:

◆ who knows more about/has a special interest in a topic?
◆ who could attract the audience's attention at the start?
◆ who is good at explaining detail?
◆ who is good at using projectors, videos, models?
◆ who is good at fielding questions?
◆ who can put forward a point of view strongly?
◆ who can appear sympathetic or open and encourage the audience to speak?

Group member	Task/role in the presentation

8 WORKING WITH YOUR AUDIENCE

8.1 Relating to your audience

Good presenters engage with the audience. You might refer back to your observations in section 1.2. How do good presenters do this?

Use the following checklist to assess your skills and add any other items you can think of. Which skills or behaviours do you use now and which could you try to do more frequently?

Audience engagement/skills/behaviours	Use now	Could use more
Maintain eye contact (not with one person, but scanning the audience)		
Ask if they can hear you or see the visual aids		
Check they are comfortable. Do the windows need to be opened/shut?		
Make references to them and their interests or needs		
Ask if they have understood		
Ask for questions		
Ask if anybody has different or additional views or information		
Watch for signs of boredom or restlessness (looking at watches/out of windows/yawning/dropped heads and slumped shoulders/putting coats on)		
Watch for signs of irritation (body language such as sitting on the edge of seats, facial expressions)		
Watch for those who want to speak (hands up, sitting forward, mouths open, interruptions)		
Use non-patronising language, avoid jargon		
Others (please list)		

8.2 Responding to audience reactions

How do you respond to an audience's reaction to your presentation? Part of the answer to this depends on your personal style.

DEALING WITH NON-VERBAL RESPONSES

You may sense your audience's reaction by observing their behaviour. If people appear bored or restless, you could:

◆ move on to another section
◆ use a visual aid
◆ ask them a question or for an opinion
◆ finish quickly.

If people look irritated, you could:

◆ ask for their opinions and deal with the irritation.

DEALING WITH QUESTIONS

If you encourage audience participation you are likely to generate questions or comments. This should not be difficult if you are well prepared.
   How can you deal with questions?

◆ Check that you understand the question.
◆ Be polite.
◆ Your responses should be appropriate and professional, *e.g. not patronising* (see Chapter 10, Ethics at Work).

◆ In a group presentation, select somebody to chair the questions session so that questioners address that person. S/he checks what the question means and then asks somebody in the group to reply. The 'chair' also decides how many questions to take, and when to end the session.

You should respond to questions in a way with which you are comfortable but you also need to be able to handle the consequences. What are other possible responses and their consequences? For example:

Possible response	Advantages	Disadvantages
Response with humour	Releases tension	The audience may feel put down
Response with a challenge	Generates discussion	May lead to an argument
Calming response	Reduces tension	The audience may feel patronised
A straight answer	Creates trust and openness	The audience may disagree
'I'm afraid I don't know, does anybody else?'	Honesty may be appreciated	There may be silence – nobody else may know
'What do you think?' (back to the questioner)	Questioner is flattered	Questioner is put on the spot
'I wonder if Jane can answer that?'	OK if Jane knows the answer	Jane may be annoyed
'Could I arrange to discuss this afterwards?'	Questioner is satisfied they will get an answer	Questioner may persist Audience may want the answer
'I don't know, but I'll find out for you'	Shows commitment	Shows your lack of information

If you waffle or answer a different question, you may cause irritation or lack of respect.

What are your concerns in dealing with questions (*e.g. you could think of questions you have been asked in the past*)? What could you do about them?

Concerns	Possible actions

8.3 Dealing with interruptions/hecklers

Interruptions may come from your audience (*e.g. chatting, hecklers*), or be from outside and beyond your control (*e.g. aircraft noise, drills, fire alarms*). You may have to think on your feet, but your manner when dealing with interruptions is important. You should appear:

◆ self-confident
◆ calm
◆ firm, yet polite.

You can often turn interruptions to your advantage, *e.g. a persistent heckler may irritate the audience so much that they are on your side.* In general your audience will be sympathetic to interruptions which are beyond your control, although it could be helpful to check out in advance if there are any possible difficulties, *e.g. flight paths, building work.*

If the interruption is from someone you know is important, you may choose to respond immediately.

The following are some suggestions for strategies:

◆ use pauses
◆ look directly at 'chatterers'
◆ use humour if you are confident
◆ be wary of patronising or belittling
◆ 'I appreciate you have a point of view, but I'd prefer to take questions at the end – thank you'
◆ 'I'm sorry to interrupt, but it would be helpful if others could hear'
◆ challenge the interrupter or chatterer (*e.g. 'Perhaps you'd like to tell us what you think?'*)
◆ ask them politely to be quiet (*e.g. 'I'd like to move on and I sense that the audience would like that too. Thank you'*)
◆ look at Chapter 14, Putting Your Case: Negotiating and Assertiveness.

What strategies could I use?

8.4 Reviewing

Ask yourself after your presentation how you responded to the audience, what worked and what you would do differently in future.

Audience reaction	My response	What I'd do in the future

9 PRESENTATION CHECKLIST

Are you prepared? The following checklist can act as a reminder.

Identify aims	
Identify audience characteristics	
Identify time allowance for the presentation	
Check out the room	
Get material together	
Decide on a format and structure	
For group presentations, divide up roles and tasks for preparation and on the day	
Make speaker's notes	
Prepare visual aids	
Prepare the delivery: ◆ the beginning ◆ the middle ◆ the end	
Prepare for the question session	
Prepare to cope with nerves	
Be organised on the day	

You might find it helpful to use some of the following strategies:

◆ watch others' presentations (there may be videos available in some libraries)
◆ look at Chapter 15, Dealing with Pressure
◆ ask others how they manage presentations
◆ attend a presentation training course.

10 REVIEWING YOUR PERFORMANCE

A way to improve your skills is to think through what you did afterwards, and ask for feedback from your audience. You could do this verbally, one to one, or you could hand out an evaluation form seeking feedback on areas to which you want to give attention. After your presentation the following checklist could help you to identify actions needed for the next one.

Preparation
Using my personal style
Timing
Combating nerves
Use of visual aids
Using group members in group presentations
Relating to the audience
Responding to the audience

11 REFERENCES AND BIBLIOGRAPHY
....

Libraries may have materials on this skill area. The following give examples.

Bernstein, D. (1988), *Put It Together. Put It Across. The Craft of Business Presentation*, Cassell.

Peel, M. (1990), *Improving your Communication Skills*, Kogan Page.

Peel, M. (1992), *Successful Presentation in a Week*, Hodder & Stoughton.

Stanton, N. (1990), *Communication*, Macmillan.

VIDEOS

The Floor is Yours Now – A Guide to Successful Presentations, GSV (24 minutes).

We Can't Hear You at the Back (part of a series: Work is a Four Letter Word), BBC, 1992 (30 minutes).

LASER DISC

Discovering Presentations, Longman Training/British Telecom, 1991 (interactive).

Contents

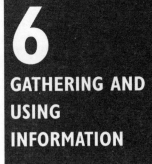

6

GATHERING AND USING INFORMATION

WHY IS THIS SKILL IMPORTANT?

We live in an information society where it is not just a question of knowing the information, but of knowing where to find it. Sources of accurate and up-to-date information are crucial because they underpin decision making. Better information can lead to better decisions.

You may be judged on the quality of the information you gather, and on the sources you use. It is important to identify and evaluate reliable sources.

We suggest you use this chapter:

◆ in relation to a particular piece of work, such as a project, report or presentation.

By the end of this chapter you should be able to:

1 find sources of information relevant and sufficient for the purpose and audience
2 use a variety of media and evaluate their usefulness for the purpose
3 use effective reading and observing strategies, e.g. skimming, scanning, in-depth reading or viewing
4 identify the meaning of professional and technical terminology
5 identify the main points or issues of relevance to the topic
6 accurately record sources of information
7 interpret information and identify factors, including your own response, which influence the interpretation, identifying any reasons for bias and distortion
8 criticise and evaluate information, using supporting evidence
9 evaluate your own effectiveness in gathering and using information and apply strategies for improvement.

See Chapter 1 for the relationship between these learning outcomes and the Key Skills qualifications.

1 YOUR EXISTING SKILLS

....

You will have used this skill already, for example in education or the workplace. It may help to begin by reviewing your existing skills.

Rate your abilities against each item below using a scale in which 1 = 'very good' and 4 = 'needs considerable improvement'.

Basic information skills	1	2	3	4
Analysing the task				
Identifying why you need the information				
Identifying who you need it for				
Identifying where you might find the information				
Meeting deadlines for gathering information				
Recording information (e.g. your filing systems)				
Using the information (e.g. reading techniques for covering a lot of material, knowing when you have enough information, answering your questions)				
Interpreting and evaluating the information				

2 WHAT IS YOUR PURPOSE?

....

It is important to start by being clear about what information you need, why and who you need it for, or you may find it difficult to stay focused.

2.1 Who is the information for? Why do they want it?

Why you want the information and for whom will influence the amount and depth of information needed as well as the focus. You may be gathering information for use by others (*e.g. in a report*) or you may be gathering it for your own purposes only to help you with a particular job.

Consider the following for the particular piece of information you have in mind:

Who is the information for?

Why do I/they want it? What will the information be used for (its purpose)?

Will the information be presented to others? If so, how? *E.g. report, presentation.*

2.2 Analysing the task

Any information seeking starts with a main question. This can then be broken down into a list of further questions. What questions do you need to address for the piece of work you need to do?

Main question
Subquestions

2.3 When do you need it by?

How much time you have can influence how you go about collecting information, and how much you can gather.

How long will it take to find the information? It is easy to underestimate this.

- If you need to write off for information, allow a minimum of two weeks for replies.
- If you need to gather information from other people, they may be busy and unable to respond immediately.
- If you are unfamiliar with computers and searching for information using them (*e.g. via the Internet*), have you added on time for learning to use them?

This implies planning ahead. You may find it helpful to refer to Chapter 2, Planning and Managing Your Workload.

3 RECORDING INFORMATION

In deciding how to record information, it is important to ask the following questions.

- How will I use it? Refer back to your purpose (Chapter 4, Report Writing, and Chapter 5, Making Presentations, may be useful here).
- Do I need it for this task only, or might I need it again?
- Will others need to find my source of information?
- Will it be presented to others? In what form?

You must also consider the following ethical and legal issues when recording information.

- **Copyright**. How much of the material can you reproduce? Will you need permission to use it?
- **Referencing**. To help you find published material again and others to find your source information, and to avoid accusations of copying others' work, you must reference it (see section 3.1).
- **Confidentiality**. Some information may be classified or you may get information from another person who does not want to be named.
- **Integrity and reliability**. Is it true? Is it accurate? Who says?

Chapter 7, Keeping Notes, Records and Minutes, may be helpful to look at.

3.1 Referencing

To help you and others find your source of information again, you need to record details which will help you do so. It is also important that others, *e.g. decision makers*, know that the source of your information is valid and reliable. Therefore, you need to reference your sources using a standard format which provides all the relevant information.

For example, if you are using the information in a formal written piece (*e.g. a report*) you need to follow accepted conventions in referring to others' work. Even if you are using it more informally, or for your own purposes, it may help to be able to find it again. For these reasons it is a good idea to get into the habit of always recording sources of information in your notes. This section tells you about the formal conventions of referencing so that you can see what information to record.

This means that you need to keep accurate records of references during your information gathering to avoid having to go back and recheck them. It is helpful to keep a note of page numbers for any information you are likely to refer to or copy, *e.g. quotations, tables of figures*.

If you are recording your information in writing (*e.g. in a report*), you will need to follow accepted conventions used to refer to others' work. The following gives examples.

If you refer to someone else's work in your text, you need to indicate where it comes from. You need to do this when you:

◆ **use quotations**. Use single or double quotation marks. Give the publication date and page number. *Drew and Bingham suggest that 'poor spelling can detract from the content of your report' (1999: 46)*.
◆ **summarise/explain the ideas of other writers**. For a general comment, give the surname of the author(s) and year of publication. *Poor spelling can affect a report (Drew and Bingham, 1999)*.
◆ **refer to a specific idea or piece of information**. Also give the page number. *The use of weak grammar, such as writing as you speak, leaves readers with a poor impression (Drew and Bingham, 1999: 46)*.
◆ **mention the writer in your text**. Do not give the name again in brackets. *Drew and Bingham (1999) suggest that poor spelling and grammar can give the reader a poor impression*.

At the end of your report you should list the works which you have used, in alphabetical order according to surname. Normally a list of **references** includes only those works mentioned on the text, whereas a **bibliography** may also contain other texts which might be helpful for the reader. (See the 'References and bibliography' section at the end of this chapter.)

Each **book reference** should include the following in this order:

◆ author surname, initial
◆ year of publication (in brackets)
◆ title (underlined or in italics)
◆ publisher
◆ place of publication (not always required).

E.g. Drew, S. and Bingham, R. (1997) *The Student Skills Guide*, Gower, Aldershot.
  For each **article reference**, you need:

◆ author surname, initial
◆ year of publication (in brackets)
◆ title of the article (in quotation marks)
◆ title of the journal (underlined or in italics)
◆ volume number
◆ issue number in brackets
◆ page number.

E.g. Parsons, D. E. and Drew, S. K. (1996) 'Designing group project work to enhance learning: key elements', *Teaching in Higher Education*, 1(1): 65–80.

For each **media reference**, e.g. video:

◆ author
◆ date of publication
◆ format and length
◆ accompanying material.

E.g. Main, A. (1987) *Study patterns: introductory programme plus units 1–4*, 3rd edn, Audio Visual Services, University of Strathclyde: Guild Sound and Vision, VHS videocassette, 3 hrs and booklet.

3.2 Storing information

Given your purpose for gathering information, what are the best ways to keep it? You could use:

◆ manual methods, *e.g. card index, loose-leaf folder*
◆ computerised methods, *e.g. wordprocessor, spreadsheet, database*. This could save considerable time and effort, particularly if the information has to be presented in some way, *e.g. as a report*. However, it may take some time to set up or learn to use the package.

Whatever your method, you need to keep it in some sort of order which will enable you to locate it easily, *e.g. by author or by topic*.
  It is important to examine critically what you are doing.

◆ Is your way of keeping information efficient?
◆ Are there better methods?
◆ Can you find information easily and quickly?
◆ If it is computerised, can you easily put it into new formats (*e.g. a table, chart or other visual display*)?

You may find it helpful to refer to Chapter 7, Keeping Notes, Records and Minutes.

Ways in which I could keep information

4 FINDING
INFORMATION
....

4.1 Current skills

How would you rate yourself on the following aspects of information-finding, where 1 = 'very good' and 4 = 'needs considerable improvement'? Where do your ratings suggest you need to improve? This section covers all these items.

	1	2	3	4
Using information sources				
Using imaginative approaches to finding sources				
Using initiative in finding information				
Using computers to find information				
Persevering in finding information				
Knowing when you've got enough information				

4.2 Information sources

Information can be divided into two categories:

PRIMARY SOURCES

This is information obtained directly from its original source, *e.g. the findings of a survey you have carried out*. It is also referred to as raw data or first-hand material. It is generally used when secondary sources are unavailable, when the problem needs the most current information, or where the situation is unique or specific to your organisation. It is usually more costly to collect information from these sources, but it can be helpful and convincing in decision-making.

SECONDARY SOURCES

Secondary data is where you are using information collected and presented by somebody else, *e.g. material from trade journals, accounting or personnel data*. Secondary data is often used to find out what other individuals or organisations have done.

The main sources you use will depend on your purpose. Some examples of primary and secondary sources are given below:

Primary sources – examples	Secondary sources – examples
Files and records, including computerised data in your organisation (*e.g. memos, reports, minutes*) Experiments Interviews Observations Questionnaires Consultants, colleagues, clients, the public Focus groups	Trade journals, periodicals, magazines, newspapers Books Documents (*e.g. government reports, bulletins brochures*) Internet Libraries Other people Directories, *e.g. Kompass*

4.3 Using imagination

For example, imagine you need to gather information on cigarette smoking. You could investigate who would be interested in smoking as an issue and identify where you would find information produced by them.

How could you become more aware of sources of information? Possibilities include:

◆ discussing it with colleagues, including those in other functional departments
◆ being alert to the media (newspapers, TV or radio programmes may spark off ideas)
◆ asking specialists
◆ asking people in relevant outside organisations, *e.g. your professional body.*

Who might be interested in smoking as an issue?	Possible sources of information
Politicians	*Hansard* and newspapers (on CD-ROM)
Health Service	Local NHS HQ, leaflets in doctors' surgeries, *Health Statistics, Medline CD-ROM, ASSIA CD-ROM, CTI PLUS CD-ROM*
Employers	Employers, employers' organisations, e.g. CBI, local Chamber of Commerce
Trade unions	Directories, Industrial Society, trade union offices
Tobacco manufacturers	Advertising directories, trade directories
People with tobacco-related illnesses, or their relatives	*Directory of Pressure Groups, Charities Digest*
Civil liberties groups	*Directory of Pressure Groups*
Pubs, transport companies, fire brigade, etc., etc.	etc., etc., etc.

4.4 People

People can be a great source of information. Networking is an important skill which can help you be effective at work. Indeed, most of the information we find at work comes via other people (Chapter 14, Putting Your Case: Negotiating and Assertiveness could help in seeing how to approach others). Others may know the information, know where you could find it or know who might know.

4.5 Using computers to find information

How would you rate yourself on the following scale, where 1 = 'very good' and 4 = 'needs considerable improvement'?

	1	2	3	4
Am I confident in using computerised systems such as a library catalogue or other databases? There are a range: bibliographic (*e.g. references to journal articles*); full-text (*e.g. a newspaper on CD-ROM*); data (*e.g. financial data about a company*).				
Can I use databases?				
Can I transfer information from a database on to a floppy disk?				
Am I confident using the Internet?				
Can I use a variety of Internet search engines?				
Do I know where I would find computer-based information, *e.g. a library, a local college etc.*?				

The above should help you identify what you need to do better. Sources of help include:

◆ your organisation may have relevant support facilities, *e.g. computing support*
◆ colleagues (most people learn IT skills from those working near them)
◆ courses/workshops which may be available through your organisation.

The Internet is an increasingly important source of information at work. If you do not have a computer which can access the Internet, could you locate one (ask colleagues, a local library)?

It may be a good use of time to spend two or three hours experimenting with computerised information. It helps to have a topic in mind and to try to locate anything on that topic. This will help you to identify which 'search engines' (i.e. systems which help you locate information) are useful and how to find routes through them.

It might help to make notes of what you did so you can remember next time. You could work with a friend or colleague to build up your confidence.

You may need to learn some 'tricks' to speed up your searches, *e.g. you may find it easier to access the Internet at certain times of day; you may find that information appears on screen quicker if you 'switch off' any visuals (these take a long time to load and may not add much to the information).*

The Internet is an area where you need to be aware of ethical behaviour (see Chapter 10, Ethics at Work).

4.6 Perseverance, or knowing when you have enough information

When seeking information are you more likely to:

◆ make a quick search and then give up?
◆ keep looking until you have every last scrap of information and not know when to stop?

Finding information is not like using a 'one-stop shop', where you get everything you need off the shelf. One source of information often leads to another, *e.g. a database may provide references to printed articles; you then need to find the articles; one article may refer to further articles.*

You may tend to search for too long and become overwhelmed by information. It helps to be very clear about your main questions and subquestions (see section 2.1). Ask yourself continually if you really need this information.

The checklist below may help.

Has the information started repeating itself?
Does the information offer anything new?
Have I covered the core material?
Have I answered my main questions/subquestions?
Is the information peripheral, not relevant to the questions, superfluous?
I can't digest any more.
I don't have any more time.

Setting realistic deadlines also helps.

Sources to use for my current piece of work	By (give deadline)

4.7 Difficulties with finding information

There are a number of possible reasons for not being able to find information. You need to know which one applies, so you know what to do about it.

Reason	Implications
People make decisions about how to organise information and they may have looked for it from an angle that is different from yours.	If in a library, try looking for it under other related subjects or try identifying other possible key words. Ask those who organise the information. Ask your colleagues.
The information might not exist.	Finding this out may mean you have to collect information from scratch yourself.
The information might exist, but not be available, e.g. it might be confidential.	This might be very useful to find out, especially if you could identify reasons for it.

5 USING INFORMATION

5.1 Covering all the information

You may have a lot of information to consider. New technology means that much more material can be found or accessed. How will you cover it all? There are three levels of helpful reading strategies. Use the first to identify what you need to look at in the second, and the second to see what you need to look at in the third.

Level	Strategy	What I currently do	What I could try
Superficial	Skimming/scanning Don't read every word, or look at every detail, instead look at: ◆ titles ◆ contents pages ◆ headings ◆ overall image (for visual items)		
Refined	Read introduction Read first and last lines of paragraphs Look at charts/diagrams Look for key words		
Detailed/in depth	Careful, thoughtful reading or observation to understand all aspects		

6 CRITICISING AND EVALUATING INFORMATION

Being critical and evaluating means not accepting information at face value, but analysing it from different perspectives – your own and other people's. The abilities to interpret, criticise and evaluate information are essential, as decisions may be based on your information.

6.1 Questioning your own assumptions

Interpreting and criticising information means questioning assumptions, including your own. Are there any possible reasons for bias in yourself about the information?

You can continually refer back to the notes you make on the next page and ask the following questions when looking at your information.

◆ Am I presenting this objectively?
◆ How would somebody with opposing views present this information?

You could ask yourself ...
Did I have a stance before I started my investigations?
What are my own views on the issue?
Why did I think like that?
Whose side am I on concerning this issue?
Are any values or political issues involved?

6.2 Questioning other people's assumptions

Might the sources of your information be biased? The following list of suggested questions could be applied to any sources of information. They will help you criticise and evaluate.

Is the information accurate? Do figures add up? Are the statistics misleading? (See Huff (1973) and Chapter 8, Using and Presenting Numerical Data.) *E.g. do they use percentages when the numbers are small; are graphs to scale?*

How up to date is the information? Is the date important? Has the information been superseded?

What is the credibility of this source? *E.g. a reputable journal may be more credible than a tabloid newspaper.*

The Internet may provide much useful information, but the sources and the information itself may not be validated or policed. You should evaluate and criticise all information carefully.

Who is the writer of the information? *E.g. do they have a good reputation in the field? What might their values/motives be and what effect would that have on the information?*

How many sources report the same findings?

Why was the information originally prepared? Was there a vested interest? *E.g. the writers of an article about a particular IT package may have a vested interest in asserting that it works well – they may be from the designing organisation.*

How selective is the coverage? Does it (perhaps deliberately) omit any information?

Are statements supported by evidence? *E.g. from primary sources.*

What is the sample on which a generalisation is based? *E.g. if it is based on a sample of two, it may be less valid than if it is based on a sample of 2000* (see Chapter 8, Using and Presenting Numerical Data).

Are there any other possible interpretations of this information? *E.g. shipment figures for personal computers may show an increase — is this because more are being sent abroad or because the data collection system has improved?*

What question was asked? *E.g.:*
Interviewer: *'Which political party do you support?'*
Respondent: *'Conservative.'*
Interviewer: *'Do you vote in elections?'*
Respondent: *'No.'*
If only the first question was used to gauge electoral support, the results might be very misleading.

Are any explanations/arguments logical and coherent? Are any steps missed out? Are there clear links from one point to another?

6.3 Distorted information

Information might be distorted intentionally or unintentionally. Can you identify distortion and the reasons for it?

Possible distortion	Example/possible queries
Highlighting an individual case and generalising from it	Child abduction – very few children are abducted, but a publicised case causes general anxiety
Personalising/anecdotes	'Trains are always late.' How often do you travel by train? Is it always the same route, or time, or day? What are the actual figures?
Graphs or diagrams not to scale	See Huff (1973) for examples of how to lie with statistics
Dubious causal relationships	If the sale of umbrellas decreased during the World Cup, would it be true to say that the World Cup caused a slump in umbrella sales, or might lower rainfall be a more plausible explanation?

You need to analyse, balance and weigh up your information.

You may find it helpful to identify what is **not** critical analysis:

◆ making assumptions
◆ making unsupported generalisations
◆ not questioning the information you have given
◆ giving information with mistakes in it or which is misleading
◆ a straight description.

It might be useful to complete the table on the following page.

What are the sources of my information?	Possible distortion/bias	What further information would satisfy me that it is useful for my purpose?

7 PROVIDING EVIDENCE

The previous section considered the questions you might ask in order to critically evaluate information. However, it may not be enough to criticise. You may need to give supporting evidence.

The information you gather is your evidence. It might consist of primary and/or secondary sources. If you have found evidence of bias or distortion you need to identify the reasons and justify why you consider the bias to exist. You may need to provide accurate references for information. Who said it? When?

What evidence can you provide for your criticisms and your evaluation of information you have gathered?

Criticism/evaluation	Evidence

8 IMPROVING YOUR SKILLS

Which aspects of gathering information do you need to improve on, and what action could you take to help you improve?

The following will help you plan ahead.

Aspects to be improved	Actions to be taken	By (deadline)

9 REFERENCES AND BIBLIOGRAPHY
....

Libraries may have materials on this skill area. The following give examples:

Bell, J. (1987), *Doing Your Own Research Project: A Guide for First-time Researchers in Education and Social Science*, Open University Press.

Cohen, L. and Manion, L. (1985), *Research Methods in Education*, Croom Helm.

Deer Richardson, L. (1992), *Techniques of Investigation: An Introduction to Research Methods*, National Extension College.

Huff, D. (1973), *How to Lie with Statistics*, Penguin.

Perry, W. G. (1970), *Forms of Intellectual and Ethical Development in the College Years*, Rinehart and Winston.

This chapter is based on 'Gathering and using information', Sue Drew, Aileen Wade and Andrew Walker, in Drew, S. and Bingham, R. (1997) *The Student Skills Guide*, Gower.

Contents

7

KEEPING NOTES, RECORDS AND MINUTES

WHY IS THIS SKILL IMPORTANT?

At work you may need to record meetings, conversations, actions agreed, project details, progress on work, information, training or conference sessions. You may consider that you have been taking notes for years perfectly adequately. Why should you reconsider this skill?

It is easy to make notes, but difficult to make good, brief, accurate notes which summarise the essence of information and which can be used and understood later. On education courses, if your notes and records are not very good only you will suffer, but at work there may be significant consequences for others. You need to have accurate records which you (and possibly others) can find and use easily.

We suggest you use this chapter:

◆ at a point when you need to make notes or minutes or to sort out records
◆ in general, to help you improve your practice in this area.

By the end of this chapter you should be able to:

1   identify the context, purposes of and the reason for the use of notes, records and minutes, including others' purposes for them (*e.g. for minutes – the main purpose of the meeting, desired goals and underlying issues*)
2   identify the main points to be noted, recorded, minuted
3   where appropriate, account for sensitive issues and hidden agendas by reporting in a way which takes matters forward constructively
4   produce notes, records and minutes with accurate information (including sources of information) and a clear meaning, which clarify the meaning of unfamiliar words, phrases and images
5   use appropriate language (*e.g. non-emotive, clear, concise, following standard conventions of grammar, punctuation and spelling*) and which emphasises meaning
6   record images which provide a clear illustration of the points
7   produce notes, records and minutes which are legible, well organised for retrieval and structured to emphasise and clarify meaning
8   produce minutes which identify follow-up action to be taken and note who will take them
9   use storage and retrieval systems and develop systems where appropriate, meeting workplace conventions
10 evaluate the effectiveness of notes and recording systems, using feedback from users and plan strategies to increase effectiveness and take action.

See Chapter 1 for the relationship between these learning outcomes and the Key Skills qualifications.

1 WHAT DO YOU DO AT THE MOMENT?

·············

1.1 Notes

It can be useful to compare your notes with someone else in a similar situation. You may find they are quite different even if you both were making notes on the same thing. Why? How?

Questions to ask in comparing notes might be:

◆ in what ways are the notes different?
◆ how are the notes organised?
◆ do you understand each other's notes?
◆ why did you include some things and not others?
◆ have they been rewritten or added to later?
◆ will the notes still make sense in a month's time? (If another person doesn't understand your notes now it is likely you won't after a time lapse.)

You may want to complete the following checklist:

> Are my notes unselective, trying to cover everything?
>
> Are my notes difficult to follow later?
>
> Do my notes highlight key points?
>
> Do my notes summarise main points?
>
> Do my notes clarify initial ideas?

1.2 Minutes

Whether you wrote the minutes or not, you could consider the following in relation to the minutes of recent meetings you have attended.

> Do the minutes tell me the main points that emerged?
>
> Do they make it clear what action is needed and by whom?
>
> Can I understand them?
>
> Could anybody who wasn't at the meeting understand them?
>
> Do they reflect what actually happened at the meeting?
>
> Did they come out soon after the meeting?

1.3 Records

It may help to discuss with colleagues what they think makes minutes good and useful.

It may help to look at what others do, *e.g. is there a central filing system you should be tapping into, do others use filing equipment which you would find helpful, could you use a computer system?*

The checklist opposite might also help.

Do I have my own filing/recording system?

Do I use a central departmental or organisational filing system?

Do I do both? Do I know what is in which?

Could others find information in my files/records (e.g. if I were on holiday)?

Do I have piles of papers on my desk or floor?

Do I have no system at all?

Can I find things easily?

Do I spend a lot of time each day looking for things?

1.4 Where to improve

Do the above checklists suggest any actions you might take to improve your notes/records/minutes?

Actions I could take

2 NOTES

2.1 Your purpose

The reason for taking notes can determine what sort of notes you make. There are examples overleaf.

Is my purpose	Examples	Possible implications	
For revision?	For professional exams	Must be understandable after a long time lapse Include all main points Make them easy to follow	
For a work project?	A project Preparation for a meeting/phone call/consultation Information for a report or other written task	Must be accurate May need to be detailed Sorted into topic areas Include basic information (to avoid having to collect it again, *e.g. if somebody wants to challenge your figures*)	
For others to use?	Projects In appraisal forms/for CPD/ professional body membership requirements (see Chapter 19) For other professionals (*e.g. as part of briefs for work*)	Must be legible Clear Use only abbreviations and words they will understand	
To record what happened?	Meetings Conversations Doctor/lawyer's consultations Appraisal meetings Interviews Focus groups	Must be accurate, detailed Others involved so may have access to them and there may be ethical issues (see Chapter 10) Record actions	
For legal purposes?	Public inquiries Tribunals (*e.g. notes of disciplinary meetings with staff*) To record accidents To provide evidence	Must be accurate Must contain information that cannot be misinterpreted	
Any other purposes?			

2.2 Selecting what to note

What do you need to make notes on and what can be omitted? If this crucial question is not addressed, you may end up with patchy notes which don't make sense or with masses of irrelevant notes.

It helps to go back to your purpose. How much detail do you need for that purpose? What are the crucial aspects of the information? Why may it be needed in future (think of recent miscarriages of justice and the role of police notes and records – your situation may not be quite so critical, but this does point to how important notes can be)?

Do you need:

◆ factual information (*e.g. costs, dates, times, amounts*)?
◆ principles, concepts, policies (*e.g. on which to base decisions or proposals*)?
◆ arguments (*e.g. justifications for decisions*)?
◆ criticism and evaluation (*e.g. to help in making decisions*)?

Correct references are required for the source of your information (see Chapter 6, Gathering and Using Information).

Are there any legal issues? For example:

◆ things you are legally required to note
◆ Data Protection Act (1984)
◆ acts relating to discrimination.

See Chapter 6, Gathering and Using Information, for help on the sort of information you need, as this will determine what to note down.

It may help to think of information in three different categories. You may not need all three – it depends on your purpose. We give an example of a project to redesign a town centre to give improved access for the disabled.

Principles, concepts, theories, arguments
Notes related to equality of provision, town planning principles, transport policies, public relations issues, standpoints of pressure groups/local traders

Relevant detailed factual information
Notes on roads, routes, shops, buildings, bus routes, car parks, paving surfaces, steps, kerbs, busiest periods, how many people it will benefit, costs

My own questions, criticisms etc.
Who stands to gain/lose, how to balance needs of the disabled against disruption/costs, who else might benefit (*e.g. people with children in pushchairs, the elderly*), what benefits are there which are hard to quantify (*e.g. improved reputation of the town*)?

How could this information best be organised? This would depend on how you were going to use the notes (*for a report to a council meeting? To help architects/planners in design work? For specifications for builders?*). Topic headings might include any of the following: pros; cons; costs; benefits; alterations needed; interest groups; etc.

For a topic you need to make notes on, it might help to try recording notes under those three categories and then to see how you might organise them into topics or sections for your purpose.

Principles, concepts, theories, arguments

Relevant detailed factual information

My own questions, criticisms etc.

How might I organise my notes into topics or sections?

2.3 *The format of your notes*

You need to consider how you wish to use the notes in order to decide how to record them. In what format would you find them helpful?

Long sentences are time consuming to write and read back. All that may be needed to reconstruct the idea are key words and phrases, or key pieces of factual information.

The following are common types of note taking.

LINEAR NOTES

Do your notes look like these?

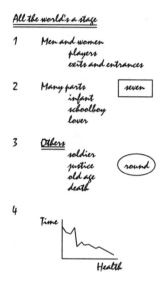

Linear notes may:

♦ contain key words and phrases
♦ use clear headings, subheadings, underlining, circles, boxes, diagrams, flowcharts and colours
♦ have margins or be written on every other line so you can return to previous parts as you get further into a document or other source
♦ have margins for your own questions, comments or criticisms (so that in the future you do not mistake your own comments for those of a trainer or author).

PATTERNS

This method uses arrows and circles to connect key words/phrases, producing a spreading pattern in all directions rather than words which start at the top of the page and work down.

It may look messy but the content can be concise and quick to read. It is also easy and quick to redraw the pattern at a later stage to make it clearer.

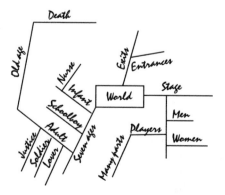

VISUAL INFORMATION It may be impossible to accurately record visual information verbally. Possibilities include:

- freehand sketches
- taking copies (but check the copyright situation, *e.g. with a library*)
- taking an accurate reference so you can find the visual again easily.

OVERALL You may want to combine linear and pattern styles in the same situation, using one piece of paper to draw patterns and another to note factual information, lists etc. Whichever type of notes you use, it helps to add a few summarising lines.

Writing notes in your own words (rather than repeating others' words) will help you to understand. It is also advisable to date and reference notes (see Chapter 6, Gathering and Using Information), *e.g. if you are making notes from text, you may need to include: title; date; author; place of publishing; publisher; chapter headings; page numbers (especially if you need to find items again).*

2.4 Sharing note taking

It can save time to share note taking – you and your colleagues can make notes on your own areas of expertise. Check that those you work with have similar purposes for their notes and make understandable, legible notes. Sharing note taking can be particularly helpful:

- in training sessions/conferences/workshops – decide who will take notes on what and discuss the notes afterwards to ensure that everyone understands them
- in team work, different people can write notes and photocopy them for the rest (but see section 3 below on minutes – the formal notes of meetings)
- divide out tasks, so that each person makes notes on different things and notes are then pooled.

2.5 Reviewing notes

You could use the following checklist to review your notes.

Short and concise? Easy to understand? Relevant? Well organised?

Review notes soon after they have been made, highlighting things you do not understand and making them clearer. It is easier to act on misunderstandings or omissions while they are fresh in your mind. Find out about things you don't understand (*e.g. from colleagues, a library, reference material, general or subject specific dictionaries, encyclopaedias, manuals etc.*). If your notes are for others in an unfamiliar context, ask them for feedback (see Chapter 17, Identifying Strengths and Improving Skills).

2.6 Retrieving notes

Will you be able to find your notes again easily? How will you store them? See section 4 below on recording information.

3 MINUTES

....

Minutes are the formal records of meetings. All formally constituted meetings have them and they are helpful for informal meetings. In formal meetings the secretary may take the minutes. This is not usually, although it may be, a secretary in the sense of somebody in a clerical role, but rather a member of the committee, working group or team (see Chapter 13, Meetings).

The main uses of minutes are:

◆ **as the basis for the next meeting**. Formal meetings start by the chairperson asking members to 'agree the minutes' of the previous meeting (to give members an opportunity to correct them).

◆ **as a record**, *e.g. of decisions and actions agreed.* The agenda for a meeting usually has 'matters arising', i.e. discussion of points from the last minutes.

3.1 Sensitivity

Minutes are a public document. All those attending the meeting and possibly others will see them. What impact might this have on the minutes for a group you are involved with (think of the actual individuals/situation)?

Suggestion	My notes
People may not like what they said being inaccurately reported	
People may not want what they said to be recorded, *e.g. criticisms of others*	
They may not want antagonisms at the meeting to be reported – it may make matters worse	
There may be hidden agendas, vested interests, 'politicking'. What might people read into the minutes?	
They may actually want others not present (who will see the minutes) to know what was said	
They may want formally to acknowledge someone's contribution	
My ideas	

Sometimes members are open about what they want (*'Please can you not minute that'*, *'Please could we minute our thanks to…'*), but often in the heat of the moment they may not think to do this, or they will assume that the minute taker will use their own judgement about what to include.

It can be very encouraging to see something important you said noted in minutes, and very embarrassing to have something you wish you had not said noted. It is important for a minute taker to be sensitive to the situation. How could you develop such sensitivity?

You could:

◆ ask the chairperson for advice
◆ find out the background to the group, to identify any hidden agendas, vested interests, or 'politicking' of which you need to be aware
◆ ask a more experienced group member to look at your minutes and alert you to any problem areas
◆ look at other minutes of similar groups in your workplace and see how they were written
◆ use the following checklist of things you might avoid.

Have I ...	
Avoided reporting word for word what was said?	
Avoided use of emotive language when expressing feelings?	
Avoided statements that attach blame to named individuals?	
Avoided humour?	
Avoided inserting things that were not actually discussed/said?	

3.2 What to include

It will help to refer back to section 2 above, as minutes are one type of notes. As with any sort of notes, they need to meet the purpose for which they are intended.

You need to know the main aim of the meeting and its goals in order to identify what to note and what are irrelevant, albeit interesting, diversions.

You need to omit unnecessary detail or repetition. Often in meetings several people may say the same thing in slightly different ways.

You need to record the main points discussed. Generally it is not good practice to report what individuals said. For example:

Jane said that the town's reputation may suffer if it shows itself to be unsympathetic to the needs of the disabled and that they might find their image suffering in comparison to other local towns and regret one day that they had not taken action earlier.

This is long winded. It may not be important who actually said it. What matters is the main point. This might be better summarised in minutes as follows, using the 'third person':

Not making better provision for the disabled might damage the town's reputation.

You must note any papers which were 'tabled'. This means papers which were distributed at the meeting rather than being sent out before with the agenda. You must note decisions taken and actions agreed, who will take the action and any deadlines.

3.3 The format of minutes

Minutes regardless of the context usually follow a standard format.

What to include	Example
Title of organisation or department. Name of group or committee.	Redtown County Council Planning Committee
Date and location of meeting (location not always required, *e.g. for internal meetings*).	22.4.99 Redtown
List of those present in alphabetical order, with the Chair and Secretary first.	Present: J. White, Chair P. Purple, Secretary A. Blue C. Green
List of those who have apologised for their non-attendance.	Apologies: K. Brown

What to include	Example
Notes using paragraph numbers that are the same as the agenda items (see Chapter 13, Meetings, on agendas). If there are several points these numbers will be subdivided. All paragraphs must be numbered to allow you to refer back to points in future meetings.	Minutes 1 Town centre access for the disabled 1.1 Building requirements Alterations will be needed to … 1.2 Traffic flow The one-way system in Market Street will …
At the end of each point actions are noted. This may be done by putting the word 'action', followed by the action to be taken/by whom/by when. Or actions can be noted in a right-hand margin.	Action. A. Blue to present a diagram of traffic flow system for the next meeting.
The penultimate item is usually 'any other business' (AOB), i.e. items not on the agenda.	8 AOB It was recommended that local groups representing the disabled be invited to attend the next meeting. Action. K. Brown to arrange by 1.5.99.
The last item is usually the date, time and place of the next meeting.	9 Date of next meeting 10.5.99, 5pm–7pm, Town Hall Chambers.

3.4 What to do with minutes

Minutes should be sent to all present, all who should have been present but could not be, and any interested parties the group decides should see them. You should attach a list indicating to whom the minutes have been sent.

Are your minutes confidential to a particular group? If so, this should be made clear in a bold way, *e.g. at the top of the minutes.*

They should be sent out as soon as possible after the meeting (*e.g. within a week*).

They should be filed with any papers which were sent out in advance or tabled and taken to the next meeting, so that the secretary can refer not only to the last meeting's minutes but to those of all previous meetings of the group.

4 RECORDING INFORMATION

....

It is important at work to keep information in a well-organised way – you can waste a lot of time looking for things, and you may lose vital information.

4.1 Your own records

How do you order notes or minutes or other information? By date order, alphabetically, numerically, by topic or subject, by 'what needs doing today/tomorrow/next week/sometime'? See Chapter 6, Gathering and Using Information, for ideas.

It is important to think about what ordering method would help you find records again most easily (or allow others to find them). How could you store your records?

Storage method	Possible advantages
Looseleaf in files	Can introduce new divisions, add extra material
Concertina file/folders	Can introduce new divisions, add extra material
Computerised database	Easy to edit
Boxed card-file system	Good for an index or references, can be stored easily, *e.g. in a card-box index you can write on the card a topic and where you have stored it*
A notebook per topic	Keeps relevant material together

How could you organise your desk and office to help you work more efficiently? What storage equipment in your office would help you? You may want to look at Chapter 2, Planning and Managing Your Workload.

4.2 Central filing systems

You may have a departmental system which you can, or are expected to, use, especially if others need access to your information. These are normally set up by people with special expertise in this area and it is important to follow their system. If you do not do so items may be lost for ever – the bigger the system the more lost it might be!

With a central or common system it is usual for an administrative member of staff to maintain it – the organisation may be worried that letting more than one person maintain it will lead to things being mislaid. In this case, the person may need guidance from you about where to file it, which means you must be familiar with the system, *e.g. you may have to write file numbers on the document.*

If you have a central or common filing system but you also keep your own records, it will be important for all concerned to know exactly what you keep where, *e.g. good labelling will mean others may be able to find things if you are not there.*

4.3 Computers

This book does not cover computer skills, but you need to be alert to the enormous possibilities they offer for recording information. The following gives suggestions. How can you find out more about computer applications?

◆ Ask colleagues
◆ Experiment with your desktop computer if you have one
◆ Ask a central computing facility in your organisation if there is one
◆ Use computer manuals.

Your computer may have templates for standard formats, *e.g. spreadsheets, databases etc.* You may use computerised databases, *e.g. for information on clients or customers.* You may use spreadsheet packages, *e.g. for recording accounts and numerical data* (see Chapter 8, Using and Presenting Numerical Data).

You might also use your computer to organise your wordprocessed work in 'folders' or 'directories' (file management). Here you create systems which are like a family tree with a main branch and subbranches. For example:

Main directory	Subdivision	Further subdivision
Sue	Employee skills Projects Publications Student skills	(for Employee skills) Keeping records, notes and minutes Gathering and using information
Rosie	Conferences Open learning Teaching	(for Open learning) Assessing open learning Writing open learning

You might organise your emails by creating 'folders', i.e. headings under which to store emails relating to a topic.

You could create a web page on the Internet for your organisation or for your area within the organisation. This might give information about your role, the role of your department, contacts etc. It would need regular updating.

5 ACTION PLANNING

Where do you need to improve your skills in keeping notes, minutes and records? There is a checklist below.

Actions to improve	By (date)
Notes	
Minutes	
Record keeping	

6 REFERENCES AND BIBLIOGRAPHY

The following give details of materials on this skill area:

Buzan, T. (1973), *Use Your Head*, BBC Publications.

Gibbs, G. (1981), *Teaching Students to Learn*, Open University Press.

Jacques, D. (1990), *Studying at the Polytechnic*, Educational Methods Unit, Oxford Polytechnic.

National Extension College (1994), *Learning Skills Resource Bank: Notes for Tutors and Trainers*, NEC.

Northedge, A. (1990), *The Good Study Guide*, Open University Press.

Stuart, R. R. (1989), *Managing Time*, The Pegasus Programme, Understanding Industry Institute.

Contents

8

USING AND PRESENTING NUMERICAL DATA

WHY IS THIS SKILL IMPORTANT?

All professionals need to use numerical information, some to greater or lesser extents. It is as essential a skill to work as is writing or communicating with others.

This chapter focuses on the sort of numerical information which any professional needs to use at work. It is not aimed at specialists using numerical data as part of their specialism, but, rather, it should:

◆ help people who have to use and make sense of specialists' numerical information
◆ help people who are not specialists but who may need to carry out a special task.

For example, it is not aimed at market researchers producing statistical data, but it might help somebody who needs to do a small market research task or to use market research information. It is not aimed at accountants who are producing financial information, but it might help somebody to do a costing exercise or to use the information provided by accountants.

The chapter aims to help you become more aware of the issues involved in using numerical data, and to identify what you need to do, rather than aiming to help you learn about mathematical or statistical operations (*e.g.* calculations). To help with this, at the end of the chapter is a list of books, with a brief description outlining how they might be useful. However, these may not be necessary, as you may be able to get all the information or help you need from those around you.

We suggest you use this chapter:

◆ when you have a specific task to do involving the use of numerical information
◆ to alert you to strategies for using numerical information and to improve your general skills in this area.

By the end of this chapter you should be able to:

1 identify a numerical task or problem
2 identify the data to be collected
3 plan and use appropriate strategies for dealing with the task or problem
4 identify sources of error and their effects
5 check that the results make sense in relation to the problem
6 evaluate the effectiveness of the strategies used
7 interpret and present data to meet the needs of the user
8 draw and justify conclusions from the data
9 evaluate your own strengths and weaknesses in regard to the above and seek support where appropriate
10 evaluate your own effectiveness in working with numerical data and apply strategies for improvement

See Chapter 1 for the relationship between these learning outcomes and the Key Skills qualifications.

1 CONFIDENCE

You may feel confident with numerical data. If so, you can move to the next section. If not (and many people are not) this section may help.

You may not feel confident with numerical data. However, you may actually be dealing successfully with numbers every day – *e.g. which of the following do you do in your personal life?*

Item	
Keep a bank account	
Pay bills	
Keep a record of bills	
Identify which financial services to use: ◆ which is the best mortgage option ◆ which bank accounts pay the best interest ◆ which holiday insurance is the best value	
Manage on a budget	
Check change	
Check bills in restaurants, shops	
Plan a journey using timetables and maps to arrive at a particular time	
Read and understand tables, graphs and charts in newspapers, journals etc.	

There are some deep-seated attitudes about numeracy, *e.g. many people believe that there is a 'right way' to do a numerical task and if they don't know that way then they can't do the task.* The reality is that most problems can be solved in various ways, using a variety of approaches, *e.g. using diagrams and charts or three-dimensional models.*

How do you normally make sense of a numerical problem? Chapter 11, Solving Problems and Making Decisions, suggests different approaches to solving problems:

◆ the logical approach – definite steps through which to go
◆ trial and error – try ideas until one works
◆ creative idea generation – think of lots of ideas
◆ rationally choose from alternatives – weigh up advantages and disadvantages.

In the context of numeracy it may be thought that the first of these is the only way, but this is not so. They can all be useful.

2 THE USES OF NUMERICAL DATA AT WORK

It may help to identify where you use numeracy at work. In considering the following, try not to be concerned with the level of numerical data or the complexity of what you had to do. Anything counts, *e.g. checking your salary slip or your tax.*

2.1 Types of task

Type of activity at work	When did I last do this at work — yesterday, last week, last month, never? What did I actually do?
Using numbers to solve a problem	
Using and understanding numerical information provided by somebody else (including graphs and charts)	
Giving somebody else numerical data, perhaps as evidence for something	
Checking numerical data, either produced by you or somebody else	

2.2 Your and other's needs

It will help to work through this chapter in relation to a task requiring you to use numerical data. The following box will help you identify a task to consider when using this chapter. We suggest you make notes in the box, using the following questions as prompts:

◆ are you likely to have to do this?
◆ why will others want the information?
◆ what will others want (*e.g. if you were receiving a request for funding, what numerical information would you want, what would you particularly look out for*)?
◆ who are the 'others' likely to be and how important will the information be to them (*e.g. will it determine whether or not you get funding or some work, or will it provide interesting background information for them*)?
◆ how familiar are they likely to be with using numerical information – what must you consider when presenting numerical information to them?
◆ where might you get guidance about these questions (*e.g. could you find examples of similar work done by others in the organisation? Could you ask colleagues for advice?*)?

Purpose	Suggested uses (you could add others)	My notes
Making decisions	As basis for decisions ... on options on needs on existing practice to project the future (trends)	
Evaluating/testing/piloting	Gathering feedback Checking on effectiveness Identifying changes needed Confirming hypotheses/concepts/ hunches	

Purpose	Suggested uses (you could add others)	My notes
Estimating costs/time/materials/ resources	Feasibility studies Tenders for work Projects Requests for funding or loans Allocating work Allocating resources	
Recording costs/time/materials/ resources	For legal purposes, *e.g. tax, annual reports* In case of queries, *e.g. payments* To maintain stock levels To identify future stock levels/ resource needs As quality control	
Providing evidence	To support a case To contradict a case	
Presentations	Reports Oral presentations Policy papers Conference, workshop, training sessions	
Others (please list)		

3 HOW WILL YOU APPROACH THE TASK?

You need to identify strategies to tackle the task. You may already be able to identify them now, or it may help to work through the rest of this chapter and then to return to the box below (section 3.2) to summarise the strategies you will use.

3.1 Getting started

The following suggests some ways of getting started in thinking about what you will do:

◆ pose the problem or describe the task in your own words (to help you understand the issues)
◆ talk about the problem or task with someone else and see how they might describe it
◆ talk to somebody else about how to tackle the problem or task. This will help you to clarify your own thinking. Do not assume that if they disagree with you in regard to how to set about the problem or task you must be wrong – there may be a number of possible routes
◆ use your intuition – your first thoughts might be very helpful
◆ think, doodle, scribble, cross out, try different ways
◆ don't immediately think 'do I know the rule for this?', it will inhibit your thinking and it is highly likely that you can use your own rules.

3.2 Identifying your strategies

The following suggests some overall strategies you might use. There will be others.

Suggestion 1	Suggestion 2	Suggestion 3
Get information/data Perhaps know some facts Make calculations Consider the results Interpret the results Consider the interpretation Present the interpretation	Order data Put things into a table Compare things Estimate Trial and error	Identify what you know and what you need to find out Identify what calculations you have to make Make the calculations Does the answer to the calculation solve the problem? Identify if you need to do something else

You can complete the box below giving your initial thoughts about your problem or task. You could return to it after having worked through the chapter to amend it.

What is the problem or task (in my own words)?	What is the aim, goal, desired outcome?	What must I do to solve the problem (e.g. subtask, processes, strategies)?	What help might I need?

You might continually review these strategies, asking yourself the following questions.

◆ Is this strategy effective? Why? Why not?
◆ What else might work more effectively?
◆ What constraints are there in relation to the strategies (*e.g. time, costs, skills*)? What could I do about these? How could I adapt my strategies to account for them?
◆ Is it the best strategy for the purpose? Why? Why not? (see section 2.2 above).

Section 11 includes a box for you to record what was effective. You could use the format of it to keep a record throughout your task, to help you when doing similar tasks in the future. This might include notes of sources of help and expertise.

4 ENSURING
ACCURACY
....

4.1 General suggestions

It is very important in using numerical data at work to be accurate, because:

◆ important decisions may be based on the data
◆ if others spot small inaccuracies it may have the effect of discrediting all your data.

How can you ensure accuracy?

Suggestions	How could I use this suggestion?
Identify how accurate you must be, in order to put in the right amount of effort. What will be the effects of any errors? Will errors in some areas of the task have more impact than in others?	
Limit the number of times you transfer data from one place to another – to reduce errors in transcription. *E.g. some computer programs enable you to design a questionnaire, read by an optical mark reader, and they then carry out calculations. If you cannot use a computer package, you can still try to reduce the number of times that data is handled.*	
Use simple rating scales. *E.g. use 1–5 rather than 1–100.*	
Ask others to check the work/a sample or part of it/your procedures. *E.g. in an audit, accountants check the methods used to process financial information and check a sample to see if they are working adequately.*	
Look at your data/answers/results and ask if they make sense or if something stands out or looks unusual. This might alert you to further checks you need to make. Or ask a colleague if it makes sense, especially someone with experience in the area.	
Use estimation to see if an answer/result looks about right. If it does not, this will alert you that there are further checks needed.	

4.2 Using a calculator

TYPES OF CALCULATOR   **Basic calculator.** This carries out the basic operations of addition, subtraction, multiplication and division. Some may be able to calculate squares and/or square roots and deal with negative numbers. In general, it may be more useful to have a scientific calculator.

Scientific calculator. This does all that a basic calculator does. It also has some mathematical functions such as sine, cosine and tangent; it allows you to input statistical data; it allows you to use brackets when inputting more complex calculations; it 'works things out' according to certain mathematical conventions.

Graphical calculators. These are mainly useful to those working with a lot of mathematics. They have a large memory, are programmable and can produce graphs.

Do you own a calculator? If so, what kind is it?	Scientific	
	Basic	
	Graphical	
What do you use it for?		

Many people do not trust the answer they get from a calculator. *E.g., what do you expect to get if you key in 5 + 3 × 2= ? Do you get 16? Or 11?*
  Can you explain how each answer is obtained?

$$5 + (3 \times 2) = 11 \qquad (5 + 3) \times 2 = 16$$

(The calculator will always give 16, as it deals with the numbers in order.)
  In dealing with numerical data you must use your own judgement and skills of estimating. You also need to experiment. One way to learn how to use a calculator is to do calculations on it for which you already know the answer.
  What sort of calculator do you need? Think about the kind of calculations you want to carry out. For example:

◆ you may wish to carry out conversions – *e.g. change quantities into percentages (in which case a percentage key would be useful; many calculators do not have one)*
◆ you may wish to substitute values into formulae that are often used in your area of work (will the calculator perform a sequence of operations in the correct order?)
◆ you may often be called on to make sense of sets of data (do you know how to use the statistical functions of a calculator?).

The explanation of the differences between types at the beginning of this section may help you to decide which sort of calculator you need.

4.3 Computers

Computers are very helpful in working with numbers, particularly where you are dealing with a lot of data. Providing that you have fed the data into the computer correctly the results will be very accurate. Many packages include a calculator and there are specialised packages, *e.g. statistical packages.* In deciding whether to use computers you might consider the following.

Question	My notes
How long will the task take to complete manually (without a computer)?	
How long will it take on the computer (including the time to obtain the software and learn how to use it)?	
If it will take me longer to do on the computer this time round, would it save me time in the future (now that I have the package and can use it)?	

Probably the most accessible type of application for most people is the spreadsheet, one of which is included in most of the packages used at work. The spreadsheet is simply a table with cells into which you insert numbers. The package can then do a variety of calculations, including adding rows and columns and changing numbers into percentages. You can usually turn the spreadsheet into graphs and charts on the computer. You need very little knowledge of computers or of making charts and graphs to do this. Once you have set up a spreadsheet for a particular task, you can use the same format again for tasks you have to repeat, such as monthly figures or accounts.

5 WHICH DATA WILL YOU USE?

....

Will you use published data (see Chapter 6, Gathering and Using Information, to see how you might identify sources of data)?

One example is the General Household Survey (GHS) conducted by the Office of Population Censuses and Surveys (OPCS). This collects information continuously from a sample of British households on issues such as population, housing, education, employment, health, family, income. Another is the Census, conducted every ten years (the local results are held in public libraries).

Will you gather the data yourself from primary sources (again, see Chapter 6)? How? You could make some preliminary notes in the following box, but we suggest that you might also find it helpful to use the rest of the chapter and then return to the box. For example, your collection of data and its analysis are closely connected. You should collect data bearing in mind how you are going to analyse it. If you do not do this you may end up with a huge task, converting information which you gathered in one way into another form.

Will you use information from published sources and also gather data yourself? How will the two be connected? It may help to see what already exists, as it may mean that you do not need to collect it yourself. Does any other department or another colleague in your organisation have data you could use?

What sort of data do I need?	Where might it already exist? (E.g. published/other departments/ colleagues.) How might I find out? (E.g. library, Internet, email to colleagues, phone calls.)	What methods might I use to collect data from primary sources? (E.g. questionnaires, observation, analyses etc.)

6 THE QUALITY OF THE DATA

....

Whether you are gathering data yourself or using data from others, you need to ensure that it is appropriate for the purpose and high quality.

The term **case** or **unit of analysis** refers to the basic unit about which information has been gathered, *e.g. if you were gathering information about cars, the unit of analysis might be a car or a particular make of car.*

In statistics, the word **population** is used to mean the total number of all the units, *e.g. the 'population' might be all the cars in the UK, or all the cars of a particular make.*

Questions (about data I am gathering or using)	My notes
What is the unit of analysis in my task?	
Can I gather information/was information gathered on all the units (*e.g. on each car in the UK, or are there too many*)?	
Do I/did they have access to each unit to gather the information (*e.g. it might be difficult to locate all the cars of a particular model*)?	

If the answer to the above questions indicates that the data cannot be gathered from all the units, i.e. the population, you will need to collect it on a sample of them. A sample should look as much like the whole as possible and share its features. These features are called **variables**, *e.g. the variables in a sample of cars might include age, make and colour.* The smaller the sample, the less likely it is that it will represent the whole.

The following questions might help you to identify if data which has been collected by others really represents what it is supposed to represent. You could also use it as a checklist to ensure that any data you gather from primary sources is appropriate (see Chapter 6, Gathering and Using Information).

Questions about the data	My notes
How big is the population?	
How many are/were there in the sample?	
What are/were the features of the units in the sample? Are these similar to the features of the population as a whole?	
How have units been grouped (somebody has decided on the grouping, *e.g. the GHS groups social classes by occupation, not by income or social background*)? Why? Could they have been grouped differently? What difference might this have made (*e.g. how have items been grouped for costing purposes*)?	
What is included in any totals? What might be missing? (*E.g. for costing purposes, has a figure for overheads been included, or for inflation, or for the unexpected — how are these calculated?*)	

Questions about the data	My notes
When was it collected? What difference might this make? (*E.g. employees might rate careers services more highly after they have found work than before.*)	
Who collected it? Might they have had a vested interest? Might their perceptions have coloured the sampling or grouping?	

Two important concepts in relation to data collection are:

◆ **reliability**. This means that data can be accurately replicated, *e.g. if you test cars and find that their gears work correctly, and when you retest them they still work correctly, your test is reliable.*
◆ **validity**. This shows that something represents what you say it represents – that it is a valid measure, *e.g. testing cars' gears while they are stationary may not be a valid test that they will work in motion.*

There is sometimes tension between these two concepts.

Questions about the data	My notes
Is my data reliable? How do I know?	
Is my data valid? How do I know?	

7 HOW DO YOU READ THE DATA?

Numbers are just a way of presenting concepts. What concept are the numbers trying to get over? Do you know what the data means? It is always worth checking out that your assumptions are correct. For example:

◆ when using computerised balance systems in accounting, sometimes a '–' sign before a figure means money which you have (income) and a '+' sign means money which has been spent (outgoings).
◆ where a complete list of data is given (*e.g. a list of individuals and their salaries*) and there is no information for a particular item on the list (*e.g. where the salary of an individual is unknown*), you need to show that this is so. In this situation an arbitrary number is usually decided on and is then always given against any items where there is no information (*e.g. '–1' against the individual's name may mean there is no information about their salary*). The list should have a note with it explaining that this is the case.

You could make your own glossary of what a symbol or a way of presenting data means in your contexts. If you want to present data to others you will have to use methods of presenting it with which they are familiar. You could check with colleagues whether there are standard symbols used in your organisation.

Symbol or way of presenting data	Context in which it is used	What it means

8 WORKING WITH AND ANALYSING DATA

Your raw data is not very useful to others, whether you have gathered it from published or primary sources. Regardless of who the data is for, they are likely to be busy and have little time to sort out its meaning, and they may not be as knowledgeable as you about the area and less able to analyse and interpret it.

You need to return here to the box in section 3.2 above, as the nature of the problem or task, who it is for and why it is needed will determine what you do with it.

This section indicates some processes for converting data into useful information.

8.1 Sorting the data

Before you can carry out any of the following ways of analysing the data you need to record and sort or order it. The ways in which you do this will be determined partly by how you want to analyse it. You therefore need to identify what you are going to do with it before you record, sort or order it. It will help if you do this before you even identify how to collect it. For example:

◆ you will see below that in order to work out a 'median' you need to list your values in order, but to work out a 'mean' you do not need to (a value is usually a number).

◆ it is quicker to analyse data from a questionnaire where respondents tick boxes than to ask them to write in response to open-ended questions, where you then have to code the answers (though the different sort of information you get from open-ended questions may be what you need).

◆ can information (*e.g. financial information*) be collected in the first place in a way which will make it easier to analyse (*e.g. directly on to computerised spreadsheets, or with all the information on one side of a form and in the order you need for analysis, to prevent you from having to rummage through several sheets of paper*)?

8.2 Making comparisons

Percentages or proportions enable you to see comparisons quickly. However, you need to be aware of the following.

◆ A simple but common mistake is to add or subtract percentages which are actually percentages of different things.

◆ You need to be careful about the sample number on which the percentages are based. You should not use percentages on a sample of less than 20, and if your sample is less than 50 you should point this out specially to the reader (Marsh, 1988).

◆ Percentages can only be between 0 and 100 (i.e. values turned into percentages become a proportion of 100). *E.g. people sometimes talk of a 400 per cent increase, but this is not really accurate and it would be better to talk of a 'fourfold increase'.*

8.3 Identifying what is typical

You may need to identify what is typical, two common methods being to identify the 'median' or the 'mean'.

The **median** is obtained by listing all the values you have collected in order of value and identifying the middle one. The points at the top and bottom of the list are known as the **extremes**. The point which is mid-way between the top extreme and the median is the **upper quartile** and the mid-point between the bottom extreme and the median is the **lower quartile**.

3
6
—
9 – lower quartile
—
12
14
—
16 – median
—
17
19
—
30 – upper quartile
—
35
40

The **arithmetic mean** is commonly known as the 'average'. It is the sum of all the values divided by the number of values – for the above values it is 18.27 recurring. It might be appropriate to round this number down to 18 (see section 10.1)

Other useful terminology:

◆ the **range** is the difference between two values.
◆ the **standard deviation** is the typical difference between the individual numbers and the mean (i.e. the typical difference between all the numbers in the above list and 18). (See Marsh (1988) or any book on statistics for how to calculate this; or it may be a function on your calculator.)
◆ The **midspread** is the difference between the upper and lower quartiles.

8.4 Measuring over time

This is a very common need at work, particularly in estimating costs/resources or monitoring costs/resources (see Chapter 9, Project Work). Visual displays are not only helpful in presenting data (see section 10 below) but in working with it.

For example, a simple way of looking at 'flow' over time is to use a graph where one axis represents amounts and the other time.

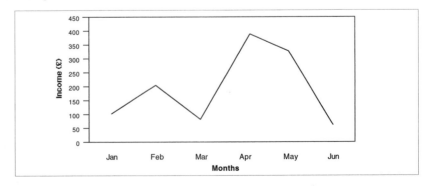

Question	Our notes
Have you given the exact wording of any questions asking for opinions?	They may be capable of different interpretations.
Have you given the base figure for percentages?	The reader must be able to convert percentages back to raw numbers (e.g. '100% of people in department X but only 25% in department Y like ginger biscuits' – what if there was one person in department X and 350 in department Y?).
Have you given totals of rows and columns?	Also acts as a check for you that you have not made any errors.
Have you pointed out any rounding up or down?	Somebody may notice that the totals do not add up.
Have you included space and used grid lines?	To make it easier to read.

Table 1 Current level of expertise by age

CURRENT EXPERTISE	BASE	EXCELLENT	ADEQUATE	LESS THAN ADEQUATE	VERY POOR
BASE	356	4%	44%	41%	11%
AGE					
18–21	240	3%	48%	39%	11%
22–24	44	5%	34%	41%	20%
25–34	58	9%	34%	52%	5%
35+	13	8%	54%	23%	15%

Source: Learning and Teaching Institute, Sheffield Hallam University, 1994.

10.3 Graphs and charts

Graphical display and charts make numerical data more understandable, as you can see the concepts the numbers are trying to convey at a glance. The following gives examples of different types of graphs and charts. In this chapter there are other examples of visual presentation – a table and an arrow diagram.

Note that most items in the checklist in section 10.2 also apply to graphs and charts, *e.g. you must give base numbers for percentages etc.*

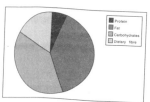
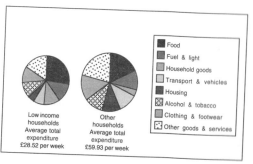

8.5 Cause and effect

Where you are considering the relationship between two variables, one may seem to have an effect on the other, i.e. a causal relationship. Care needs to be taken here, as statistical correlations may not actually represent cause and effect and you may need to make careful judgements and look for other possible reasons for the correlation – the box below gives examples. There may be multiple causes for something. You may need to do further investigations, to check if the relationships are real, or if they are positive or negative.

It may help to consider the following questions and make notes in relation to your own task. Common sense/existing knowledge might tell you the answers to the questions in relation to your task, or there are statistical operations to help (see Marsh (1988) or other books on statistics).

Question	Example	My notes
What actually causes what? Which of two correlating factors is the cause and which the effect?	Marsh (1988) gives as an example a correlation between old age and poverty, where it is not poverty that causes old age but rather old age that causes poverty.	
Is an apparent causal relationship real?	Marsh (1988) gives as an example a statistical correlation between the number of storks and the number of human births in the Swedish population.	

You may want to represent causal links diagrammatically:

Scatter graphs (see section 10 below) are one way of showing cause and effect visually.

8.6 Deciding what to use

How do you decide which operations or calculations to use? It can help to consider the following:

◆ What will make most sense to the user or reader? *E.g. is it better to use a standard deviation or to use a range?* It may be harder in some situations for users to grasp the idea if you use a standard deviation rather than a range – *e.g. in looking at height of men, to say the standard deviation was 6cm may be less meaningful than to say the range is 161–184cm (Marsh, 1988).*

◆ How you will use the information? *E.g. is it better to use a median or a mean?* Medians are more useful where you need to be very accurate, and means where you want to describe or explore something or where you may have doubts about the accuracy of all your values.

◆ What will give the best interpretation of the data? E.g., *again, is it better to use a median or a mean?* If you have one number which is very different from the rest, it may alter the mean considerably but it will not alter the median much. (See the list in section 8.3 above and see what happens to the mean if you change one or two of the numbers by a large amount.)

What do I need to do with my data? How will I analyse it?

9 INTERPRETING DATA

. . . .

You will find it helpful to look at Chapter 6, Gathering and Using Information, for guidance on interpreting information. You may also find it helpful to look at Huff (1973) whose book on how to lie with statistics gives ideas about what to look out for (see also Chapter 10, Ethics at Work, in case you are tempted to borrow the ideas).

The following is intended to spark off ideas about what you might look out for, rather than being a comprehensive guide.

- Look for the unusual. Unusual values may need to be highlighted, may indicate that further investigations are needed or that your data needs to be regrouped. Is it a fluke? Does it help you diagnose the problem? Could it be an error?
- Data might be unimodal (i.e. with one peak on a graph) or bimodal (with two peaks on a graph). The latter might mean that you are actually depicting two different groups.
- It may help to look again at section 6 above on the quality of data. *E.g. while we were writing this chapter, the way unemployment statistics are gathered was changed to include those not in receipt of benefit, increasing the number of unemployed at a stroke. If the number of crimes decreases, is it because people have stopped reporting them or because there are fewer crimes? If more women die from breast cancer in some geographical areas than others, is this because of environmental factors or differences in medical treatment?*
- Data can have far-reaching effects. There could be ethical issues involved (see Chapter 10). *E.g. retail price indices are used in wage negotiations and to set pensions. All items cannot just be added together because people use some items more than others, so that some items, e.g. food, are weighted. What is included, how are they weighted, who decides — e.g. x may be used twice as often as y, so if x=7 and y=5, you need to weight x by multiplying it by 2 (x becomes 14)?*

We suggest you look at Chapter 6, Gathering and Using Information, before completing the following:

What questions do I need to ask when interpreting the data?

The questions you ask will lead to your conclusions. Th...
needs and aims of your task (see section 2.2 above). Decis...
of your information (or you may have to make recommen...
– see Chapter 11, Solving Problems and Making Decisio...
and resources. They may be quite significant for your or...

Your conclusions will therefore not only have to be...
dence but capable of being justified to others.

What conclusions have I drawn from the numerical information?	What is my... conclusions

10 PRESENTING DATA

. . . .

10.1 Detail

People are confused by too much detail. For mo...
many decimal points of accuracy. *E.g. for the list of...
recurring. Would using 18.27 recurring have added an...
rounded down to 18.* You may need a high level of...
at the final presentation stage this may not be...
creates the impression of scientific accuracy. W...
Chapter 10, Ethics at Work)?

You can round either up or down, or you ca...
cut and doing so on all the data, *e.g. 95.1, 97.5,...
leading to 95, 97, 99.* This is quicker than roundin...
You must make clear what you have done or...
and work out that they do not come to the to...

Whatever your data and its level of detail,...
visual display, to make the data more unders...

10.2 Tables

The following checklist will help in mak...
(1988) pp 140–42 and adds others).

Question	Our notes
Have you given the table a number?	So readers know... top of page 3'...
Have you given the table a title?	This should cle...
Have you given the sources of the information?	See Chapter... referencing... data gather... questionna...
Have you indicated any missing information?	E.g. give...

EXAMPLE TA...

PIE CHARTS

BAR CHARTS

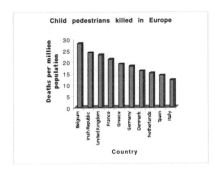

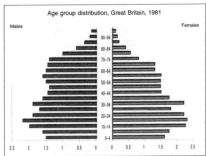

LINE GRAPH AND SCATTER GRAPH

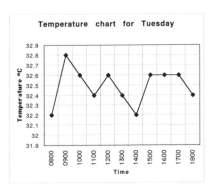

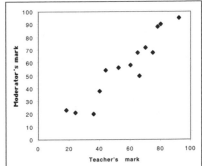

The above examples of graphs are adapted from Routledge (1998).

If you are producing a chart or graph by hand all you need is the simple equipment you were familiar with at school – a pencil, a ruler, a protractor, compasses, squared paper. However, you may not need to do this as you may be able to produce what you need on a computer (see section 4.3 above). Do you have a colour printer with your computer? What help might that be (*e.g. in colouring sections of a 'pie' to make them clearer*)?

What would best show, very quickly, the information you would like to get over? You could consider:

◆ your information
◆ the concepts you want to express
◆ the people who will use it (including yourself – we all have personal preferences for how we like things to be displayed)
◆ how important 'image' is (does it just need to convey the information or is there a public relations function too?)
◆ how will it be reproduced and what are the costs (*e.g. colour printing is expensive*)?

The following gives a list of common types of charts and graphs. We suggest you add your own notes to ours in the central column about general usage, and notes about usage for your particular task in the final column.

Type of chart/graph	Uses	My notes
Pie	Best where there are few categories Shows proportions	
Bar	Shows comparisons between categories	
Line	Shows peaks, troughs, trends	
Scatter	Good for causal relationships	
Arrow diagram	Good for causal links	
Gantt chart (see Chapter 9, Project Work, for an example)	Shows activities/resources/costs over time	
Others (add your own)		

11 IMPROVING YOUR SKILLS. ACTION PLANNING

We suggest that you return to section 3.2. How well did the strategies you listed there (and others you used) work in this particular situation? What would you do the same or differently in future?

The strategies I used	How effective they were

Where do you need to improve your skills and how might you do so? The options for sources of help include:

◆ **yourself** – numbers are only a way of expressing concepts. This chapter is full of numerical concepts yet it has very few actual calculations. Working out your issues and problems is what matters – the actual calculations can easily be looked up (or done on a calculator). You may just need practice in thinking through numerical tasks.

◆ **this chapter** – were any sections of it particularly helpful, *e.g. any of the self-completion boxes*? If so, could you use those processes again, on other tasks you have to do?

◆ **colleagues at work** – a valuable immediate resource (unless you work in an extremely small organisation).

◆ **books** can show you how to do calculations and operations.

◆ **computers** – you may not need to be able to do the calculations and operations yourself but instruct the computer to do them (colleagues at work may be able to help, include those who know about computers).

◆ **training courses** – your organisation may offer these, or may be able to send you on an external course.

◆ **equipment** – do you need to buy a calculator, or a computer package?

What can I do? What have I realised, having worked through this chapter, that I am good at or find easy?	How can I make the most of this?

What do I still find difficult? Where do I need to improve?	Actions I could take (be as specific as possible)	By (date)

12 REFERENCES AND BIBLIOGRAPHY
....

With thanks to John Routledge, on whose SkillPack parts of this chapter are based.

Huff, D. (1973), *How to lie with Statistics*, Penguin.

An entertaining book on how statistics can distort information. Useful both in helping avoid some of the pitfalls but also in interpreting published information.

Learning and Teaching Institute, Sheffield Hallam University (1994), *Final Report, Skills Pack Project*, Sheffield Hallam University.

Marsh, C. (1988), *Exploring Data: An Introduction to Data Analysis for Social Scientists*, Polity Press.

Routledge, J. (1998), *Confidence with Numbers: Starter Level and Development Level of the Student SkillPacks Masters*, Gower.

9

PROJECT WORK

Contents

WHY IS THIS SKILL IMPORTANT?

Because of the changing way in which organisations operate, project work is becoming increasingly important. Project work requires the coordination of varied activities and tasks, and needs to be well planned to be cost effective.

We suggest you use this chapter:

◆ when you have a project to carry out, to help you plan in advance and to carry out the project
◆ to draw up a project proposal and feasibility study.

Your project may be generated by yourself or it may be given to you.

By the end of this chapter you should be able to:

1   identify and agree purposes, aims and targets based on relevant information
2   identify constraints, resources, influencing factors and audience requirements
3   plan action to meet targets
4   use resources most effectively
5   implement actions, resolve difficulties and achieve targets
6   seek and use feedback on performance and progress
7   monitor and review progress and amend targets and plans appropriately
8   communicate effectively with all stakeholders, present project outcomes appropriate for the target audience
9   evaluate effectiveness of your own communications, identify areas of improvement and implement action.

See Chapter 1 for the relationship between these learning outcomes and the Key Skills qualifications.

1 WHAT IS PROJECT WORK?

....

A project generally has the following characteristics:

◆ it is unique, a one-off, rather than routine or repeated operations
◆ it has a definite start and end point
◆ it has clearly identifiable goals or outcomes
◆ it must be completed within cost limits and it uses resources.

Projects can vary in size from very small, involving one or a few people, to very large, involving thousands of people and many organisations. Project work is increasingly common and complex – set in a context where there is rapid change and a demanding market.

   Since this book is aimed at graduates or those with diplomas in the first few years of employment, we assume that your project will be small, or that you are working on part of a large project. 'Project management' is a term which may be used. In this context it does not necessarily mean managing people, although it may involve overseeing all or part of the process, to achieve the desired goals.

2 WHAT DOES YOUR PROJECT AIM TO ACHIEVE?

....

2.1 Aims, goals, deliverables

It is crucial to start with a clear idea of the desired end point, whether you are working on a project already agreed or drawing up a project proposal. Without having clear goals, you will be unable to plan or monitor progress.

◆ What is the overall purpose of your project or of a project in which you are involved? Why are the outcomes desirable? Why is this project important to your organisation? *E.g. it will increase efficiency.*
◆ What are your goals? Here you need to be as precise as possible. If you are working on part of a project, what are the goals for your aspect? *E.g. to develop and implement a new ordering system.*
◆ What will you have at the end of your project, or your part of the project? What will be your 'deliverables'? This is a useful word, as it suggests something well defined which you could actually give to somebody else. *E.g. a fully operational ordering system and all its component parts; documentation to help staff use this system; staff fully trained in operating the new system.*

It will help to make notes in the following table in relation to your project:

Overall purpose	Goals	Deliverables

2.2 Judging success

How will you judge success? It may simply be to meet your goals and produce your deliverables, or there may be other factors. If you want to develop a new product, success may relate to how well it subsequently sells, to user feedback, or to the views of writers in trade magazines. Might your project enhance people's lives, or the status of your organisation, or your own job or career prospects? The criteria for success may relate to the purpose you noted in section 2.1 above.

What are your criteria for success?

2.3 Background information

If you had difficulty in completing sections 2.1 and 2.2, it may be because you have insufficient information. It will help to clarify exactly what is required. Who could you gather information from and what information do you need? It may be unwise to plan a project based on assumptions which you haven't checked out (*e.g. is a product actually needed?*).

In the following table you could make brief notes relating to your project (*e.g. the names of people to contact, or the specific information you need*).

Source of information
Client
Customers
Users
Managers (immediate, senior)
Colleagues
Technical experts

Source of information
Written briefs
Those providing funding
Relevant literature (trade journals, books, Internet)

Type of information needed from the source
Client/user needs/aims/motivations
Market research (who might buy it, where, how much for etc.?)
Motives of the funder. What will they get out of it? What do they need to know about the project? Have they any special requirements or constraints?
Hidden agendas, vested interests, why do people really want this project?
Any overlaps with colleagues' areas of expertise, toes that might be trodden on? Who might the enthusiasts and supporters and antagonists be?
Has it been done before? By whom? How? Did it work? What were the problems? Why are you doing it again?
What are the main technical issues or challenges? Is solving these a main aim of the project? Who has vested interests in these?

You will need good recording systems for your project and could start by recording all the background information needed. Chapter 7, Keeping Notes, Records and Minutes, will help.

2.4 Amending your goals and deliverables

As you move further into your project, you may need to amend your notes in this section, but it helps if your goals and deliverables are as clear as possible at the start. Making changes to projects mid-stream can be costly.

You will need to refer back to section 1 when planning, carrying out and controlling or monitoring your project, and to refer to your criteria for success in reviewing performance and quality.

3 CONSTRAINTS

AND LIMITS

....

You must identify the constraints or limits within which you have to operate. At this point you may be able to identify some of these, although you will be able to identify more once you have done more detailed planning. It may help, therefore, to return to this section while using the rest of this chapter and to add further notes as ideas occur to you.

You could make notes on the constraints and limits of your project under the headings below.

Time – Must it be completed in a given time? Do you/others have only a certain time available?
Money – Do you have a budget or cost limits?
People – Can a limited number of people work on this? Do they have the right skills/expertise/knowledge?
Resources – e.g. equipment, accommodation
Geographical location
You – Your own skills/expertise/knowledge
Other constraints (please list)

4 PLANNING

....

Good planning is vital and may take up a considerable proportion of the project's time – perhaps 10 or 20 per cent. The prevailing economic conditions are tough, regardless of whether you work in a market driven or publicly funded organisation. Time and costs will be critical. Poor planning is likely to waste both.

4.1 Getting started

You need to refer back to your goals and deliverables (section 2) and list the work needed for them. It may help to do this at increasing levels of specificity, and here you may like to consider who needs the information:

◆ Level 1   Senior managers may need only the broad outlines of the plan and work to be done.
◆ Level 2   Those responsible for the work need to know in more detail what is required.
◆ Level 3   Those carrying out the work need specific instructions ('job cards').

Even if you carry out the project alone, breaking it down in this way will help you see your main areas of work and help you in monitoring and controlling them (see section 8).
   Where could you start? You could:

◆ brainstorm (alone or with others) activities needed to carry out the project, then group them into activities which look similar
◆ look at project plans produced by others and use their categories as a starting point
◆ ask advice from colleagues (*e.g. who have carried out similar projects, who are experts in certain functional areas etc.*)
◆ show draft notes to others and ask for feedback, *e.g. on what you have omitted*
◆ find out if your organisation uses a particular project management and planning method – it may also have computer software to help. If you are carrying out one aspect of a large project, you may need to fit in with overall planning methods.

4.2 Initial plans

Once you have notes on the tasks needed you could break them down into subtasks, using the following level structure.
   Our example:

Goal – To develop and implement a new ordering/procurement system
Deliverables – A fully operational ordering/procurement system and all its component parts; documentation enabling staff to use this system; staff fully trained in operating the new system

Level 1 Broad areas of work	Level 2 More detailed breakdown (Example of item 1 only)	Level 3 'Job cards' (Example of item 1.1 only)
1 Investigate current system and user needs	1 Investigate current system and user needs 1.1 Gather information on operation of existing system 1.2 Gather information on end-user requirements 1.3 Gather information on operator requirements	1.1 Gather information on operation of existing system 1.1.1 Gather existing system documentation (*e.g. order forms*) 1.1.2 Gather information on documentation usage (*e.g. end-users, operators*) by observation/interviewing 1.1.3 Gather information on operational costs 1.1.4 Identify benefits/ difficulties of current system

Level 1 Broad areas of work	Level 2 More detailed breakdown (Example of item 1 only)	Level 3 'Job cards' (Example of item 1.1 only)
2 Investigate other commercial systems 3 Develop/acquire new system 4 Pilot new system 5 Produce user documentation 6 Staff training 7 Full implementation and monitoring of new system	…and so on for items 2–7 at Level 1	1.1.5 Summarise information (e.g. constraints, operational requirements, costs etc.) …and so on for item 1.2 at Level 2 and subsequent items

Project planning is a developmental process. You may be unable to complete level 3 at this stage. You also may find that you now need to revise your notes in section 1, *e.g. you may now realise that the project is too big, or that there are crucial goals you have omitted.* Plans are not set in concrete, but are to be used to help as the project evolves. However, the further you get into a project, the more costly any changes may be.

You may find it helpful to identify another strategy which might work better in your situation, *e.g. by asking colleagues what they do.*

Level 1 Broad areas of work	Level 2 More detailed breakdown	Level 3 'Job cards'

4.3 Milestones and scheduling

'Milestones' are interim events or products at which to aim and funders of projects will often ask for them. For the example we are using throughout this chapter, 'milestones' might include: *the summary of the current system; a summary of user requirements; recommendations for what the new system would include; recommendations on whether to purchase a commercial system or develop an in-house system; etc.*

You also need to identify when you might reach the milestones. How long will it take to carry out the work you have specified at level 3? You may be able to estimate this yourself, or you could ask colleagues. Are there factors outside your control which will influence the timescale, *e.g. time for parts to arrive?*

What are my milestones?	By what date should each be completed?

'Float' is the time for which a job can be delayed without affecting the overall completion date. Can you have any 'float' in your plans?

4.4 Planning techniques

There are many sophisticated tools for project planning, often using systems developed by the oil industry or American defence organisations, and usually involving computer applications. Your organisation may use these and if so you need to find out about and fit into its systems. If not, the following simple tools may help.

Bar charts or **arrow charts** can be used to indicate timescales and milestones. A visual summary can help you see whether your plans are feasible and is also useful in monitoring whether you are on target.

BAR CHART

	Jan	Feb	Mar	Apr	May	Jun	Jul
Gather information	▭						
Identify needs	▭						
Review commercial systems		▭					
Pilot system				▭			
Produce documentation				▭			
Training				▭			

Timescale ⟶

*ARROW DIAGRAM
SHOWING SEQUENCE
OF TASKS*

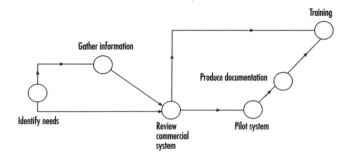

A bar chart (or Gantt chart) enables you to see at a glance what work needs doing when and helps you see if your timescales are possible. You can amend bar charts to make the bars black for work completed to date and clear for work yet to be done. An arrow diagram shows what work follows on from what, or the tasks which need to be done together, and can help in identifying the relationship between major phases of the work.

Could you now develop bar charts and arrow diagrams for your project? Our examples are simplified and your own charts and diagrams may be more complex.

It may help to go back over your work plan and identify what is essential and what is desirable. If you have tight time limits you may need to focus your energies. **Critical path analysis** is a planning technique used to identify the critical events or activities with deadlines for when they must be completed. This works best for projects where you can assume that the plan you develop at the start will not alter and be subject to changing circumstances. Even if this does not apply to your situation, it may focus your mind to draw a critical path through the activities and milestones identified in sections 4.2 and 4.3 above.

4.5 Constraints and risks

It will be helpful to return to section 3 and look again at your constraints and limits. You may now have a clearer idea of what they are. How can you plan to allow for them? *E.g. if your constraint is that you have very limited time, how could you make the best use of it (miss out some activities, use other people, work overtime)? If the project team do not have the expertise needed how could this be overcome (training, can somebody else be employed)?*

It can also help to identify the risks in your proposal and to plan for them. In the example we are using in this chapter, one risk might be problems at the handover stage between the old and the new system. Is the risk so great that the project must be abandoned? Often the timescale is such that mistakes can't be compensated for.

You may want to return to sections 4.2 and 4.3 and amend them.

4.6 Your plan

You should now be at the stage where you have:

Clearly identified goals and deliverables
Criteria for judging success
A list of work activities needed, grouped appropriately (*e.g. so that they can be carried out by functional specialists*)
Milestones
A timescale for when these milestones will be achieved

Your plan may change when you start work on your project.

5 RESOURCES

·················

5.1 Resource needs

You must identify the resources needed to carry out the project. If you are making a project proposal, it will be essential to do so in order to see if it is feasible. You need to know what actual resources you need and their availability and how much these resources will cost. How could you estimate costs? Suggestions are:

◆ your organisation may have fixed percentage charges for overheads
◆ your personnel or human resources department may have standard figures for the costs of certain personnel
◆ you could look at previous project plans as a starting point
◆ for some items you will be able to make very accurate estimates, *e.g. if you are running a workshop for 20 people, you will know the rate per head that your organisation charges for lunch*
◆ functional areas in your organisation can provide certain costs, *e.g. the print unit for printing costs, stores for stationery*
◆ you may be able to draw on your own experience of how long work tasks take and then calculate the cost in person-hours.

You could complete the following, or use it as a checklist against the plan you made with the help of section 4. For each work activity identify the resources needed.

Resource	Issues	Resources needed and costs
People	How many people/person-hours? Who? Skills/expertise/knowledge needed, in-house or bought in? Training needs Who must be consulted about their availability? Administrative support?	
Accommodation	For how many, or what type? Will clients or customers use it? Location Specialist needs	
Equipment	Computers, phones, fax, technical equipment, projectors, screens, stands	
Consumables	Photocopying paper, computer disks, pens, flipcharts, acetates	
Overheads	Heating, lighting, rates, accommodation, phones, modem	
Money	VAT, other taxes, *e.g. corporation tax* Foreign exchange rates	
Travel and subsistence	Car/rail/plane travel Hotels Meals, entertaining	
Use of company infrastructure	Finance department Personnel/human resources IT Porters Receptionists	
Others (please list)		

Ideally, an organisation needs to 'level' resources to avoid severe peaks and troughs (*e.g. needing to lay people off*). How might you 'level' your resources?

5.2 Scheduling costs

It is likely that you will need to know the phasing of your resource requirements. You may have to work within financial years, your funder may give you money in instalments, your organisation must plan its cash flow, payments may need to be made.

Return to your list of work activities and bar charts of your milestones (section 4.4). Can you now put cost estimates for each phase up to each milestone? You need to know what each item will cost and the total costs. This will help your planning and control, as you can use this information to see if you are on target in budgetary terms. You could draw a bar chart to show costs over time.

You may need to identify tolerance levels, i.e. the overspending level past which you will not continue without agreeing more funding. If at the end of the project you are overrun by 10 per cent it may not be too bad, but it would be very bad at the start of your project, as it could indicate severe future overspending.

How often will you consider costs? The more critical they are, the more frequently you need to look at them.

5.3 Agreeing resources

With whom must you agree resources? Can you clarify resource provision in advance? Looking for extra resources at a later stage may use up considerable time and goodwill.

You may remove potential problems if you agree contracts with resource providers. This makes what is required clear to all involved. If you are using outside resources, you should draw up formal and legally binding contracts and you may need legal advice or to use procedures already in existence in your organisation. Your company secretary, solicitor or procurement department may be able to help. Internally you may need a less formal agreement, something in writing confirming what resources you need and when.

6 PROJECT PROPOSAL

If you are developing your own project proposal, as opposed to working on a project already agreed, you will now be in a position to put this proposal together.

Who will receive and decide on this proposal? What they will want to know and what will persuade them? You may need to become familiar with their terminology, or with what would currently grab their attention. If you are applying for funding from public bodies, there will be forms to complete and procedures to follow. Your recipient is unlikely to need your level 3 information. They will certainly need your level 1 information and possibly level 2.

It is always helpful to seek advice from others who have been through the same process or from the funders themselves, who are usually only too happy to provide advice which will lead to good proposals and avoid them in the necessity of going through incomplete bids. If your proposal is to an internal person, you are more likely to know what will appeal to them.

The formats of proposals differ (Chapter 4, Report Writing, may give you some ideas), but you are likely to need the following:

- overall aim, and possibly rationale
- goals
- deliverables
- project plan with timescales and milestones
- costs and resources needed.

7 CARRYING OUT THE PROJECT

7.1 What helps projects succeed?

Harrison (1992) suggests that the main factors which cause failure in project work are poor coordination and human relations, and that the main aspects contributing to success are adequate and appropriate structures, planning and control. Other factors affecting success or failure include commitment to the goals, participation by those involved in decision making and frequent feedback from the client or senior management. Harrison summarises the three most important factors as being organisation, human factors and planning and control. The last two are dealt with in sections 4 and 8.

7.2 Organisation

In most organisations people work in functional areas (such as sales or accounts) with responsibility to a line manager. Grouping people together according to function is efficient and provides mutual support.

Projects tend to be organised differently, and a project team may consist of people from a variety of functions. The project manager or leader has responsibility for the project but often does not have line management authority for its team members.

Features of project organisation which you may like to consider include:

◆ an accountable project manager who can coordinate what is happening.
◆ the traditional pyramid structure in organisations is not the best structure for projects, where people, often of similar levels, need to work together across functions rather than having to go up and down lines of hierarchy to obtain decisions or instructions
◆ there is a need for considerable delegation to project team members
◆ often tasks have to overlap to achieve a short timescale
◆ there needs to be an orientation to goals rather than operations or tasks (i.e. each person has deliverables to which to work)
◆ work can be grouped in a way which can be parcelled out to individuals or groups
◆ there is a need to look ahead, anticipate problems and needs, and take decisions.

7.3 Making decisions

How will decisions be made on your project? Where the organisation is very hierarchical only a few people make the decisions. In flatter organisations (i.e. short lines of management) more people are involved in decision making. Involving everybody in decision making can motivate people but you need to ensure that as well as making them happy you also achieve the goals.

You might find it helpful to look at the current situation in your organisation. How are decisions made? What effect does this have?

How are decisions made?		What effect does this have?
All made by senior managers		
Most big decisions made by senior manager, small ones by manager		
Group discussion by work team		
I make my own decisions		
Varies, unclear		
How will decisions be made on my project?		

How could the separate individuals involved in your project best be coordinated?

Coordination method		How could this work in my context?
Via a senior manager		
Via regular group meetings of the functional managers involved		
Via coordination committees		
Via steering groups		
Via project team meetings		
Via subworking groups		
Via computer conferencing or email		
Via planning, control and monitoring systems		
Others (please list)		

What is the best organisational structure for your project? Who will be responsible to whom? You could now sketch out an organisation bearing in mind the areas you have considered in this section (see section 7.2).

7.4 Human relations

Project work has characteristics which tend to place a spotlight on human relations. Projects are temporary and staff may have little time to get to know each other or may be thrown together in an intensive working relationship. They may be from functional areas with very different cultures.

The project manager's responsibility often exceeds their authority, as they may not be the team members' line manager.

Different attitudes are needed from those in more traditional functional areas to cope with what may be considerable change, with flexible approaches, with commitment to goals rather than to functional areas (there may be divided loyalties), and with the need to see the whole picture.

If you are working on an aspect of a larger project, how will you deal with the following?

Issue	How will I deal with it?
My commitment to the project goal	
Ways of working effectively with professionals from other functional areas	
Meeting the demands of the project and my other work	
Ethical practice in dealing with others (see Chapter 10, Ethics at Work)	
Others (please list)	

If you are managing a project with a team of people from different functional areas, how will you deal with the following?

Issue	How will I deal with it?
Gain the commitment of others to the project	
Exerting power without authority – what strategies will you use to get things done (see Chapter 14, Putting Your Case: Negotiating and Assertiveness)	
Agreeing matters with the line managers of those involved	
Creating a team out of diverse groups, building a team spirit	
Team members may have to change their working methods	
Others (please list)	

How can you deal with conflict? Conflict may arise not from personal dislike but because of things you can avoid.

Possible source of conflict	How could I avoid conflict arising for this reason?
Schedules/timescales	
Priorities	
Resources	
People not delivering work of the right quality on time	
Technical issues	
Administration	
Costs/money	
Personality clashes	

8 PROJECT CONTROL, MONITORING AND REVIEWING PROGRESS

Project control is critical. Without it, you will not know whether you are on target or spending within your limits. With a project plan and costing schedule, you can check how you are doing against them.

Project control enables you to pick up difficulties early and deal with or anticipate them. You need to know as soon as possible how all the aspects of the work are progressing in order to help you amend your plans. Control can also have a motivational function – the equivalent of making yourself lists and ticking off what you have done.

The control cycle is more complex than just plan–carry out–control. Most projects do not work so simplistically and in reality the interaction between planning, execution and control is much more complex. *E.g. if you are running out of time, what further plans could you make? Could you use overtime, buy in people on a temporary basis, take short cuts etc.?*

8.1 Data collecting

What sort of data do you need about your project? How important is this data? Given the likely demands on your time, you should avoid collecting data for no good purpose.

Does somebody else need data from you, such as for tax purposes? How will you know if you are on target? Look again at your bar chart project plan and milestones (section 4.4). What information would you need to tell you if you were on target? Look again at your criteria for success (section 2.2). What information would you need to tell you you were succeeding? To help you here, refer to Chapter 7, Keeping Notes, Records and Minutes.

There are some project control strategies which could help (given here in very simplified form).

♦ Identify two factors of importance to you (*e.g. money and time*) and subtract one from the other. This gives you a negative or positive 'variance'. *E.g. look at the time you allowed and subtract what you have actually used. If it is negative you are under time and if positive you are over time.*

♦ Analyse your performance based on earned value (value in terms of person-hours or costs of work actually completed). Look at what you budgeted for (*e.g. £100*), what you have spent (*e.g. £80*), and the value of the work already completed (*e.g. £50 worth of a person's time spent on it*). You can then do the following calculation:
Cost = £50 (earned value) − £80 (spent) = −£30, i.e. you are £30 overspent
(See Harrison (1992) for more detail − there are also other formulae which you might use.)

Who may need data from me?	What sort of data?	How could it easily be recorded and by whom?
Personnel or human resources		
Finance department		
The funder		
Resource providers		
My line manager		
Senior managers		
Clients		
Colleagues		
Project team members		
Procurement or buying department (lack of materials can cause delays)		
Others (please list)		

The strategies suggested are guides only. It may not, for example, be good that you are underspent – it may mean you are behind with the work. For most small projects it may be sufficient to track your progress against bar charts.

Any analysis of data must be easily understood, and must highlight problems or identify trends.

8.2 Change control

You may need a 'change control system', a way of recording changes made to your original plans and their likely effects and costs. Changes may be beneficial if you find quicker or cheaper ways of doing things, but they may also incur extra expense. Problems can be multiplied if changes are made at the building or manufacturing stage. Your changes may be essential, *e.g. if there are health and safety considerations*. If you are working in a team constant changes may frustrate and demotivate people. Your record could look something like the following:

Proposed change	Is it essential or desirable?	Likely effects and costs	Actual effects and costs

Will you need approval from somebody else for changes? Will you give approval for the changes that others make? Would a formal change approval system help (*e.g. a form like the above table but with a column for 'authorised by'*)?

8.3 Review procedures

How often do you need to review progress and with whom?

◆ yourself
◆ your manager
◆ your project team
◆ a steering group
◆ a planning group
◆ your funder (this might be from within your organisation as well as outside)
◆ an outside organisation which has commissioned your project.

Feedback from others on the progress of your project will be very helpful. How will you encourage others to give constructive feedback and how will you respond to it? See Chapter 17, Identifying Strengths and Improving Skills.

8.4 Quality control and assurance

The above sections relate to meeting targets but not necessarily to carrying out work to a required standard of quality. You may need to return here to section 2.1 and your criteria for success. What, in terms of this project, does quality mean?

What criteria will I use to know if my deliverables are of an appropriate quality?	How will this be checked?	Who will check it?	When?

8.5 Amendments

It may be that you now need to return to your plans and revise them, or even to your goals and deliverables – but always remember to look at section 8.2 on change control.

9 REPORTING AND COMMUNICATING

. . . .

A major cause of project failure is lack of communication. Who needs to know what and when? What are the likely effects of their not knowing?. You may want to consider here how much detail people need and what will be extraneous detail likely to get in the way of good communication. It is tempting when you are committed to something and pleased with it to tell everybody everything about it.

All managers need information which is interpreted for them. They will rarely want raw data. What do the cost figures show? What do any difficulties actually mean in terms of delays?

Who wants to know?	What do they want to know?	When do they need to know?	How will I tell them?

You may need to change and develop your ideas in this area as your project progresses.

You are likely at the end of a project, and perhaps at interim stages, to produce a report (see Chapter 4, Report Writing). The structure of this chapter should suggest what you need to include. Your report may have to include recommendations for future action. You may also at stages be required to present your work orally, *e.g. to clients or colleagues.* Chapter 5, Making Presentations, and Chapter 14, Putting Your Case: Negotiating and Assertiveness, will help here.

10 IMPROVING YOUR OWN EFFECTIVENESS IN PROJECTS

....

At the end of your project, it will help you for the next project if you review what you did well and can build on, what you did less well and need to improve, and what action you intend to take. You could then note when you have taken that action, *e.g. you could go on a short course, seek advice, read books on project management or buy a computer package to help you monitor your projects.*

Area	My strengths and weaknesses	What I need to do in future projects (building on or changing)	Actions I will take to develop this in myself	Taken

11 REFERENCES AND BIBLIOGRAPHY

....

Harrison, F. L. (1992), *Advanced Project Management: A Structured Approach*, Gower.
Skinner, M. P. (1992), *Elements of Project Management: Plan, Schedule and Control*, Prentice Hall.

Contents

10
ETHICS AT WORK: ETHICAL PRACTICE AND CODES OF CONDUCT

WHY IS THIS SKILL IMPORTANT?

In order to operate together, people develop and follow certain rules of behaviour which allow them to understand and interpret each other's behaviour and enable relationships to run smoothly.

We suggest you use this chapter:

◆ to help you become more generally aware of ethics at work and how to work within them
◆ if you are facing a particular situation which poses ethical issues.

By the end of this chapter you should be able to:

1 identify your own personal ethical practice and code of conduct, drawing on evidence
2 identify formal or informal ethical practices and codes of relevant individuals and organisations, using appropriate evidence
3 identify possible outcomes and results of these ethical practices
4 identify similarities and differences between ethical practices and codes of conduct
5 identify areas requiring ethical judgements
6 make judgements about what you consider to be appropriate ethical practice for your work context and act on those judgements
7 take responsibility for your ethical practices and codes and their outcomes
8 evaluate the appropriateness and effectiveness of your ethical practice and codes, using feedback from others, identify areas where improvement is needed and take action.

See Chapter 1 for the relationship between these learning outcomes and the Key Skills qualifications.

1 WHAT IS ETHICAL PRACTICE AND WHY IS THIS AN ISSUE?

········

1.1 What are ethics and codes of conduct?

Business practice and judgements are often based on 'rules' regarding conduct. These 'rules' may be implicit, based on assumptions shared by those who operate them. Those new to a workplace or profession or facing an unfamiliar situation need to find out about them in order to behave appropriately. Where they relate to values and standards (such as moral standards) they can be seen as 'ethical practice'.

Values are significant beliefs which underpin behaviour – your values may relate to your views on these standards (*e.g. honesty is generally regarded as a value, but standards of honesty differ and what you regard as dishonest another person may not*).

Ethics can be seen as 'common decency', as relating to justice and fairness, as adhering to a set of principles.

In some professional areas ethical practice and codes of conduct are very explicit and openly discussed. The medical profession provides a good example of an ethical code of conduct, which includes confidentiality between a doctor and patient and obtaining the agreement of an individual before treatment.

Many other professional bodies also have explicitly stated codes of ethical conduct, *e.g. British Computer Society, Royal Town Planning Institute, Chartered Institute of Marketing*. These can be seen as promises made by the profession to regulate itself for the benefit of society. However, this is not just a question of obeying the law or following written codes of conduct, since ethical practice also includes those informal rules, stated or implicit, which relate to the values in the workplace.

Ethical practice not only allows people to operate with a shared understanding, but it has a particular function which is related to protection. If individuals follow the 'rules' of ethical practice, they protect those with whom they come into contact, themselves and their organisation.

1.2 Ethics/codes of conduct in practice

Actions and decisions at work, made by you or your organisation, are likely to involve ethical issues and codes of conduct.

The following suggests some areas where ethical issues may arise and gives examples which are **applicable to the UK**. This is a very important point. Ethical practice and values are set within a culture and other cultures may operate differently. The table below is not intended to suggest that UK practice is 'right' but rather that there **are** UK practices.

In some professions ethical practices cross cultural and national boundaries (*e.g. in the medical profession*), but in others they may not. Different work areas (*e.g. retailing, construction, the legal profession, public bodies*) within one country may have different ethical practices.

Area	Examples of ethical issues	Examples of what is generally considered poor ethical practice in the UK
Working relationships (colleagues, clients, competitors)	Health and safety Justice, privacy Equality Respect Trust Confidentiality	Nepotism (getting jobs because of who you know rather than ability) Scapegoating (blaming everything on one person) Discrimination on the grounds of gender or ethnicity Misuse of power (*e.g. strong vs weak, bullying*)
Finance	Takeovers Release of financial (clear and accurate) information Inducements Shareholders' demands	Bribery Insider dealing (using privileged information to further own finances) 'Cooking the books' Theft
The environment	Effects of products produced, resources used	Product 'dumping' Breaking environmental laws Falsifying information

Area	Examples of ethical issues	Examples of what is generally considered poor ethical practice in the UK
Advertising, marketing, sales, sponsorship, public relations	Legality Decency Honesty Truthfulness	Stereotyping Misleading information Persuading the vulnerable (e.g. children) to buy what they do not need which may be harmful
Wider community	Effects of research and development (e.g. genetic engineering) Relocation (e.g. effects on jobs, housing market), sponsorship (vested interests)	Failure to consult (e.g. using research information without agreement by the subjects) Secrecy

For most of our examples there might be completely different practices in other cultures – *e.g. in some countries it is accepted that you get jobs because of who you know, or that you need to offer inducements to those with whom you want to close a deal (seen as gifts rather than bribery).*

These examples illustrate the possible effects of your operating to one code of conduct while others operate to another (*e.g. you may never get a job in a particular country if you look for advertisements rather than using your contacts*). You may need to make personal decisions about how far you wish to adopt other people's practices (see section 6 below).

You need to identify ethical practices and codes of conduct in any contexts in which you operate and among the people with whom you come into contact.

2 WHOSE RESPONSIBILITY?
....

Responsibility and ethics are interrelated.

You are responsible for your ethical behaviour within the organisation, as any unethical practice will damage you at work. In the extreme, it may lead to your dismissal, but what is more likely is that it will affect your standing with others, in particular the respect and trust they have for you.

This is not to absolve the organisation of responsibility. Any organisation is responsible for the conduct of its employees, and unethical behaviour can be potentially damaging to it. The ethical tone of an organisation is set by its management, from the top downwards – what sort of role model are you setting for staff for whom you may be responsible?

3 WHAT ARE THE POSSIBLE OUTCOMES AND RESULTS OF ETHICAL PRACTICES AND CODES OF CONDUCT?
....

Good ethics is good business.

It may be easier to identify the effects of poor ethical practice than those resulting from good practice. Following what is accepted as good practice in your workplace may simply result in smooth running. The effects of poor practice may, however, be much more observable.

These effects may be quite drastic. *E.g. in a recent case the misuse of funds by a bank employee led to the collapse of the bank, with all the attendant repercussions – for the employees, the investors, the banking sector in general and the person who misused the funds (a jail sentence).*

This was a dramatic situation, but we are all involved in much smaller events or issues each day which have ethical implications. The following table deliberately uses such possible events, and invites you to consider what might be good or poor ethical practice and what the possible results might be in your workplace.

You might consider the immediate results of your actions (*e.g. if you are late for a meeting will they have to delay the start?*) and the more long-term effects (*e.g. if you are late for a meeting will others be unconcerned or will they regard it as a discourtesy to them and will this influence their view of you?*).

Scenario	What might be poor practice in my workplace? What might the results be?	What might be good practice in my workplace? What might the results be?
Arrival at a meeting (on time? late?)		
Your reaction to a colleague who is on a lower grade than you and who is uncooperative		
Your reaction to a colleague who is rude to you in public		
An external person asks for information about one of your clients/colleagues		
Travel and subsistence expenses		

Poor ethical practices and not following an accepted code of conduct may cause offence, result in bad feelings or lack of trust, or transgress clearly stated professional codes (*e.g. related to confidentiality*). Good ethical practices may do the reverse.

4 ETHICS, CODES AND DECISION MAKING

One area where ethics and codes of conduct may be brought into sharp relief is that of decision making. Chapter 11, Solving Problems and Making Decisions, looks at this whole area in more detail, but it may be worth considering it here specifically in relation to ethics. For example:

◆ *an unemployed friend wishes to apply for a job where you (who are already employed) are the only other candidate. Would you go through with your application?*
◆ *a colleague in your workplace has closed a sale with somebody whom you know of via your sister. She has been told in confidence that that person is in debt and will be unable to pay. What will you do?*

Because ethics and codes are bound up with values, decisions involving them can create strong feelings in us. You may not see any ethical issues in the above two scenarios. In the first example, you may think that the interviewer will decide on whom to appoint for the job and the best person will succeed. In the second, you may think that your colleague should check out her or himself whether a customer can pay before agreeing a deal. Or you may feel emotions such as guilt, anxiety, competitiveness.

It is important to be aware of ethical issues in decision making in order to avoid making unintentional blunders with damaging repercussions. You might also want to consider your self-respect and ensure that you are not left with bad feelings.

In order to help increase your awareness of the place of ethics, values and standards in workplace decisions, you might find it helpful to complete the following – either for decisions you or others have recently made or for decisions which must be made shortly (small or large decisions).

Decisions I or others have made or are about to make	Ethical issues/values/standards involved; actual or possible repercussions	What decision was/will be made? What does it indicate about actual ethical practice? How do I feel?

5 OTHER PEOPLE'S ETHICS AND CODES OF CONDUCT

5.1 Whose ethics and codes of conduct?

An important skill at work is to be able to quickly work out what the norms are from which any group of people operate. Without knowing this, you could behave inappropriately in small or more significant ways.

You need to know what others' ethical practice is. If you don't you may commit all sorts of unwitting blunders (at the worst you may even lose your job or professional status).

Whose ethics matter to you in your work and how important are they to you (who do you not want to offend, or whose interests are important, or whose opinion of you matters)?

	Very important	Quite important
The company/employing organisation		
My managers		
Colleagues on my level		
Colleagues on lower levels		
Clients		
Competitors		
Professional body		
The public		
Interest groups (please specify)		
People from other countries		
People from other cultures		
Others (please list)		

5.2 Formal codes of conduct

Ethical codes, systems and standards may be recorded as formal statements.
Where might you find them? Possibilities include:

◆ professional body or company codes of practice or ethics
◆ mission statements
◆ organisation policies (*e.g. equal opportunities policies*)
◆ guidance notes (*e.g. from embassies about appropriate behaviour*)
◆ contracts (*e.g. some contracts with building contractors have statements about behaviour towards women*)
◆ legal documents or Acts of Parliament (*e.g. concerning data protection, consumer protection, patents, copyright, trades descriptions, health and safety, discrimination etc.*)

Can you summarise the main points of any formal statements? Do you understand them – if not, how might you clarify them?

How do these points work in practice?

5.3 Informal practices

If there are no formal statements of ethical practice, how else could you find out what the requirements are?

Suggestion	
Ask experienced staff in your own organisation	
Ask a contact person in other organisations	
Ask specialists (*e.g. in other professional areas or who are familiar with other cultures*)	
Ask members of your ethics committee (if your organisation has one)	
Attend any available ethics training	
Observe practice in your workplace and that of others. What clues could you look for? ◆ How do people speak to/treat each other? ◆ Do they treat different people differently? ◆ What is treated as confidential? ◆ What sorts of decisions do people have to check out with superiors? ◆ Have any colleagues found themselves in difficult situations? ◆ What do people worry about, get upset or annoyed about? ◆ What do people omit to do? ◆ What sorts of statements do people make about others or their work?	

Observing what happens and drawing your own conclusions about what is acceptable and effective is not only important in terms of ethical practice, but also in terms of being generally sensitive to the culture of your organisation.

5.4 Summarising ethical practice and codes of conduct

Could you summarise the main 'rules' which seem to be observed in your work context? You may just need to consider the 'rules' from which your work colleagues operate, or those of other professionals, clients, customers or the public. You may find it helpful to look back at your notes on sections 5.1, 5.2, 5.3 above.

Area	Formally stated codes of conduct	Informal 'rules' or codes of conduct	What actually happens?
Commitment to work (e.g. hours worked, how agreements are honoured etc.)			
Working relationships (colleagues, clients, competitors)			
Finance			
Advertising, marketing, sales, sponsorship, public relations			
The environment			
Wider community			
Other areas important in my organisation (please list)			

What would you say are the underlying principles on which those you come into contact with at work base their ethical practice?

Contributing to the well-being of society
Contributing to the well-being of a particular group in society
Avoiding harm to others
Being honest and trustworthy
Respecting property rights
Respecting others' rights and values
Effective use of resources
Proper recognition for abilities/work
Others (please list)

6 YOUR OWN ETHICAL PRACTICE

6.1 How does it relate to those of others with whom you come into contact?

Throughout your life you have developed certain values on which you base what you do – influenced by family, friends, school or work situations. You probably operate from these values without thinking about it, until you come up against a situation which challenges them in some way.

It may help to begin by looking back at the table in section 5.4 above. How do your own values and standards of behaviour fit against those of others at work?

◆ Are they similar?
◆ Are they different? How?

If they are different, it may help to make notes in the following box. They may differ but not in ways which really matter much to you, or the difference may actually be quite significant for you (are you shocked at their standards, are they shocked at yours, may they see you as over-fussy about areas they see as unimportant, or vice versa?).

How do they differ?	How much does it matter?	What could I do about this?

6.2 What is your own ethical practice at work?

You may want to consider not what you aspire to but what you actually do (your intentions may be good, but what matters to others is what you actually do).

Area	Examples of aspects you might consider	My actual practice	Where I need to amend my practice
Commitment to work	Attendance Timekeeping Completing tasks Keeping agreements		
Working relationships	Dealing with managers, colleagues, those on lower grades, men, women, clients, customers, competitors, the public Privacy Motivation Manipulation Abuse of privilege/power		
Finance	Personal expenses Money – organisation's/clients'/customers'/public Fair remuneration Takeovers Insider dealing Pricing policies		
Advertising, marketing, sales, sponsorship, public relations	Your interests (*e.g. commission*), those of your organisation, clients/customers The public Respecting the buyer Compulsion or pressure The Internet Imitating other products		
The environment	Pollution Congestion Public safety Enhancing the environment Future generations International aspects		
Wider community	Housing Employment Leisure Health Security Safety		
Other areas important in my organisation (please list)	Copyright Intellectual property Legal positions		

7 ACTION

PLANNING

....

In identifying the action you might take to improve your ethical practice, you might consider:

◆ where could you get support?
◆ from whom could you get feedback? See Chapter 17, Identifying Strengths and Improving Skills.
◆ how could you develop strategies for improvement?
◆ what skills do you need?

Areas where I need to improve	Actions I could take
Finding out more about what appropriate ethical behaviour is in my context	
Resolving possible differences between my own ethical practices and those of others	You may find Chapter 14, Putting Your Case: Negotiating and Assertiveness, helpful
Improving my own ethical practices	

How will you judge your success in improving your practice? It might be helpful to return to this section from time to time to review your progress.

8 REFERENCES AND

BIBLIOGRAPHY

....

Carmichael, S. and Drummond, J. (1989), *Good Business Guide to Corporate Responsibility and Business Ethics*, Business Books.
Donaldson, J. (1989), *Key Issues in Business Ethics*, Academic Press.
Donaldson, T. (1984), *Case Studies in Business Ethics*, Prentice Hall.
Vallance, E. (1995), *Business Ethics at Work*, Cambridge University Press.

Contents

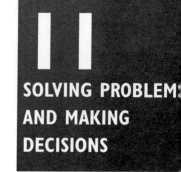

SOLVING PROBLEMS AND MAKING DECISIONS

WHY IS THIS SKILL IMPORTANT?

Problem solving and decision making occur in all areas of life, in simple situations and more complex ones. They involve making a choice. Some decisions will be risky, others will be more predictable.

Problem solving and decision making are important skills for effective working and are crucial in all professional areas. You will be expected to deal with both unanticipated, e.g. how difficulties between people could be resolved, and anticipated problems, e.g. how systems or processes could operate more effectively.

This chapter aims to help you solve the problems likely to be encountered in your work.

We suggest you use this chapter:

◆ in relation to a particular work activity or task which involves solving a problem
◆ before you start work on that activity or task
◆ then while you are working on it.

By the end of this chapter you should be able to:

1 collect sufficient information to
    ◆ clarify critical features of the problem
    ◆ identify possible solutions
2 select relevant information
3 identify critical features of problems which include a broad range of factors and a range of possible solutions
4 where appropriate, accurately follow set procedures to clarify the problem, seek information and identify solutions
5 identify and select efficient and effective procedures to clarify the problem, seek information and identify solutions
6 identify and use criteria to select an effective solution (e.g. short- and long-term benefits).

See Chapter 1 for the relationship between these learning outcomes and the Key Skills qualifications.

1 HOW DO YOU CURRENTLY SOLVE PROBLEMS AND MAKE DECISIONS?

How do you usually solve problems and make decisions? Add your own items to the list.

I respond immediately with an impulsive reaction

I avoid taking any action

I put off making a decision

I use my intuition

I use past experience

I use a logical approach

I use trial and error

I try creative techniques

I allow myself thinking time

I discuss it with others

Others (please add)

It may help to ask others how they normally solve problems. There can be a tendency to think that our way is the only way.

How effective are you at solving problems?

I would like to solve problems in less time (be more efficient)

I would like to find better solutions (be more effective)

I would like to feel less anxious or enjoy solving problems more

2 PROBLEM-SOLVING PROCESSES
....

There is a range of different ways to solve a problem. There are no right or wrong techniques, only those which are best for the situation and for you. How you generate solutions will depend on your preferences, personality and the way your mind works.

You might start:

◆ by generating possible solutions
◆ or by identifying what procedures you will use
◆ or by identifying the essential elements of a problem.

There are general milestones in the problem-solving and decision-making process, and at some stage you will need to give attention to them. The following is presented in a circular rather than a linear form – since it is important to acknowledge that there is no single right way.

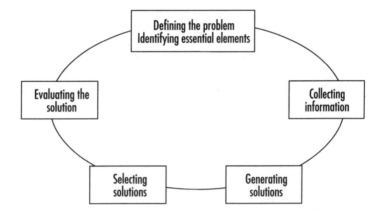

You may find that you need to move around the circle, backwards and forwards, *e.g. once you have selected a solution, you may need to collect further information.*

The skills you may need to use involve the following.

◆ **Analysing**. Breaking down a problem into smaller parts, *e.g. asking questions such as who, which, why, when, where, how?*
◆ **Synthesising**. Putting parts together to make the whole, *e.g. seeing the whole, the pattern.*
◆ **Valuing**. Thinking it through in relation to values and standards.

You might ask yourself the following questions in relation to your problem.

3 IDENTIFYING THE ESSENTIAL ELEMENTS OF A PROBLEM
....

What is the problem? (put this in your own words as clearly as you can; describe it to others to help you clarify it)
For whom is it a problem?
What makes it a problem?
Are there any related problems?

What does the solution have to achieve?
By when?
Who will need to use/apply the solution? Who is involved?
What is the context or background to the problem?
Are there any constraints which might limit your solutions, *e.g. cost, time, facilities*?
Who has vested interests in it?
What are your own feelings about the problem?
Others (please add)

4 COLLECTING EVIDENCE

. . . .

4.1 What do you need to know?

What do you need to know before you can solve your problem? This might include factual information and data, people's perceptions, opinions and needs. The type and quantity of information you need to collect will differ according to the problem. You may find it helpful to identify the main questions you need to answer and to break down your problem question into a series of smaller ones.

Questions I need to answer about my problem

You might find it helpful to look at Chapter 6, Gathering and Using Information.

4.2 Conflicting aspects

It can help to identify any conflicting or contradictory aspects. For example:

◆ a meeting, *e.g. one person is entertaining and interesting but talks too much and prevents the meeting from achieving its goals*
◆ an energy project, *e.g. the cheapest fuel is also the most environmentally damaging*
◆ work, *e.g. you need to revise for your professional exams, but you need to balance this with work activities and priorities.*

What are the contradictory aspects of your problem? Why are they contradictory? Resolving these contradictions may be crucial to the problem-solving process.

Conflicting elements	Reasons for this

You need to weigh up the effects of any contradictory aspects in order to make a judgement. There are several possible strategies.

◆ Identify the advantages and disadvantages of each aspect.
◆ Identify the costs and benefits of each aspect.
◆ Consult others who have an interest in the issue.
◆ Identify your immediate gut reaction/feelings and then question the reaction (*e.g. if somebody told you to concentrate solely on your revision for a professional exam, regardless of the effect on your work, would you be relieved or worried?*).
◆ Gather more information. It might swing the weight of evidence in one direction.

What other strategies have you or your colleagues tried?

4.3 Reviewing your information

You may need to continue to gather information to clarify the problem. One of these pieces of information may lead to a new question or angle.

The following suggests three stages to the information review, but there could be more or fewer.

Initial questions	Information/answers

Secondary questions	Information/answers

Final questions	Information/answers

4.4 How do you know that you have enough information?

Ask yourself the following questions:

> Is the information repeating itself?
>
> Is it really relevant?
>
> Is it worth the time taken to gather it?
>
> Is it adding anything?
>
> Will it make a big difference?

5 POSSIBLE PROBLEM-SOLVING TECHNIQUES

There are a variety of approaches to problem solving used in the working environment. Your choice will be influenced by the problem and its context and by what you feel comfortable with.

5.1 Methodological approaches

Structured methods can be helpful as they may:

◆ help ensure no important steps are left out
◆ give you more confidence
◆ mean it is easier to evaluate something which is methodical
◆ aid communication
◆ enable documentation of the process.

They may, however, encourage you to be less flexible.

A DESIGN PROCESS

This approach is often used to design manufactured products and organisational systems.

1 **Needs evaluation** (*e.g. What is the purpose of the object or system?*)
   ◆ What are the user's needs?
   ◆ What are the circumstances in which it will be used?
   ◆ What might be the benefits of having or using it?

2 **Design specification** (*e.g. What are the requirements of the design?*)
   ◆ Cost factors
   ◆ Evaluation of other products
   ◆ Safety standards
   ◆ Quantities required
   ◆ Manufacturing facilities available.

3 **Concept or solution generation.** This is the creative part of the process – generating a wide range of possible solutions.

4 **Solution evaluation.** This involves detailed consideration of how well each solution or concept satisfies the needs identified and design specifications.

5 **Detailed design.** This takes the selected solution and ensures that it will work.

6 **Review.** This ensures that the final product satisfies the criteria in 1 and 2 above before moving to implementation.

FOLLOWING SET
PROCEDURES

For some areas, particularly where safety is involved, you need to follow set procedures accurately.

In this case you should clarify exactly what the procedures are, who will know, whether they are written down anywhere. If you fail to find a solution, you may have to backtrack to see if you have followed the procedures correctly.

5.2 Trial and error

If you find it difficult to get started or you become anxious when confronted with a problem, it can help to first try something – anything – to remove the block. Possibilities are:

◆ do it now. Scribble down ideas immediately then return to them later to review them.
◆ 'quantity not quality'. Get plenty of scrap paper and write as many ideas and thoughts about the problem as possible.

In certain situations trial and error may be dangerous, *e.g. with electrical equipment*. Using trial and error can also be more time consuming than thinking things through in advance.

5.3 Creative idea generation

According to some theories, the two sides of our brains have different ways of handling information.

LEFT BRAIN/
RIGHT BRAIN

Left brain	Right brain
Connects with the right hand	Connects with the left hand
Analyses, abstracts, counts, marks time, plans step-by-step procedures, verbalises, makes logical, rational statements	Understands metaphors, dreams, creates new combinations of ideas, makes gestures to communicate

The aim in **creative** problem solving is to encourage the right-brain process. You could try the following.

◆ Work at the best time and in the best place for your creative thinking. This will be very personal and you will have to work this out from experience. We all work better at certain times of the day – can you adjust your working hours? Some work best in silence, others while listening to music (*could you take a personal stereo to work?*).
◆ Use a different communication process, *e.g. if you have been talking about a problem, stop talking and draw, generate computer images.*
◆ Don't think about it, *e.g. since ideas often emerge when you least expect them.*
◆ 'Reframe' the problem or look at it from another angle, *e.g. if an object is involved, look at it upside down or see the spaces or voids in it rather than the solid parts; look at positives rather than negatives; look at it from somebody else's standpoint.*
◆ Use unrelated objects to 'unblock' yourself, *e.g. after brainstorming a problem for a while, add one or two completely unrelated objects or ideas and consider how they could be used to solve the problem.*

BRAINSTORMING

You can do this alone, although it often works better with a group of people with differing experiences and approaches. If you are in a group, ask one person to write what is said on a board or flipchart where everyone can see it. It can be helpful to set a time limit and not allow interruptions. Use the following steps.

◆ Write down any ideas, however unusual, impractical, impossible or crazy (don't judge or select at this stage).

◆ Encourage 'piggy backing' (adding ideas to other people's ideas, even if at this stage they seem to be far off the point).
◆ Encourage lateral thinking.
◆ Do not make judgements about the ideas. Your concern is to generate ideas creatively at this stage.

When you have finished generating ideas:

◆ if in a group, start to check what people meant
◆ whether in a group or alone, group similar ideas together
◆ judge which items look suitable and which ones don't.

A variation on this theme is a 'collective notebook', in which people record their thoughts and ideas in a notebook over a given period. Any ideas count and can be anonymous if necessary.

MIND MAPS

These can be a powerful creative tool as a way of representing your mental patterns in visual form. You start by writing down everything you can think of around a central idea, in a box in the middle of the paper. You then put related ideas around it, growing outwards and connected by lines. See the example in Chapter 4, Report Writing.

DECISION/ RELEVANCE TREES

This is a representation of the dominant idea, broken down into its component parts:

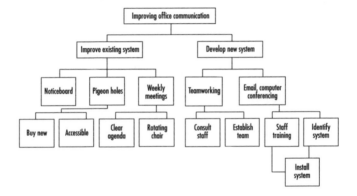

GRIDS, BOXES AND MATRICES

Some people find it helps to think in boxes, either two- or three-dimensional. A matrix may help you by listing and examining all the possible combinations which might be useful in solving a problem and the relationship between them. The following example would help you identify criteria against which to judge options.

Option A – Good for a limited budget where quality is not important
Option B – This is a poor option
Option C – The best, providing you have available funds
Option D – This is not as good an option as C

CHECKLISTS

These challenge you to think creatively about a problem in relation to specific questions. They bring the problem into sharper focus and may help you look at it from different angles and check that you have covered the main points. They can be useful for finding new ideas.

Example 1	Example 2
For a marketing strategy or a production line	For an engineering model or an office communication system
Who? What? Why? How? Where? When?	Can it be simplified? Can it be adapted? Can it be modified? Can it be substituted? Can it be reversed? Can it be combined? Can it be rearranged?

5.4 Which approach would suit you best?

With the exception of those areas which require you to follow a set procedure, there is normally no single best way to solve problems. It may therefore be helpful to try out an approach which is different from the ones you normally use. You can then see if it works better, if you prefer your usual approach, or if you could merge the approaches in some way.

Using an approach which is totally alien can inhibit your creativity – but so can failing to try new ones.

Which strategy/strategies would be most useful for me and my problem?

Once you have decided how to generate solutions, you need to set aside time to do it. Problem solving can be time consuming.

What are my possible solutions? (At this stage, it helps to identify as many as possible)

6 EVALUATING YOUR OPTIONS (SELECTING A SOLUTION/MAKING A DECISION)

....

6.1 What might influence your decision?

Your choice of solution may not only depend on practical considerations such as cost, time, space or the demands of your organisation. You may also be influenced by, for example:

◆ other people
◆ organisational politics
◆ strong emotion
◆ personal values
◆ personal goals
◆ stress and tiredness (here you may not produce quality decisions).

What might influence me?

There may be a value or ethical consideration (see Chapter 10, Ethics at Work) which has overriding importance.

For example, if staff work from home, it may be very helpful for clients to be able to contact them by telephone, but the invasion of staff privacy may make this unacceptable. Managers may decide that privacy is more important than ease of communication and so will not give out personal phone numbers.

For a decision you need to make now, are there any values or ethical considerations to take into account? How ethical are they?

Values/ethical considerations	Importance

6.2 Criteria

What criteria will you use to judge your possible solutions? These will vary from problem to problem and may include criteria which must be judged in both the short and long term.

Take the example of a new filing system:

Criteria	Important in the short term	Important in the long term
A Can find items easily	✔	✔
B Degree of difficulty and time to set up	✔	
C Ease of maintenance	✔	✔

This indicates that criteria A and C are the most important.

Refer back to section 2 where you identified the essential elements of the problem, before you decide your criteria.

Criteria against which to judge solutions for my problem	Important in the short term	Important in the long term

6.3 SWOT analysis

A SWOT analysis can help to identify the strengths and weaknesses of a solution as well as the opportunities offered and the threats posed.

The following is an example of a SWOT analysis for a possible new filing system.

Strengths	**Weaknesses**
Easy to find items Easy to maintain All can access it	Difficult to set up Lack of in-house expertise to establish it
Opportunities	**Threats**
Openness Better communication Ownership	Some items may be confidential (accessible to all?) If everyone has access they may not file items properly

6.4 Pros and cons

According to Edward de Bono (1982), we tend to make decisions about problems in an emotional, rather than rational, way.

De Bono's method is to think of solutions to a problem and then write down in three columns the **plus**, **minus** (these can also be pros and cons) and **interesting** aspects of each solution (these can also be 'pros' and 'cons').

By 'interesting' he means any consequences of the decision that are neither negative or positive. The plus and minus columns can focus on facts and the interesting column allows the mind to wander over consequences.

Possible solution	Plus	Minus	Interesting

6.5 But is the grass greener?

Any choice means that you reject at least one other solution. One difficulty in deciding may be that you do not want to lose the other option. To make a decision, you need to come to terms with your rejection of the other option. You may come to an informed decision but still feel uncomfortable.

You could, for example, do this by focusing on the positives of the option you have selected, *e.g. you may need to choose between staying in your current job and moving to a new one.* This may not be a clear-cut decision.

7 EVALUATING YOUR SOLUTION

·················

An effective solution is one which meets the goal and criteria and which also takes into account the consequences and the unexpected. There is an element of risk in all decision making and it should be carefully calculated. What might be the best outcome? What is the worst that could happen? Can you reduce the risks?

How can I improve the chances of success?

Have I selected a solution? If not, what else do I need to do to help me?

8 EVALUATING YOUR EFFECTIVENESS

What are your strengths in solving problems? Where do you need to improve? You could adopt a problem-solving approach to your own skill development. For example:

◆ what evidence is there of your problem-solving skills?
◆ what does this tell you about your strengths and weaknesses in solving problems?
◆ how could you improve your problem solving?
◆ which ways of improving your problem solving will you select?
◆ how will you implement them and review their effectiveness?

You could begin at any point with the above questions and then complete the following.

Areas I need to improve	Actions to take

9 REFERENCES AND BIBLIOGRAPHY

Libraries may have materials on this skill area. The following give examples:

Ackoff, R. (1978), *The Art of Problem Solving*, John Wiley and Sons.
Cowan, J. (nd), *Individual Approaches to Problem Solving*, Department of Civil Engineering, Heriot Watt University.
de Bono, E. (1982), *De Bono's Thinking Course*, Ariel Books, BBC.
Rickards, T. (1990), *Creativity and Problem Solving at Work*, Gower.

Contents

12

WORKING IN TEAMS

WHY IS THIS SKILL IMPORTANT?

In organisations, most work is carried out by a team of people working together to share resources, perspectives, ideas and abilities. You may be working in:

◆ an overarching team with a general responsibility/overall focus, e.g. a technical or sales department
◆ a subteam of a larger one, with a more specific focus, e.g. sales of a particular nature.

You may be working in a number of teams at any one time. These could be:

◆ temporary or long term
◆ small or large
◆ with people from within your organisation or outside, e.g. other professionals, members of the public
◆ for an activity with a specific purpose.

Whatever the purpose and composition of the team, it will be effective not just because of luck, or because of the particular mix of members, but because the individuals work together to make the team productive.

While team work can be exciting and enjoyable, a group that is not working well can be frustrating and ineffective. Team-work skills can be developed and improved. This chapter aims to help you think about what is happening and to identify strategies which will work for you.

Working in groups or teams can be formally constituted, very informal or somewhere between the two extremes. For the sake of simplicity, this chapter will refer throughout to 'team work'.

We suggest you use this chapter:

◆ when a particular team first forms
◆ and then throughout that team's work.

By the end of this chapter you should be able to:

1 clarify, agree and understand team goals and collectively review them at appropriate points
2 identify your own personal goals and those of others in relation to collective goals, and develop strategies for managing them
3 plan working arrangements and actions to meet goals within available resources and review team and individual progress; review and agree amendments to goals and plans as necessary
4 agree and amend responsibilities and allocation of tasks, taking into account individual skills, expertise and knowledge and encouraging flexibility; make appropriate offers of action; agree appropriate leadership if needed
5 feed relevant information and suggestions to ensure collective goals are met
6 carry out tasks within agreed limits, using the different perspectives, skills, expertise and knowledge of other team members to improve personal performance

7   actively seek and listen to the contributions of others
8   identify possible difficulties and areas of conflict and deal with them con-
    structively and appropriately
9   request feedback on individual performance (relating to task and behaviour)
    and act on it; give constructive feedback to others
10 monitor progress towards collective goals
11 identify elements of personal performance which are effective or less effective
    in team work; plan action to implement appropriate behaviour.

See Chapter 1 for the relationship between these learning outcomes and the Key
Skills qualifications

1 INTRODUCTION

Before you start working in a team, it may help to think about how you feel about team
work in general. What are the main issues you want to consider when you work in
teams?

Main issues
E.g. will everyone contribute? Will the team work as effectively as an individual would?

After you have worked through this chapter, you can return to this box to check
whether your concerns have been addressed.

2 CLARIFYING THE PURPOSE

2.1 Team goals

Being clear about the goals of your team is an essential first step. It will help to discuss
and clarify them with the team members so that each person understands and accepts
a commitment to them, and everyone knows what is expected. These goals are better
expressed in straightforward language to prevent misunderstanding.

Formally constituted teams often work within terms of reference or are given a remit.

◆ **Terms of reference** put limits around the proper concerns of the team.
◆ A **remit** is the task and responsibility given to the team.

*For example, the remit may be to devise a new ordering system. The terms of reference may be to
report to the managing director, to work within a given budget and to meet the needs of specific
departments.*

What is the main remit/goal/purpose of the team?

What are the terms of reference?

What is the timescale?

2.2 Individual goals

A team is made up of a number of individuals, with differing personalities, skills, knowledge and motivations. The strengths of team work lie in combining these to work effectively. Just as the team itself will have goals, so each person will have their own expectations and needs. These may be the same as the team's or different.

What do I want to achieve as an individual? (*E.g. gain experience, demonstrate my performance, a high appraisal grade, promotion*)

3 ESTABLISHING WORKING PRACTICES

....

Your team is likely to start with a meeting, whether face to face or via technology (*e.g. videoconferencing, teleconferencing*). For how to organise and manage formal and informal meetings, see Chapter 13, Meetings.

How the team is structured and organised will depend on its role in the organisation and how much authority it has, *e.g. whether it is a subgroup of another group with authority, or whether it will be a central decision maker.*

3.1 Team leadership/team coordinator

What sort of leadership would be appropriate for the situation? If vital decisions must be made quickly, you may need a leader. In other situations – *e.g. where gaining everybody's agreement and sharing responsibility are important* – the team might operate collectively.

A team leader may be appointed by your organisation, or the team may be able to elect an appropriate person.

Leadership style may influence the effectiveness of the team. This involves giving focus and direction and requires personal skills and abilities, *e.g. communication, vision, commitment.* Team leaders should be able to inspire and mobilise the team.

Team leaders may be given 'authority' in a hierarchical sense, *e.g. they may be in a managerial position to make decisions, commit resources.* They may have authority and influence because of their position.

It may be that the leader has limited authority and positional 'power' and will need to use other means to get things done. They may be a more participative leader, using personal skills such as persuasion rather than autocratic strategies (see Chapter 14, Putting Your Case: Negotiating and Assertiveness, for some help).

The team may need a coordinator to monitor who is doing what.

What would work best in my team?

3.2 Team members

Individuals' responsibilities, their authority and accountability may be spelt out by your organisation. Whether in writing or not, each team member has a responsibility to the team to work in a way which enables it to meet its goals.

Individuals within teams are often motivated by achievement and target setting. Each member will be able to offer expertise in an area and may need to look at their own targets in the context of others and the overall goal. The team members may need to be flexible in their approach to team tasks, *e.g. multi-tasking*, and how the team functions *e.g. negotiating, delegating.*

Section 4 below looks at allocating tasks. If you are leading a team, who do you need on it to carry out those tasks? If you are part of a team, what can you contribute and who else on the team can help you with your task?

Team members (including myself)	What can each contribute?

3.3 Organisational structure

How does your team fit into the organisational structure? You need to know this whether you are organising it or part of it. The following box may help.

Issue	My notes
Who does the team ultimately report to?	
Who will make team decisions? How? Will they have to be approved? Who by?	
What departments/functions will the team come into contact with?	
What resources can the team use (this includes people's time)? Are you working to a budget?	
Other organisational issues (please list)	

Would it help to draw a diagram showing the reporting structure and links to other departments? It might help to raise the issues above in a team meeting – to ensure that everybody shares the same understanding.

3.4 Communication systems/structures

Effective communication is essential for team work. It is helpful to write down clearly laid out and simple systems, so that all team members have the same information.

When communicating with others, *e.g. managers, support staff, technical personnel or other teams*, keep the number of links as short as possible.

	Managers	Support staff	Other teams
Who must the team communicate with? (names)			
What will it be about?			
What is the communication system? (meeting, interim reports, email etc.)			
Who will do the communicating? (names)			
How often?			

How do team members communicate between themselves? *E.g. via meetings, email, computer conferencing, computer forums or bulletin boards*

4 PLANNING ACTIONS AND ALLOCATING TASKS

....

Planning how to meet your goals is essential to avoid wasted effort and problems, and to make the most of your resources. Answering the following questions may help.

◆ How can the main task be subdivided into smaller tasks?
◆ When must each subtask be completed?
◆ Who can do which subtasks?
◆ Does the workload seem appropriately distributed?
◆ If you carry out all the subtasks by the time agreed, will all your goals be met?

4.1 Dividing up tasks

When allocating tasks to team members, you could consider:

◆ personal interests.
◆ members' expertise. Members might want to use their existing expertise or develop new expertise by attempting new tasks. Team members are a resource and it is important to use them effectively.
◆ members' available time. They may have other workloads to consider.

Suppose you cannot agree who will do what? Negotiating is an important skill in working with others. Depending on the structure of the team, either the team leader could allocate the tasks or the whole team can work together to:

◆ identify preferences
◆ identify conflicts of preferences
◆ identify any solutions, *e.g. redivide or redefine the subtasks; work together on a subtask.*

You may find other chapters of this book useful in planning your work:

◆ Chapter 2, Planning and Managing Your Workload
◆ Chapter 9, Project Work – many teams are formed to carry out projects.
◆ Chapter 11, Solving Problems and Making Decisions
◆ Chapter 14, Putting Your Case: Negotiating and Assertiveness – to help in agreeing who does what

Task	To be done by (team member)	Deadline

4.2 Monitoring progress

There may be penalty clauses for non-delivery of targets written into a contract which will cost your organisation money, or another team's project may be dependent on your team's producing work on time. The team, or some of its members, may be under threat if you do not deliver by the deadline. Monitoring and reviewing progress will be an essential aspect of the team's action planning. (See Chapter 9, Project Work.)

How will the team monitor progress to check that everybody has completed their agreed tasks? Possibilities include:

◆ writing down what was agreed, *e.g. minutes should show actions to be taken by whom and when* (see Chapter 7, Keeping Notes, Records and Minutes)
◆ regular progress review meetings, which team members are expected to attend
◆ nominating a member of the team as a progress chaser, who keeps in contact with and chivvies team members
◆ informing others early if there are particular problems, *e.g. that you won't be able to complete by the deadline, that another team has not completed its work, so the information is not yet available*
◆ working together on problematic tasks, *e.g. combining team members' expertise*
◆ using Chapter 14, Putting Your Case: Negotiating and Assertiveness.

How will you ensure that **you** do what you have agreed? (See Chapter 2, Planning and Managing Your Workload, and Chapter 15, Dealing with Pressure.)

If you work on your subtask mainly on your own you will miss one of the main benefits of team work – getting ideas, new perspectives and information from others to improve your work. Have you:

◆ discussed how you will go about your subtask with other team members and checked progress with them?
◆ asked them for information or ideas to help you?
◆ discussed how your subtask relates to theirs?
◆ discussed their subtask and reviewed their work?

4.3 Reviewing goals and plans

Circumstances change. New information comes to light and new angles emerge, *e.g. you may need to extend or develop your project, a team member may leave.*

In these cases, you may have to rethink your goals, the division of subtasks and their allocation to individuals. Progress may produce unexpected issues – you will have to decide, as a team, how to respond to these (but see Chapter 9, Project Work – changing things may have costs associated with it).

You may need to return to basic principles, review them and agree those from which you are operating. These principles might refer to how you operate as a team or to the task (*e.g. principles relating to your project, criteria for judging the effectiveness of the project*).

The following should help you carry out regular reviews, *e.g. at every team meeting.*

Initial goals	Amended goals

Initial subtasks	Amended subtasks	By (team member)	Deadline

5 IDENTIFYING YOUR OWN TEAM SKILLS

This chapter focuses not on other people's behaviour but on how you work with other people. Your behaviour will influence others' behaviour and you have a better chance of changing what you do.

5.1 How you behave in teams

The following will help you to clarify your behaviour in teams and gives examples of skills you could consider:

◆ communicating
◆ flexibility
◆ contributing your share
◆ punctuality
◆ giving/seeking help when needed
◆ being courteous, *e.g. thanking people for their contribution*
◆ doing what you say
◆ meeting deadlines.

The last two items are essential to the team's effectiveness and performance, and indicate a commitment to the team goals which requires members to do what they say by the given deadline.

You might like to ask those you have worked with or your manager:

◆ what they thought about how you did the work
◆ what they thought about how you behaved in the team.

Aspects I am confident about, things I do well in teams	Aspects I find difficult, things I need to improve in teams

5.2 Team roles

A great deal of work has been done on identifying the roles that people play in teams and some organisations now use psychometric testing or personality inventories to help determine team membership. They try to ensure that the composition of the team includes all the characteristics which make an effective team.

An understanding of the different roles involved in teams and of the role preferences of the members will help you work with your team.

Team role refers to a tendency to behave, contribute and interrelate in certain distinctive ways. The following role descriptions are taken from work by Belbin (1993). You may disagree with these role descriptions, but they may help you think through the sort of roles you think people do have in teams.

- ◆ **Plant** – Creative and imaginative. Sometimes unorthodox. Solves difficult problems.
- ◆ **Resource investigator** – Extrovert, enthusiastic and good communicator. Explores opportunities and develops contacts.
- ◆ **Coordinator** – Confident and mature, a good chairperson. Clarifies goals and promotes decision making. Delegates.
- ◆ **Shaper** – Challenging, dynamic and good under pressure. Overcomes obstacles.
- ◆ **Monitor evaluator** – Strategic and discerning. Sees all options and judges accurately.
- ◆ **Teamworker** – Cooperative, perceptive and diplomatic. Listens, averts friction and calms.
- ◆ **Implementer** – Disciplined, reliable and efficient. Turns ideas into practical actions.
- ◆ **Completer** – Conscientious. Looks for errors and omissions. Delivers on time.
- ◆ **Specialist** – Single-minded and self-starting. Dedicated. Provides unique knowledge and skills.

Do you recognise yourself and others in these descriptions? Do you fit into more than one? Do you play the same role in all the teams you are in or take on different roles?

6 HOW THE TEAM WORKS

....

6.1 Team stages

A team goes through a number of stages during its development, from its initial formation to reaching its full potential. There may be stages where the team is not as effective.

Tuckman and Jenson (1977) suggest that teams go through four stages.

Forming. This is a period when the team comes together, gets to know each other and evaluates each other's personalities, abilities, goals and power. The team is unlikely to be able to carry out demanding tasks and members may be concerned about whether they will be accepted.

Storming. As members establish roles within the team, there may be a period where members express their views more freely and disagree. Conflict may arise and leadership may be challenged. Alliances and factions may form. (However, it should be noted that a certain level of disagreement can be productive and lead to effective problem solving and decision making.)

Norming. This is a period of greater cooperation, with views expressed and issues raised without emotions running high. Team members have identified their role and found their position in the team. At this point, any individual challenge to team decisions may isolate that person.

Performing. The team performs effectively, with a high level of commitment and a strong team identity. It is aware of its potential and any differences of opinion and challenges are listened to as a way of improving the effectiveness of the team.

Your team may not go through all these stages, but it will go through its own stages because of different phases of work, different pressure, members leaving/joining and interpersonal issues.

What is crucial is to identify what is currently happening in your team and what you can do to help it work better. Other chapters in this book that could be useful here are:

◆ Chapter 2, Planning and Managing Your Workload
◆ Chapter 9, Project Work
◆ Chapter 14, Putting Your Case: Negotiating and Assertiveness
◆ Chapter 15, Dealing with Pressure.

What stage is your team at? It may be at a helpful or less helpful stage, *e.g. agreement/conflict, productive/inactive, all contribute/some avoid it by fooling around.* All team members can influence what happens, not just the team leader.

What stage is my team at?	Why?	What could I do, *e.g. to build on the stage or improve it?*

6.2 Team process

The following may help you think about what is happening in your team. It has a scale of 1–4, where 1 = 'very helpful behaviour' and 4 = 'very unhelpful behaviour'.

In our team, do we ...	1	2	3	4	
express views openly?					grumble afterwards?
ask others for views/ideas?					fail to ask others for their views/ideas?
listen/respond to others?					ignore others/their ideas?
share work evenly?					fail to share work evenly?
participate equally in discussions?					dominate, or keep quiet?
use team members' abilities well?					fail to use team members' abilities?
help each other?					form cliques/act uncooperatively?
trust each other?					feel suspicious of each other?
show enthusiasm?					show apathy?
understand team goals?					not understand team goals?
accept team goals?					not accept team goals?
achieve team goals?					fail to achieve team goals?
use resources well?					not use resources well?
all agree decisions?					not make decisions or not involve all?
use time effectively?					not use time effectively?
treat each other courteously?					behave rudely or inconsiderately?

If there are problems between team members (*e.g. somebody not pulling their weight or being domineering*), it can help to:

◆ identify the cause (*e.g. are there any internal/external pressures?*)
◆ focus on the team, not the person (*e.g. 'We've got a problem, what can we do about it?'*)
◆ identify actions that members could take, rather than criticise them (*e.g. 'We need to sort this out in this way …'*)
◆ express your view of things before they get out of hand in your mind (*e.g. 'I am getting concerned about …'*)

Chapter 14, Putting Your Case: Negotiating and Assertiveness, may help here.

7 DEALING WITH TEAM ISSUES

It is important to deal effectively with any problems or you may not achieve the team goal. If you fail to meet your goal, it may have repercussions on:

◆ the organisation, *e.g. it may lose a client, money, its reputation*
◆ the team, *e.g. missing important deadlines, loss of credibility, power, valuable team members*
◆ individuals, *e.g. end up with too much work, become resentful, poor appraisal.*

Good team-work skills are the means by which to deal with such situations.

The following are examples of typical problems and suggested ways of dealing with them; but they are suggestions only and you may have other ideas.

Problem	Suggestions
Uneven workload, 'passengers', people not pulling their weight	Agree who does what at the start and write it down to avoid confusion. Ask those not pulling their weight why not – they may have good reason. Discuss the effect it is having on the team. Use Chapter 14, Putting Your Case: Negotiating and Assertiveness.
Wasting time, not achieving targets on time	Ensure that the team is using members' skills efficiently. What could you do differently (*e.g. set deadlines, appoint a timekeeper for meetings*)? See section 4.2
Too much work involved	Review your goals – are you focused enough? Are there more efficient ways of carrying out the task? Use Chapter 2, Planning and Managing Your Workload.
Confusion	Discuss your goals as a team and keep referring back to them. Use Chapter 11, Solving Problems and Making Decisions.

What are the reasons for any problems you have identified by using the above list? What is your part in any problems? What could you do personally to improve things? You could return to section 6.2 at intervals to see if there is any improvement.

The team's main problem	Action to be taken by the team	Action to be taken by me

Your team may conflict with another team for a variety of reasons, *e.g. competitiveness, power struggle*, and the result may be a lack of trust, reduced cooperation and communication. This conflict could have the effect of enhancing each team's unity, but may not meet the organisation's overall goals.

What is the cause of the conflict?	What is the effect of the conflict?	What could be done?

If you or your team encounters a problem which you are unable to deal with, you may need to seek further help from your organisation.

8 ACTION PLANNING

Are there aspects of your behaviour when working in teams that you'd like to change? If so, you might wish to try out new behaviours. You could seek feedback (see Chapter 17, Identifying Strengths and Improving Skills) from team members or managers where relevant, about:

◆ how well you carried out your elements of the work
◆ how you behaved in the team
◆ how flexible you are when you operate in a team. Are you able to take on different roles or tasks if necessary?

In completing the box below you could consider sources of help:

◆ your organisation may have staff development opportunities, *e.g. team-building courses*
◆ other chapters in this book
◆ books on team skills (see bibliography – libraries may have many more, including videos)
◆ colleagues, mentors (see Chapter 18) and managers (they may help you monitor what you are doing)
◆ a diary (you could keep a record of what you do).

Return to section 1. Has this chapter met your needs? If not, what else do you need to do? What further help do you need? From where or whom?
   Please complete the box opposite.

What do I do that is helpful to both me and the team?

What do I do that is unhelpful?

What would I like to do differently?

Actions I could take to change things in the future

9 REFERENCES AND BIBLIOGRAPHY

....

Libraries may have materials on this skill area. The following gives examples:

Belbin, M. (1993), *Team Roles at Work*, Butterworth Heinemann.

Johnson, D. W. and Johnson, F. P. (1991), *Joining Together: Group Theory and Group Skills*, Prentice Hall.

Rackham, N. and Morgan, T. (1977), *Behaviour Analysis in Training*, McGraw-Hill.

Tuckman, B. and Jenson, M. (1977), 'Stages of Small Group Development', *Group and Organisational Studies*, 2(4).

13
MEETINGS

Contents

WHY IS THIS SKILL IMPORTANT?

Meetings are an essential aspect of work and need to be well organised and efficient in order to be effective and avoid wasted time and cost.

This chapter aims to help you participate more effectively, plan meetings and review in order to improve your skills.

We suggest you use this chapter:

◆ before you participate in a meeting
◆ before you organise a meeting
◆ in conjunction with other chapters in this book:
    7   Keeping Notes, Records and Minutes
    9   Project Work
    12   Working in Teams
    14   Putting Your Case: Negotiating and Assertiveness.

By the end of this chapter you should be able to:

1 identify in advance the purpose of the meeting, possible goals, context and personal role and prepare appropriately
2 agree purpose, collective goals and any specific roles at the start of a meeting and review these at the appropriate points in the meeting
3 identify the conventions applying to the meeting and work with them
4 provide at appropriate points information of evidence which is relevant, accurate and concise
5 recognise your own role/responsibilities and those of others and contribute within them
6 contribute in a way which:
    – is equal and recognises your own role/responsibilities and those of others
    – supports the meeting's purpose and collective goals
    – is sensitive to the other participants
    – encourages the contribution of others and makes use of others' skills, expertise and knowledge
7 keep records of the meeting
8 clarify your own responsibilities and actions, note appropriate offers of action and carry them out.

See Chapter 1 for the relationship between these learning outcomes and the Key Skills qualifications.

1 INTRODUCTION

....

1.1 Purposes of meetings

Meetings may be:

◆ formal, informal
◆ one to one, small or large
◆ face to face, via video/teleconferencing (see Chapter 3, Communicating at Work).

You may need to have meetings with a range of people, *e.g. your colleagues, managers, clients, members of the public, contractors, other professionals*. There are different types of meetings – sales meetings, contract meetings, project meetings, meetings at conferences or to plan conferences. Each meeting will have a different purpose and you will need to respond to other participants appropriately to achieve that purpose.

Meetings may be held for a variety of reasons:

◆ share information
◆ brief teams
◆ generate ideas
◆ review/monitor progress
◆ coordinate teams
◆ motivate
◆ sell/persuade.

Can your purpose be served by other means of communication, *e.g. telephone calls, memos, teleconferencing, videoconferencing*? Time and money may be saved.

Type of meeting I attend	What is the main purpose?

Whether you are organising, leading or participating in a meeting, you need to know in advance what you want from it, in order to prepare for it. You could complete the box below for a meeting you are about to have:

What are the aims/objectives of the meeting?	What do I personally want to get from it?	What preparation do I need to do in advance? E.g. information to gather, handouts to prepare

2 OPERATING PROCEDURES FOR MEETINGS
··············

2.1 Formal roles

In smaller meetings, formal roles may not be necessary. In larger ones or where more structure is needed, it can help to have a chairperson and a secretary. These roles could be fixed or you could rotate them. It may be helpful to encourage flexibility in team members.

A chairperson:

◆ agrees an agenda (asks for items from the group), either in advance or at the start of a meeting
◆ helps the group work through the agenda and keeps an eye on time
◆ encourages contributions, involves quiet people, asks talkative people to let others speak
◆ makes people feel comfortable.

A secretary:

◆ takes accurate notes (minutes) of meetings. It can be helpful to ask the chairperson to use the final five minutes to check what has been said and to clarify the actions to be taken
◆ arranges meetings, venues.

DURING THE MEETING: THE PROCESS

The chairperson should normally:

◆ welcome the participants and make any necessary introductions
◆ confirm start and end times. Always stick to time. People become bored and frustrated if you over-run
◆ give information about breaks, location of toilets etc.
◆ confirm 'groundrules' (see section 2.2)
◆ work through the agenda, keeping a record of any decisions and recommendations. If any action is to be taken, keep a record of by whom and by when
◆ arrange the next meeting, if appropriate
◆ thank the participants.

MANAGING/LEADING THE MEETING

The chairperson needs to provide direction and 'manage' the participants to ensure an effective meeting. You may have organisational authority over participants, or may need to use other means to lead, *e.g. persuasion* (see Chapter 14, Putting Your Case: Negotiating and Assertiveness). Whatever your position, you will need to use your skills to:

◆ keep control of time, *e.g. give two-minute warnings when the allocated time for an item is near to the end*
◆ maintain the focus of the topic – meetings can sometimes wander off the point and you will need to bring discussions back to the purpose
◆ 'manage' the participants, *e.g. using your communication abilities to ensure that everyone is contributing what they can, inviting people to speak, maintaining order if necessary.*

AFTER THE MEETING

◆ Minutes are important as a record and action plan (see Chapter 7, Keeping Notes, Records and Minutes). They should be brief and circulated as soon as possible.
◆ It will be helpful to review and evaluate the meeting to help you improve how you work in meetings in the future (see section 6 for guidance on how to do this).

2.2 Groundrules for meetings

It is very helpful to agree a set of rules ('groundrules') to guide the way in which the meeting will operate. Following groundrules will help make meetings run smoothly, prevent problems and give you some control if there are difficulties. The groundrules should be discussed at the start of the meeting wherever possible. Your organisation may have procedures for this.

EXAMPLES OF ITEMS
FOR GROUNDRULES

◆ Start and end meetings on time.
◆ Agree an agenda for meetings.
◆ Meetings are confidential (if appropriate).
◆ Everyone has the right to contribute.
◆ Encourage everyone to speak.
◆ Nobody to dominate discussions.
◆ No interrupting.
◆ No putting others down. Criticise the ideas, not the person.
◆ Identify and agree actions to be taken and by when.

What groundrules would be helpful for your meeting?

Groundrules for the meeting

2.3 Formal meetings

Council meetings in a local authority, governors' meetings in public organisations, board or shareholder meetings and trade union meetings will all have set procedures and you need to find out about them in advance.
   Examples of such procedures are:

◆ *participants may have to address all questions or comments to the chairperson, who then re-directs them all to others.*
◆ *an individual may be invited to make a presentation. There may be a general discussion about the presentation in which the presenter does not take part. The presenter may then be asked to comment on the discussion.*
◆ *agreement may be obtained by somebody 'putting a motion' which must be seconded by another and then there must be a vote.*

3 HOW YOU OPERATE IN MEETINGS

You are likely to behave differently in different meetings, according to the purpose and the other participants, *e.g. you may choose to behave differently in an appraisal interview, than in a team meeting with colleagues.*
   The following list, from Turner (1983), describes how people may operate. You could use it to identify how you behaved in a particular meeting, *e.g. a project group meeting.*

Roles	Behaviour	My notes
Task roles	Initiates	
	Seeks opinions	
	Gives opinions	
	Elaborates	
	Coordinates	
	Summarises	

Roles	Behaviour	My notes
Maintenance roles	Encourages	
	Gatekeeps (keeps the group to the task)	
	Sets standards	
	Expresses group feelings/reactions	
Task and maintenance roles	Evaluates	
	Diagnoses	
	Tests for consensus/agreement	
	Mediates	
	Compromises	
	Relieves tension	
	Makes jokes	

Source: Turner, C. (1983) *Developing Interpersonal Skills*, The Further Education Staff College (now Further Education Development Agency).

You could also use the following list, also from Turner (1983), to identify any of your behaviours which are unhelpful in a group.

Unhelpful behaviour	
Being overly aggressive	
Blocking (rejecting ideas without due consideration, going off at tangents)	
Self-confession	
Competing	
Seeking sympathy	
Special pleading (for own concerns or interests)	
Horsing around	
Seeking recognition (excessive/loud talking, unsociable behaviour)	

Does your behaviour as an individual contribute to the meeting's effectiveness? Score yourself on the chart overleaf using the following scale, after meetings. It has a scale of 1–4 where 1 = 'very positive' and 4 = 'very negative'.

Positive behaviour	1	2	3	4	Negative behaviour
Listening to others, asking for clarification (e.g. 'did you mean …?')					Ignoring others
Allowing others to speak					Interrupting
Expressing relevant views positively and openly					Being negative, disruptive, being irrelevant
Asking others for their views and ideas					Ignoring others' views, being dismissive
Contributing equally to discussions					Keeping quiet, dominating
Asking what others think about your contributions					Unconcerned about others' views
Showing enthusiasm					Showing apathy
Offering to take action if you have the expertise					Not volunteering

NON-VERBAL SIGNALS   People will not only hear what you say, they will observe what you do in meetings. The way you look and act will give them an impression of you. They will 'read' your signals and interpret them. You also need to be aware of other people's non–verbal signals. Some examples are given below.

◆ Your **clothes** may suggest what your professional approach is, *e.g. wearing casual clothes when meeting an important client, wearing inappropriate shoes on a building site.*
◆ **Facial expression**, *e.g. yawning shows boredom*
◆ **Body language**, *e.g. folded arms may suggest that you are immovable, leaning forward may indicate interest.*
◆ **Mannerisms**, *e.g. tapping fingers can indicate impatience.*

You may offend people from other cultures by being unaware of their protocols. You will need to check what they are in advance, *e.g. the Japanese find it offensive to blow your nose in public, most cultures have different practices in terms of the distance they stand from other people or touching others (they may feel crowded out if you stand too near, women from some cultures would be offended if a male touched their arm).*

Areas I need to be careful about	Action I could take

4 DEALING WITH PROBLEMS IN MEETINGS

··············

There may be times when problems arise, *e.g. disagreements, people not contributing, losing focus.* Whether you are leading the meeting or a participant, you need to use your skills to help the meeting deal with any difficulties and move forward.

The following are examples, with suggestions for ways of dealing with them. You may have other ideas and strategies. You could also look at Chapter 14, Putting Your Case: Negotiating and Assertiveness (particularly the section on dealing with conflict).

Problem	Suggestions
Quiet group members.	Ask for their views, encourage them to speak, be positive about their comments.
Disruptive group members, *e.g. excessive lightheartedness, negativeness, overtalkativeness, aggression, rudeness.*	Possibilities include ignoring jokes, asking 'talkatives' to let somebody else have a say, pointing out when someone is negative and asking for positives.
Nobody contributes/ideas are not forthcoming.	Invite people by name, if you feel/know they could contribute. Suggest that others who could contribute attend the next meeting, *e.g. a specialist in a particular field.*

How can you help a meeting deal with difficulties? You can influence what happens if you are leading the meeting or if you are just a participant. It is helpful to identify the causes of problems.

What is the difficulty?	What is the cause?	What could I do?

5 ORGANISING A MEETING

....

You may need to arrange a meeting. Effective meetings are well planned in advance. Careful planning and preparation are very important to their effectiveness.

5.1 Planning a meeting

PURPOSE

◆ Why are you having a meeting? You need to be clear about your aims and objectives.
◆ What do you want to achieve?

PARTICIPANTS

If possible, keep these to a minimum:

◆ Who can contribute? *E.g. who can generate ideas, who shares your views, who can make decisions or offer information?*
◆ Who should be invited as a matter of courtesy?
◆ Will you need specialists, *e.g. secretary to record the minutes, legal representative, interpreter, or guest speaker?*

FORMAL OR INFORMAL?

Whether the meeting is formal or informal will influence your venue and the organisation you need to do.

TIME AND VENUE

◆ Will anyone have to travel? Arrange the time and place accordingly. Will you need accommodation?
◆ What is a good time? Friday afternoon may not be, before lunch may be.
◆ How long will the meeting be?
◆ What venue would be appropriate for your purpose? *E.g. internal meeting room, conference centre, hotel, on site.*

AGENDA

The agenda gives a framework for the meeting and prevents time wasting.

◆ What topics are to be covered, in what order? The most important items should come early in the meeting.
◆ Each item should have a time allocation and the names of anyone giving a presentation about it.
◆ If it is a long meeting, you may choose to have a coffee break or lunch.

Depending on your purpose, the agenda might be:

◆ prearranged and circulated beforehand, to allow people to prepare relevant material
◆ prearranged, presented at the beginning of the meeting, with opportunities for participants to add items
◆ open, generated at the beginning of the meeting by participants.

An example of a prearranged, formal agenda might be:

I	Chairperson's opening remarks
II	Attendance and apologies
III	Approval of the minutes from the previous meeting
IV	Matters arising from the last meeting
V	General business
VI	Any other business (AOB)
VII	Date and time of the next meeting

5.2 Before the meeting

SENDING OUT INFORMATION

People are busy. They will need all the necessary information in advance so that they can plan accordingly.

The following gives the information that participants will need.

The purpose of the meeting	
List of those attending	
Location (with map if necessary), date and time	
Agenda (send this out only a few days in advance, so participants don't lose it)	
Any background information you need to send out beforehand, *e.g. minutes of last meeting*	
Do participants need to prepare any material beforehand? If so, what?	
Other information needed	

MAKING ARRANGEMENTS

This checklist may help.

Have I booked a venue (costs?). Have I arranged accommodation if needed?	
Have I arranged transport if needed (costs?)?	
Have I booked refreshments/meals (costs?)?	
Have I organised equipment needed, *e.g. OHP, video/teleconferencing facilities?*	
Have I arranged for any specialists who need to attend?	
Have I agreed costs with those responsible?	
Have I confirmed any arrangements before the meeting?	

5.3 On the day

Check that everything is organised, *e.g. the room is set out appropriately for your purpose, resources are available and working, name tags, spare copies of any material, agendas, papers.*

6 ACTION PLANNING

·············

How could you improve your performance in meetings? You could seek feedback from others in the meeting (see Chapter 17, Identifying Strengths and Improving Skills).

When completing the box below, you could consider sources of help:

- ◆ other chapters in this book
- ◆ information on meetings, *e.g. books, videos*
- ◆ colleagues, mentors, managers
- ◆ a diary to keep a record of how you operate in meetings (you could jot down notes during the meeting or afterwards on what you did).

	Action I could take	By (date)
Identifying the purpose and conventions of a particular meeting		
Recognising my role and responsibilities in meetings		
Recognising others' roles and responsibilities		
Operate in a way that helps the meeting move forward, *e.g. contributions, behaviour*		
Offer appropriate action		
Keeping notes/records/minutes		
Organising a meeting		

7 REFERENCES AND BIBLIOGRAPHY

···················

Harrison, F. L. (1995), *Advanced Project Management: A Structured Approach*, 3rd edn, Gower.
Moss, G. (1991), *Survival Skills for New Managers*, Kogan Page.
Turner, C. (1983), *Developing Interpersonal Skills*, The Further Education Staff College (now Further Education Development Agency).

Contents

14

PUTTING YOUR CASE: NEGOTIATING AND ASSERTIVENESS

WHY IS THIS SKILL IMPORTANT?

Our effectiveness in most situations depends, at least in part, on how well we deal with other people.

In many work situations you need to put your case: explaining things to colleagues or clients; selling or persuading; in interviews. Note that Chapter 5 deals with making more formal presentations to audiences.

What we and others want from a situation is rarely identical and all people at work need to agree things with others. This process, known as negotiating, is sometimes formal but more usually informal. In many jobs (surveying, social work, contract management, buying, selling etc.) it is crucial.

Assertiveness is about getting what you want, while respecting the needs of others.

We suggest you use this chapter:

◆ when you are in a situation where you need to put your case to others, to agree things with others, to be assertive
◆ when you are in a situation where you need to deal with conflict
◆ when you need to give feedback to others
◆ on an ongoing basis to help you review and monitor what you do.

By the end of this chapter you should be able to:

1 identify your own needs, goals, responsibilities, rights, check on others' understanding of your position within working arrangements
2 clarify your understanding of others' needs, goals, responsibilities, rights within working arrangements
3 know of strategies and their possible effects in given situations
4 implement strategies and review their effectiveness in meeting mutually acceptable goals
5 work with others in a way which is consistent with resources, responsibilities and the context
6 give constructive feedback to others where appropriate
7 give relevant information and evidence to others to meet their needs and responsibilities
8 make offers of appropriate and relevant action, accept responsibilities agreed and carry out actions within working arrangements
9 identify areas of difficulty and conflict and deal with them constructively
10 identify strengths and weaknesses of your own dealings with others, using feedback from others, identify and take actions to build on strengths and improve weaknesses, and review progress.

See Chapter 1 for the relationship between these learning outcomes and the Key Skill qualifications.

1 YOUR NEEDS

....

What situations are you likely to find yourself in?

Situation	How frequently will I meet this?	Do I find this easy/difficult?	How important might it be?
Agreeing things with others			
Asking for something I want			
Selling something			
Persuading somebody about something			
Giving feedback to others			
Resolving conflict/settling disputes			
Being interviewed			
Being in meetings			
Being appraised (see Chapter 19, Professional Development)			
Others (please list)			

Making presentations to others is covered in Chapter 5, Making Presentations, and is also partly covered by Chapters 3 and 4 (Communicating at Work and Report Writing) – although this chapter can help you work out the wording and content of your communications. It focuses on direct dealings with individuals.

It will help to work through this chapter with a particular situation in mind. Perhaps one of the above is currently facing you or has faced you recently?

2 GOALS

2.1 What do you want?

Whatever the situation, in dealing with others you need to be clear what you want. This will enable you to be more coherent and to identify your approach to the situation. It will help to ask the following questions before talking to others.

What is the basic issue or problem?
What are my feelings about it?
Do my feelings really relate to the situation/other person(s) involved? (They might do so, or they could really be about something else, *e.g. your general stress level or feeling of well-being/dissatisfaction*)
What do I want to happen?
What is my responsibility?
What is their responsibility?
What is someone else's responsibility?
What rights do I have in this situation?

2.2 What do they want?

What are 'the others' likely to want? What might the situation look like from their perspective? You cannot accurately know what another person thinks, but what is your best guess? Can you put yourself in their position?

What is likely to be their basic issue or problem?
What will they want?
What are their feelings likely to be about this?
What information do they need in order to deal with the issue or problem?
What is rightly their responsibility?
What rights do they have in this situation?

2.3 Putting it together

Difficulties with others often arise from misunderstanding. Are others clear about what you want? Are you clear about what they want? How will you clarify this with them?

◆ Should you put all your cards on the table immediately? What effect would that have?
◆ Should you begin by asking the other person what they want or how they see things?

The best approach depends on the situation. To whose advantage is it to begin?

One approach is to lay out the issue generally so that both parties are aware of the 'agenda' (*e.g. 'I need to talk to you about my workload'*). You could then ask the other person for their views (*e.g. 'What do you think my priorities should be?'*) before stating what you want.

Try to check that others have understood you (*e.g. 'Do you need any more information?'*) and that you have understood them (*e.g. 'Did you mean …?'*)

3 AGREEING THINGS WITH OTHERS

3.1 When might you need to do this?

This section uses the term 'negotiation' to mean any situation when you have to agree something with somebody.

When might you have to do this? Consider the situations on the list opposite.

Situation	
Agreeing work with colleagues: – on lower grades – at your own level – at a more senior level – in other departments or functions	
Resolving disputes: – with a colleague – between colleagues – with a group	
Agreeing prices or services with others: – clients – customers – providers of products or services	
Agreeing your own development needs, *e.g. via appraisal* (see Chapter 19, Professional Development)	
Others (please list)	

You may find it helpful to mark those items on this list which you find difficult. You could then complete the rest of this section in relation to such a situation, or perhaps to a situation currently facing you.

3.2 Your approach

There are various approaches to negotiating. These include (based on Steel, Murphy and Russill, 1989):

◆ coercion (*e.g. 'if you don't agree then …'*)
◆ use of emotion (*e.g. 'I've struggled here on this broken leg, the least you could do is …'*)
◆ brinkmanship (*e.g. 'I'll resign unless …'*)
◆ divide and rule (*e.g. 'but Fred didn't say that …'*)
◆ deliberate misunderstanding (*e.g. 'It's 40p for one', '40p for one hundred is quite reasonable'*).

This chapter assumes that such 'tricks' are counterproductive. You may have to work again with those with whom you negotiate and your organisation may need to maintain goodwill or a reputation (see Chapter 10, Ethics at Work).

How do you normally try to agree things with others? Does it work? What effect does it have on others?

Techniques I use	Effects

Why do you think you sometimes fail to agree things with others at work? Identifying the reasons may help identify what to do about it.

	Often	Sometimes	Never
I dislike the other people			
I'm wary of the other people			
I find them difficult			
I try to please others			
I get side-tracked			
I have misunderstandings with others			
I fall into conflicts with others			
I do not know what I want			
I don't think about/know what they want			
I find it hard to think of solutions			
I find it hard to make decisions			
I like having things my way			
I get anxious when things get out of my control			
I dislike losing face			
Others (please add your own)			

3.3 An approach to negotiating

One approach is proposed below. After each suggestion (based on a book by Fisher and Ury, 1987), a box is provided for your notes about how you could use it in a situation confronting you.

SEPARATE THE PEOPLE FROM THE PROBLEM

Identify problems and issues rather than focusing on personalities (*e.g. not 'It's his fault the job is behind' but 'Why hasn't he been able to meet the deadline? What do we need to do now?'*).

Consider the people not as 'the other side' but as individuals. How do they see things? You don't have to agree with them, but acknowledging it helps. What are their attitudes/feelings? Involving them can encourage commitment (*e.g. not 'This is what we've agreed; what do you think?' but 'How should we go about it?'*).

How could you use this suggestion in your situation?

The problem	The other people's perspective

FOCUS ON INTERESTS NOT POSITIONS

If you take up a firm position it can be hard to shift from it without losing face (*e.g. 'If you don't support me, I'll resign'*).

An alternative is to explore interests. This might reveal commonalities as well as differences. You could ask everybody to list their interests and see where they coincide. You can find out others' interests by asking 'Why?' instead of 'Why not?'.

How could you use this suggestion in your situation?

What are the interests of those involved (including me)?

GENERATE OPTIONS BEFORE MAKING DECISIONS

It can help to have several options. Obstacles to generating options include a 'bottom line' which limits your thinking, although you may need one (*e.g. the project deadline*); looking for a single answer; assuming a fixed situation; seeing the problem as somebody else's; making judgements too early. It helps to generate ideas first without evaluating them.

It also helps to know what you'll do if you don't agree, and to work out other alternatives (the better the alternative, the greater your power — *e.g. if somebody else could do the work a colleague has not done, this puts you in a stronger position than if only s/he can do it*).

How could you use this suggestion in your situation?

What options are there?

AGREE CRITERIA AGAINST WHICH TO JUDGE SOLUTIONS

Agreeing the principles by which you operate and criteria for judging if the solution was successful can prevent face-saving problems (*e.g. not 'Did you win or lose?' but 'Was the end result of our project good?'*).

Establishing criteria in advance can forestall problems (*e.g. agreeing a job must be done to a certain standard or by a deadline gives you some comeback if standards or deadlines aren't met*).

How could you use this suggestion in your situation?

What are my criteria for success?

YES, BUT...

What if there is an argument or somebody just digs their heels in? See sections 4 and 5 below.

3.4 Other suggestions

There are further suggestions on the opposite page.

Suggestions	What could I actually do in my situation?
Aim for win/win, avoid win/lose ◆ How could all involved get something they want? ◆ How could you avoid anybody having to give way completely? ◆ Could any option meet everybody's needs?	
Build in leeway ◆ Identify where you could give way. ◆ Avoid tying things up absolutely right at the start – leave room for manoeuvre.	
Identify what really matters ◆ Avoid making a stand on things that are not really important. ◆ Devote time to the things that really matter. ◆ Avoid getting bogged down in detail.	
Compromise ◆ Where could you give way? ◆ What could you offer? ◆ Where might they give way?	
Avoid emotional or bad language (It can give others the moral high ground or antagonise them.)	
Focus on 'we' ◆ Ask what we can do about it. ◆ Identify what we want.	
Add your own	

You could return to your replies to section 3.2 above. Do you have any attitudes which get in the way of these suggestions (*e.g. wanting to win, needing to be right, not wanting others to see weaknesses etc.*)?

You may also return to section 1 to reconsider your goals. Might your attitudes stop you achieving them? (*E.g. you need the expertise of others but you like to be 'right', you need others' collaboration but you like to win, you have no authority over others but you get anxious when you lose control.*)

How much do you really need to keep your attitudes? Would other attitudes be more productive? (*E.g. is it better to be right or happy? Is it better to get the job done or for justice to be done? Does it matter if you do what they want? The answers to these questions might be yes or no, but asking them will clarify what you need to pursue and what to drop.*)

You can change an attitude by:

◆ being aware of it
◆ wanting to change it
◆ stopping yourself when you start to think in that way (*e.g. pin up a notice to remind you, keep notes in meetings of your attitude, keep a diary, reward yourself when you stop yourself thinking that way, talk out loud to yourself, repeat a phrase to yourself which is the opposite – e.g. 'I like others to win'.*)

These may sound like an effort or 'silly', but they work. If it is important to you to change your attitude they may be worth trying (it may take some time – it depends how deeply embedded your attitude is).

4 ASSERTIVENESS

4.1 What is assertiveness?

Our behaviour towards others may fall into the following categories. These are not fixed, as we may behave differently in different situations with different people.

◆ **Passive**. Allowing others to get what they want, not expressing your needs (*e.g. 'You have the chocolate cake'*).
◆ **Aggressive**. Imposing your will or needs on others (*e.g. 'Give me that chocolate cake'*).
◆ **Manipulative**. 'Scheming' to get what you want (*e.g. 'No, no, you have the chocolate cake, I'll go without'*).
◆ **Assertive**. Expressing your needs openly without imposing on the other (*e.g. 'I like chocolate cake, do you? Should we divide it up?'*).

How do you tend to use the above behaviours at work, with whom and in what situations?

Situation	People	Behaviour

Your behaviour can affect others.

◆ Being **passive** can make others feel powerful or frustrated.
◆ Being **aggressive** can make others feel angry or intimidated.
◆ Being **manipulative** can make others feel powerless or as though they are being taken advantage of.
◆ Being **assertive** allows others to know where they stand and to feel respected. It also encourages them to be assertive rather than be forced to react to one of the other behaviours. People sometimes equate assertiveness with aggression, but these are very different.

Just because you are assertive does not mean that the other person will necessarily be assertive back. They may continue to behave in one of the other ways. But you stand more chance of them being assertive with you if you are so with them, and assertiveness may be a productive response to the other behaviours.

Do you need to be more assertive? Looking at two main areas may help:

◆ why you behave non-assertively
◆ assertiveness techniques.

4.2 Reasons for not behaving assertively

There are many reasons for not behaving assertively, including lack of confidence or thinking that others are better than you. Assertiveness is about thinking 'I am OK and you are OK'.

A starting point might be to identify why you tend to behave non-assertively in certain situations and then what you might do about it. For example, if you are **non-assertive**:

◆ when you feel **negative** about something, you could try to rephrase negative thoughts positively
◆ when you are **under stress**, you could identify what causes stress and take action to reduce it (see Chapter 15, Dealing with Pressure).
◆ because you are **trying to please others**, you could begin to think also about your own needs.

Reasons for my non-assertive behaviour (i.e. if you are passive, aggressive or manipulative)	Possible solutions

Sometimes people behave non-assertively because they have never considered the alternative. The following 'bill of rights' may help here (from Townend, 1991).

I have the right to	
1	express my thoughts and opinion
2	express my feelings and be responsible for them
3	say 'yes' to people
4	change my mind without making excuses
5	make mistakes and be responsible for them
6	say 'I don't know'
7	say 'I don't understand'
8	ask for what I want
9	say 'no' without feeling guilty
10	be respected by others and respect them
11	be listened to and taken seriously
12	be independent
13	be successful
14	choose not to assert myself

Which of these rights do you find difficult to claim? Why? Could you challenge your existing assumptions and views?

Rights I feel difficult to claim. Why?	Actions to take. Challenges to my own assumptions.

4.3 Goals

To behave assertively, you must know what you want. It will help to return to section 2 above and review the notes you made.

Being assertive involves acknowledging others' needs and goals, to find solutions which are acceptable to those concerned. Section 2 above looked at the needs and goals of others and it will help to return to it.

If you have difficulty knowing what you or others want, what could you do?

In relation to your needs, you could:

◆ identify your gut or first reaction to the situation. What does it suggest about your needs?
◆ look at the 'bill of rights' in section 4.2 above. Are your attitudes stopping you from knowing what you want?
◆ look at Chapter 11, Solving Problems and Making Decisions.

In relation to others' needs, you could:

◆ ask them
◆ look at what they say or do. What does this suggest about their needs?
◆ imagine yourself in their situation (but remember that you may be very different).

4.4 Assertiveness techniques

Being assertive is partly about attitudes and partly about behaviour. If you begin to behave in a way which is assertive, even if you don't feel assertive, it 'rubs off' and helps to build confidence. The following techniques could help.

'BROKEN RECORD'   This is repeating what you want, without being drawn into an argument.

Statement	Response
'You agreed to produce information and we need it for tomorrow's meeting.'	'I haven't got time.'
'Yes, but we need it for tomorrow.'	'I've had a lot of other things to do.'
'I appreciate this, but the meeting is tomorrow.'	'Can't somebody else do it?'
'We agreed that you would do it, and the meeting is tomorrow.'	'OK, I'll do it tonight.'

If you do get drawn into an argument you are lost. For example:

Statement	Your response
'I haven't got time.'	'You've had lots of time.'
'No I haven't.'	'Yes you have,' etc., etc.

ACKNOWLEDGING CRITICISMS

Accepting criticisms, but without grovelling, can defuse matters. For example:

'That's right, I should have produced the information.'

ACCEPTING COMPLIMENTS

Accept compliments without putting yourself down. For example:

Statement	Your response
'That graph looks good.'	'Thanks.' (not: 'It's not as neat as I want!')

ASKING FOR CLARIFICATION

Ask others to be specific. If they are giving you feedback, look at Chapter 17, Identifying Strengths and Improving Skills, for a section on seeking feedback.

AVOIDING PREAMBLES

Long preambles to a simple request or statement can confuse the listener and weaken the statement. For example:

'I don't want to trouble you, and I know you are very busy, and you've had a cold but the meeting is tomorrow and the managing director and all the shareholders will be there and please could you give us the information?'

A direct request is better. For example:

'Could you provide the information please?'

ACKNOWLEDGING AND RECOGNISING YOUR FEELINGS

It is important to recognise your feelings. What was your initial gut reaction? Interest? Happiness? Panic? What does this tell you that you should do?

You need to 'own' your feelings (i.e. say they are yours not somebody else's). This will remove the impression that you are making global criticisms of another person (they may react aggressively or lose confidence, think 'everybody' is talking about them etc.). For example:

'I am worried that you might not deliver that work on time and about what effect it will have on our work.'

rather than:

'Everybody is really worried about you not delivering that piece of work on time.'

'GOING UP THE GEARS'

If you don't get what you want at first, become increasingly firm. This means not starting off at a maximum position but allowing yourself some room. *E.g. if somebody owes money:*

- ◆ *ask for payment*
- ◆ *then give them a deadline*
- ◆ *then say you will take further action if you have not received it by …*
- ◆ *then say you are putting it the hands of a solicitor (it is best to mean what you say)*
- ◆ *then put it in the hands of a solicitor.*

**BEING AWARE OF
YOUR APPEARANCE**

How you dress can increase your confidence.

Non-verbal signals give other people messages about how you feel. Some non-verbal behaviour makes you look assertive – *e.g. facing another person on the same level (if the other person stands while you sit they may appear dominant).*

Examples of non-assertive non-verbal behaviour:

◆ stooped posture
◆ no eye contact
◆ a soft, angry or loud voice
◆ gestures, such as pointing fingers and biting nails.

Examples of assertive, non-verbal behaviours:

◆ upright posture
◆ eye contact
◆ firm, clear voice
◆ relaxed gestures.

**PRACTISING SAYING
'NO'**

Practise saying 'no' without excuses. It will get easier. For example:

'I'm sorry I won't be able to meet the deadline.'

not:

'I'm really sorry but I've had another urgent job to do and I've been off with a cold and I've got behind and now it's the month end and I've got the monthly report to prepare and …'

4.5 What is effective for you?

It might help to think of the approaches you could use in a situation you currently face, in relation to the following questions.

◆ Have you used similar approaches in the past?
◆ What effect would it have on you if you were on the receiving end?
◆ What short-term effect might it have on the other person?
◆ What long-term effect might it have on your relationship with them?
◆ Will it lead to a solution which is mutually acceptable?

Approach/strategy	My notes

5 USING YOUR PERSONAL ATTRIBUTES

. . . .

5.1 Strengths

Which of your attributes help you deal with others? Identifying them can increase your confidence. Beware of using your strengths manipulatively – *e.g. charm used to manipulate others can appear as 'smarminess'.*

Possible strengths	
Humour	
Relaxed manner	
Trustworthy, reliable	
Good listener	
Ability to explain clearly	
Patience	
Others (please add your own)	

5.2 Weaknesses

Which of your attributes might cause problems in dealing with others? (*E.g. impatience, not listening, interrupting, being pushy, being tentative, being irritable, being very quiet etc.*)
   What could you do to:

◆ avoid them?
◆ change them?
◆ allow for them?

Weakness	Actions to take

6 DEALING WITH CONFLICT

....

It may be best to avoid conflict arising in the first place. If your attempts to agree things with others and to be assertive succeed, you should avert conflict.

However, conflict cannot always be avoided.

You may face a situation very likely to result in conflict.	Work through sections 3 and 4 above in advance.
You may have worked through sections 3 and 4 above and still find conflict has arisen.	See below.
You may suddenly find yourself in the midst of conflict.	See below.
You may need to help others resolve a dispute.	Use sections 3 and 4 above and also section 7 below on giving feedback.
You may feel stressed because of the conflict.	Look at Chapter 15, Dealing with Pressure.

Sections 3 above and 7 below will be helpful in a conflict situation. Section 4 above on assertiveness will be essential. The following give more specific suggestions about conflict resolution.

WHAT IS IT ABOUT?

Identifying what the conflict is really about can help you work out strategies for its resolution. If there is conflict, it is likely to be because it matters to those concerned - it has engaged their feelings in some way.

OVERALL STRATEGIES

◆ You could just leave it. People may calm down, see it as unimportant in the cold light of day, bringing it up again may make things worse.
◆ You could confront it. Try to talk about it to the others involved. You might start by acknowledging their feelings or asking for what they are – this might diffuse anger (*'What do you think/feel about this', 'You seem to be mad about this'*). Use sections 3 and 4 above.
◆ You could work around it. *E.g. if the problem is to do with pressure of work, you could reallocate tasks.*

DEALING WITH YOUR OWN ANGER

These suggestions are based on Goleman (1996).

◆ Do not vent anger. There is a view that expressing anger is good, but Goleman suggests that venting anger makes you angrier. This does not mean not speaking of what caused the anger (see sections 4 above on assertiveness and 7 below on feedback), *e.g. 'You're not meeting the deadline is delaying our work'* may be helpful but *'How could you not meet the deadline? What do you think you were doing? You are useless'* is unlikely to be.
◆ When you start to feel angry stop and write it down. Then challenge your assumptions. Is the basis for your anger well founded? Are you really angry about something else? How might the other people see it?
◆ Reframe the situation positively. How could you describe it positively?
◆ See this as a separate incident caused by a particular circumstance which may change (as opposed to yet another piece of evidence of a fatal flaw in somebody's character or in the organisation)
◆ Do something pleasant to distract yourself (*e.g. switch to a work task you enjoy*)
◆ Take time out, but not to fume. Use the time out to think about it positively or to distract yourself. Fuming makes it worse.

If you can get your own anger under control, it will be much easier to use the strategies suggested in sections 4 above and 7 below.

DON'T ASSUME HOSTILITY OR THREAT

Assume that others are well meaning. This will help you go into the situation non-defensively and non-aggressively.

ASK FOR FURTHER INFORMATION BEFORE MAKING ASSUMPTIONS

Try to avoid jumping to conclusions before you have all the information. You could check with others involved to see what information you need.

USING THE SUGGESTIONS

Which of the above suggestions (or those in sections 3, 4 or 7) could you use? This may depend on the reason for the conflict. You could complete the following in relation to a situation you have faced or are currently facing.

Possible cause of conflict	Particular aspects/needs in this situation?	What could I try?
Pressure (see Chapter 15, Dealing with Pressure, and Chapter 2, Planning and Managing your Workload)		
Personal dislike or antagonism		
Misunderstandings		
Differing views on how things should be done		
Poor performance/quality		
Others (please list)		

Dealing successfully with conflict can make you feel really good!

7 GIVING FEEDBACK TO OTHERS

··········

People at work constantly give each other feedback in all sorts of ways – via humour, facial expressions, throw-away remarks, cutting or sarcastic remarks, outbursts. These methods may undermine the confidence of others, make them feel bad and give you a reputation as being critical, insensitive or rude.

7.1 Positive feedback

Giving positive feedback is often seen as less of a concern than giving negative feedback, but it might still help to think about the following questions and make notes for yourself.

For example, if receiving positive feedback makes you feel good but you never give it to others, you might want to start doing so. If you don't like others being patronising, you could think about how you speak to others.

Beware of inferring too close a relationship between your reactions and those of others. *E.g. if you lack confidence you may distrust others' compliments, whereas other, more confident people may react favourably.*

Question	Possible issues/reactions/methods	My notes
How do I feel when others give positive feedback to me?	Pleased Embarrassed (why?) Confident Makes you like the person Makes you not trust the person (why?)	
How do I like others to give me positive feedback?	Patronising With humour Straight To you alone In public By thanking you	
How often do I give positive feedback to others? When did I last do so?	By thanking them About particularly good things About anything good Very rarely (why?) Never (why?)	

7.2 Negative feedback

When might you need to give negative feedback to others?

To whom?	In what situations? Suggestions	What would I find easy/ difficult/be concerned about in such situations?
To those for whom I have responsibility	In a staff appraisal meeting (see Chapter 18 on appraisal) On aspects of their work On their attitudes On their relationships with colleagues On their performance at interview	
To those with responsibility for me	In your own staff appraisal meeting, to your appraiser (see Chapter 18) To your mentor (see Chapter 18), e.g. about lack of support To your line manager, *e.g. about lack of support, things s/he has done that made things difficult for you*	

To whom?	In what situations? Suggestions	What would I find easy/difficult/be concerned about in such situations?
To those at my level, to colleagues in my own or other departments	On an aspect of their work On the way they relate to you On their attitudes	
To clients or customers	On their product On the information or help they have given On how others perceive them/their actions	
To suppliers of products or services	On the quality of the provision On costs On delivery times On the helpfulness of their staff	
To the public	On their complaints	
To others (please list)		

'RULES' OF FEEDBACK

There are some 'rules' which can be very helpful:

◆ Give feedback as soon after the event as possible – while it is still fresh in the minds of those concerned, before it can fester or fade.

◆ Give feedback on areas the person can do something about. If they cannot alter an aspect of their physical appearance or an aspect of their work is beyond their control, it is unhelpful to mention it.

◆ Give specific feedback which helps them take action. Not 'The report was poor' (why? how?) but 'The report didn't have a structure you could follow – it didn't have an introduction and conclusion and it had no paragraph numbers.'

◆ Avoid personal, judgemental comments and language. Not 'You are selfish, you only think about yourself' but 'If you do not turn up to the meetings it creates problems for the rest of us.' Critique the deed, not the person.

◆ Give feedback where it is your responsibility to do so and 'own' it (see section 4 above on acknowledging your feelings). Giving feedback on somebody else's behalf can be problematic – the receiver has to deal both with the feedback and with thinking that others have been 'conspiring' or 'talking behind my back'. The person who should have given the feedback may lose respect if they are seen as lacking the courage to do so – and you could encourage them to give it themselves. It may, however, be your responsibility to give feedback on behalf of others, e.g. you may be their representative or have line management responsibility for someone or functional responsibility for a job.

◆ Identify the best place to give it – your place (will give you confidence) or theirs (will give them confidence)? Feedback needs to be immediate, but what if that means giving it in front of others? It is often not appropriate to do so, but there may be exceptions (e.g. if somebody is behaving unhelpfully in a meeting, or if they are rude to you in front of others). If you have to give feedback in front of others, bear in mind the above 'rules' and be very short, e.g. 'Your focus on negatives is stopping us move forwards, can we think about the positives', 'I don't think it is very helpful for us to pursue that here. Please can we meet later?' This may be an issue in open-plan offices with little privacy. Could you go for a coffee, or a drink, or for lunch?

◆ Identify the best order for what you will say. Some writers advocate giving positive feedback first, but if the other person is expecting negative feedback they may not listen to the positive and may want to get the negative over (*e.g. feedback on a promotion they did not get*). It may help to identify the expectations of the other person and order what you say accordingly. You certainly need to inject positives and it may be helpful to end on a positive – what is going to happen or positive feedback.

How could you apply these 'rules' in practice? You could identify a situation and make notes on what you might do, what you actually did and, finally, how well it went.

'Rules' – give feedback …	What I will do	What I did and what worked
as soon after the event as possible		
on areas the other person can do something about		
on specifics to help somebody to take action		
avoiding personal, judgmental comments and language		
where it is your responsibility to do so and 'own' it		
in the most appropriate location		
in the most appropriate order		

8 ACTION PLANNING

....

You will continually encounter situations where you need to deal with others. It is important to build on your experiences to become increasingly effective. You could keep a diary to record and review progress, or you could return to this chapter at regular intervals to do so.

Questions you could ask yourself include the following:

What works for me?

What doesn't work for me?

What are the effects of my approaches or strategies?

Am I feeling any better about my dealings with others?

Are others reacting any more positively to me?

Are my needs/goals being met?

Having answered these questions, what do you need to improve?

Areas for improvement	Actions to take	By (date)

9 REFERENCES AND BIBLIOGRAPHY

....

Dickson, A. (1982), *A Woman in Your Own Right*, Quartet Books.

Fisher, R. and Ury, W. (1987), *Getting to Yes: How to Negotiate to Agreement Without Giving In*, Arrow Books.

Goleman, D. (1996) *Emotional Intelligence: Why It Can Matter More than IQ*, Bloomsbury.

Moores, R. (1989), *Negotiating Skills*, Industrial Society.

Scott, B. and Billing, B. (1990), *Negotiating Skills in Engineering and Construction*, Thomas Telford.

Steele, P., Murphy, J. and Russill, R. (1989), *It's a Deal: A Practical Negotiation Handbook*, McGraw-Hill.

Townend, A. (1991), *Developing Assertiveness*, Routledge.

With thanks to Olga Lane of Sheffield Hallam University for ideas gathered from her workshop on feedback and to Jane Steer, final year student, BA Women's Studies, 1998.

Contents

15

DEALING WITH PRESSURE

WHY IS THIS SKILL IMPORTANT?

Developing the ability to cope with pressure makes you more likely to succeed in your work and be more effective, healthier and able to enjoy what you do.

Inevitably you will experience pressures – employment is likely to bring its own pressures, as may other areas of your life.

This chapter aims to help you cope more effectively with those pressures which you can anticipate as well as those which you can't.

We suggest you use this chapter:

◆ when a period of pressure is approaching
◆ when you are in a difficult situation
◆ to handle ongoing pressures.

You may also find it helpful to talk to others about the chapter.

By the end of this chapter you should be able to:

1 identify, using appropriate evidence, your own reactions and usual responses to pressure, and recognise signals of your own stress at an early stage
2 seek and use feedback constructively
3 anticipate and identify possible sources of pressure at an early stage
4 monitor the effectiveness of your own reactions and responses, and identify needs for change
5 identify and prioritise long-term and short-term goals, review and revise them regularly
6 plan and implement actions which allow for changing circumstances to manage pressure effectively
7 identify at what point there is a need for support and actively seek and use it
8 record and review progress in relation to changing circumstances
9 evaluate your own effectiveness in coping with pressure, identify areas for improvement and take action.

See Chapter 1 for the relationship between these learning outcomes and the Key Skills qualifications

1 SOURCES OF PRESSURE AND STRESS

....

Different people react differently to pressure and even have different views on what causes it. It is our perception of our ability to cope in a given situation that matters, not the situation itself.

Excessive stress may be caused by one or two major occurrences or by a cluster of several small ones.

Generally, we feel stressed by things which are very important to us, changes which impose new pressures, continually facing situations or people we don't know how to handle.

Any change in general life events – even welcome ones – can be stressful. The table below gives some indication of the wide range of stressors in our lives.

Stress may be caused by work situations or outside – there may be a cumulative effect. Stress at home may make you less able to deal with pressure at work and vice versa.

Look through the list below and add notes on your own experiences of events or situations in the right-hand column, where you feel it appropriate. Those at the top of each section have the highest impact on our stress levels.

Events/experiences	My stressors (experienced within the past year)
Relationships Death of a partner Divorce/separation/break-up of relationship Death of a close family member/friend Marriage Marital reconciliation Sex difficulties Gain of new family member Children leaving home Difficulties with in-laws Partner starts/stops work	
Personal Prison term Personal injury/illness Pregnancy Outstanding personal achievement Change in living conditions Moving house Change in recreation activities (*e.g. sport*) Change in personal habits (*e.g. sleeping/eating*) Holiday/Christmas	
Work/education Loss of job (*e.g. dismissal/redundancy*) Retirement Change of work role (*e.g. different work, responsibilities*) Begin or end school/college Difficulties at work Change in work hours or conditions	
Financial Change in financial state Large mortgage Foreclosure of mortgage or loan Small mortgage or loan	

Use the following to make notes on your current pressures – *e.g. in your life at work or outside.*

> **In my life at work or outside, what is particularly important to me at the moment?**
>
>
> **What do other people want from me and who wants it?**
>
>
> **What is happening that is new or different in my life?**
>
>
> **Has my workload or level of activities changed?**
>
>
> **Are there people who upset or annoy me? Why?**
>
>
> **Do I experience stress symptoms in particular situations?**

2 EFFECTS OF PRESSURE AND STRESS

....

POSITIVE EFFECTS

Pressure and stress will have effects on both you and your organisation, on performance, costs and relationships.

Human beings respond to, and are encouraged by, challenges, and a certain amount of tension is positive. The great advances in civilisation have been made by individuals dealing with and overcoming challenges or problems.

Pressure may be useful when it enables us to achieve the best results and high performance. A surge of the hormone noradrenalin by the adrenal glands in a pressurised situation can heighten alertness and clarity of thought, *e.g. dealing with difficult meetings.*

Each person has their own threshold in coping with pressure. The challenge is to find the right amount of pressure which will enable you to be efficient and effective, with some reserves to cope with unexpected situations.

NEGATIVE EFFECTS

The effects of pressure become stressful when you perceive that you can't cope with the situation and the human body's biochemical processes respond to a challenge or threat by releasing adrenalin – the 'fight or flight' hormone – into the blood stream.

Modern society's rules of behaviour often prevent us from fighting or fleeing, so there is no release of physical tension. Unrelieved tension causes stress. We all experience stress and deal more or less effectively with it.

Certain illnesses can be stress-related – *e.g. heart disease and high blood pressure.* Long before we reach that extreme stage, stress can impair our performance.

People react to stress differently, but common **psychological** responses include: changes in sleep patterns; irritability; loss of temper; excessive worrying; recurring minor ailments. Common **physical** symptoms of stress include: butterflies in the stomach; shallow breathing; minor illnesses such as sore throats, or more serious ones such as ulcers.

3 IDENTIFYING YOUR OWN REACTIONS TO PRESSURE/SIGNS OF STRESS

. . . .

3.1 Positive reactions to pressure

In what positive ways do you tend to react to pressure? It is worth reminding yourself of your strengths. How will you know if you are reacting negatively and feeling stressed? It is worth being able to identify the signs so that you can take remedial action.

Add your own items to the following checklist.

When under pressure I ...	
Think more clearly	
Work faster	
Discard or ignore what is unimportant	
Take a step back and think before acting	
See the pressure as an opportunity	
See the pressure as a challenge	
Enjoy meeting targets	

3.2 Negative reactions to pressure

How often do I ...	Often	Sometimes	Rarely	Never
Feel irritable/angry?				
Feel restless?				
Feel frustrated at having to wait for something?				
Talk fast?				
Feel rushed?				
Slump?				
Become easily confused/have memory problems?				
Find it difficult to concentrate?				
Think about negative things without wanting to?				
Have marked mood swings/emotional outbursts?				
Feel weepy/upset?				
Smoke?				
Drink alcohol?				
Eat too much/eat when I am not hungry?				
Go off my food?				
Not have enough energy to get things done?				
Wake up early?				
Find it difficult to fall asleep?				
Find it difficult to get out of bed in the morning?				
Feel I can't cope?				
Find it hard to make decisions?				
Feel sorry for myself?				
Worry about the future?				
Feel I have lost my sense of humour?				
Take tranquillisers/non-prescribed drugs?				
Have minor accidents?				
Total number of ticks				

We all feel or do most of these things from time to time, but if most of your ticks are in the 'often' or 'sometimes' columns it might be time to review your lifestyle. It is easy to fall into destructive behavioural habits, accept them as 'normal' and fail to realise that they are indicators of stress which can be removed or reduced.

When I am stressed, what are the most significant signs for me?

3.3 The effects of your reaction to pressure

How you react to pressure will have advantages or disadvantages. *E.g. putting things off may make you feel better in the short term but cause longer-term problems.* You may find it helpful to discuss with friends how they think you react to pressure. What advantages or disadvantages can they see in your reactions? How effective are they?

In the past, have you encountered pressures you hadn't anticipated? *A sudden rush of work? An increase in demands placed on you? A crisis?* What did you do? Was it effective or not?

What might have made things better? Here the focus should not be on factors over which you may have no control, but within yourself.

You might like to consider:

◆ your goals (what were you trying to achieve?)
◆ your attitudes (were they helpful?)
◆ your feelings (were they justified?)
◆ your behaviour (did it meet your goals?).

Source of pressure	My behaviour, actions, feelings	Advantages	Disadvantages	Effectiveness

4 HOW CAN YOU COPE WITH PRESSURE?

....

The following suggests a range of strategies to help. Some of these may suit some situations and you better than others – you need to pick and choose. You could refer back to your notes on current pressures.

4.1 Recognising pressure early

Recognising pressure early, or even before it starts at all, can be very helpful. Pressure can creep up on you. Once you get to the point of feeling overwhelmed, it is harder (though not impossible) to cope.

What one person considers pressurising, another might not. What sort of things do you usually tend to find pressurising?

How can you spot pressure early or anticipate it?

◆ Although exactly the same situation may not recur, you could look out for situations similar to those you have found pressurising in the past – *e.g. being required to meet several deadlines close together; having to deal with certain sorts of people.*

◆ You could become more sensitive to your own possible reactions to pressure and consult this chapter when you feel you need to think things through.

◆ Stress can occur if you find it difficult to react positively or to use up the tension caused by pressure. What are your early warning signs, *e.g. positives may include excitement and exhilaration; negatives may include not sleeping and irritability?*

Are you experiencing any current pressures? Can you spot any pressures building up now or any which may occur in the near future? You need to maintain a balance between being prepared in a positive way and negatively expecting the worse.

Please use the boxes below and overleaf for your responses.

Areas I tend to find pressurising

My own early warning signs of stress (refer back to section 3.2)

Current pressures	Pressures just beginning	Possible future pressures

The earlier you use techniques to deal with stress, the better, and the following sections give suggestions. They can also be helpful if stress has crept up on you.

4.2 Treat the symptoms of stress

Some simple techniques can reduce the symptoms of stress.

BREATHING EXERCISES

If you are anxious you may tend to breathe shallowly, only using the top of your lungs. Breathe fully out, pulling your stomach in. Then breathe in by letting your stomach out, allowing air to fill the bottom of your lungs. Breathe out to a count of 4, 6 or 8 and in to the same count. This technique should control the butterflies in your stomach and calm you and nobody will know you are doing it.

RELAXATION EXERCISES

If you are at home, lie down or, at work, sit in a comfortable chair. In turn, tense and then relax your muscles. Start with your foot, then your calf muscles, and move up through the whole body, finally relaxing the facial muscles and the scalp. At work, you could do at least some of these relaxing in your chair.

OTHER FORMS

Other forms of relaxation include meditation, massage and yoga. There are plenty of yoga classes around and being in a group can make it easier to become involved. You may feel it is appropriate to visit your doctor, who will advise you.

PLEASANT THOUGHTS

Think about something pleasant – a holiday location or a room you like. See it with your mind's eye and concentrate on it.

NOT SLEEPING

If you can't sleep, count backwards aloud from 500 to stop your mind racing. Keep a pad by the bed and write down what you are thinking. Getting it on paper can help to stop you churning it over.

4.3 Remove the cause of the pressure

You could remove yourself from the situation – *e.g. could you limit contact with those who cause pressure, could you discuss your workload with your manager and try to reduce it?*

However, sometimes it may be better in the long term to stay and sort the problem out.

4.4 Find a better way of dealing with the pressure

What could you do differently?
For example:

◆ **be clearer about what you want** and tell people in an assertive way (see Chapter 14, Putting Your Case: Negotiating and Assertiveness).

- **take a fresh look at the situation.** Write the problem down, list the options, then think about the alternative approaches (see Chapter 11, Solving Problems and Making Decisions).
- **talk the situation over** with someone else to help clarify things.
- **plan ahead.** It might help to draw up a plan for the short term (*e.g. this week*), the middle term (*e.g. this month*), the longer term (*e.g. this year*). It is important to build into each stage an allowance for the unexpected (even at a relatively simple level, *e.g. allowing for longer queues than you expect*).
- **prioritise** (see Chapter 2, Planning and Managing Your Workload). What else can be put aside or abandoned?

Things nearly always take longer than you think – and if the unexpected doesn't materialise you'll have a bonus in terms of extra time and energy!

Type of pressure	What could I do differently?
Short-term pressure	
Medium-term pressure	
Long-term pressure	

If you find planning difficult, refer to Chapter 2, 'Planning and Managing Your Workload'.

4.5 Look after yourself

You are more likely to cope if you feel well. Regular exercise can use up 'fight or flight' hormones. It does not have to be strenuous – little and often is the key, but aerobic exercise like swimming or fast walking is particularly good. Making short journeys on foot instead of catching the bus may make the difference between feeling tense and relaxed.

Eat healthily – there is evidence that certain foods cause stress. The healthy diet advocated nowadays comprises lots of fruit and vegetables and less junk food.

It may not feel like it at the time, but drinking alcohol and smoking increase stress. They are stimulants which add to the agitation caused by the 'fight or flight' hormones.

Take a lunch break, even if it is a short one. Try to get out of the workplace for a short time.

Am I ...	
Doing things I enjoy as well as things I have to do? At work, could I negotiate this with my manager (see Chapter 14, Putting Your Case: Negotiating and Assertiveness).	
Giving myself treats?	
Letting myself off the hook, giving myself a break?	
Resting, relaxing, sleeping?	
Having fun, pursuing interests?	
Keeping fit?	
Eating properly?	
Not drinking too much alcohol?	
Not smoking too much?	

4.6 Put things into perspective

What is the worst that could happen? How likely is this, and how important would it be in six months' or a year's time?

Are there positive consequences? Humour is therapeutic – can you laugh things off?

4.7 Seek help

It may be appropriate to talk things over with someone else. Are you identifying at what point you need support and where you could get such support? This will vary from individual to individual. What is important is knowing what your 'point' is.

If you feel under stress you could seek help from the following sources. In a working situation, you will need to consider who you can trust to discuss this area with:

◆ Consult your mentor or manager: s/he may help you prioritise, or plan your time more effectively.
◆ Consult your colleagues: they may have ideas they have tried out.
◆ Consult friends or family members: 'a problem shared is a problem halved'.
◆ Consult the personnel or human resources department, if your organisation has one.
◆ Look at Chapter 2, Planning and Managing Your Workload, and Chapter 14, Putting Your Case: Negotiating and Assertiveness. A lot of work stress is caused by either workload or difficulties with other people.
◆ Join others with similar concerns: you may find lists of groups in a local library or you could form one yourself.
◆ Attend a stress management course: this may help manage situations more effectively.
◆ Join in recreational activities: your organisation may have sports facilities or use local authority amenities.
◆ Consult a local careers service: they can help you consider your work options.
◆ Consult a counselling/guidance service: these can provide support and an opportunity to talk things through.
◆ Visit a medical centre/doctors: this can help if the symptoms have made you ill, or help you to prevent them making you ill.
◆ Consult your church.
◆ Contact the Citizens' Advice Bureau.
◆ Contact Relate (supports pressure caused by relationship difficulties).
◆ Contact your trade union.

This list of suggestions will act as a stimulus for ideas. You may find that these people and agencies know of other organisations and groups which may be helpful. Contact numbers will be in your local phone book.

For example:

Pressure	Possible point at which support is needed	Possible support
Several coinciding deadlines	Can't see how to meet them all	Manager
Health problems	Recurring, persistent, interfering with effectiveness	Doctor

You could fill in the table below in relation to your own circumstances.

Pressure	Possible point at which support is needed	Possible support

5 WHAT CAN YOU DO DIFFERENTLY?

It could be helpful to review this chapter and your notes on it, to summarise the main areas you want to change, what actions you could take and who or what might help. It may be useful to keep notes on your progress. Use the chart below.

Areas to change	Actions to take/sources of support	Progress notes

6 REFERENCES AND BIBLIOGRAPHY
....

Libraries may have materials on this skill area. The following gives examples:

Atkinson, J. M. (1988), *Coping with Stress at Work*, Thorsons.

Cooper, C., Cooper, R. and Eaker, L. (1988), *Living with Stress*, Penguin.

Farmer, R., Monahan, L. and Hekeler, R. (1984), *Stress Management for Human Services*, Sage.

Fontana, D. (1989), *Problems in Practice: Managing Stress*, The British Psychological Society and Routledge.

Froggat, H. and Stamp, P. (1991), *Managing Pressure at Work*, BBC Books.

Looker, T. and Gregson, O. (1989), *Stresswise*, Hodder & Stoughton.

Patel, C. (1989), *The Complete Guide to Stress Management*, Optima.

Contents

16
REVIEWING YOUR EFFECTIVENESS

WHY IS THIS SKILL IMPORTANT?

Reviewing your effectiveness is important all the time at work. Professionals need to know they are doing a good job, to learn from their experiences and improve. It is not just common sense, it is a skill you can develop. It is often known as the skill of reflection – and it is seen as increasingly important, e.g. in appraisal, professional bodies' membership schemes and Continuing Professional Development (CPD) (see Chapter 19).

This chapter takes you through a process of reflecting and reviewing your effectiveness in a structured way. If you prefer a less structured way of reflecting, you could note what might work better for you. Reflection is a personal thing. Some people continually question what they have done, said, or thought, while others find this uncomfortable or difficult.

We suggest you use this chapter:

◆ if you are asked to review your effectiveness or reflect on your experience for a specific purpose, e.g. for membership of a professional body, for an appraisal meeting, for Continuing Professional Development (CPD)
◆ if you have had a particularly successful or difficult experience at work, to help you build on it or learn from it
◆ generally, to help you think through what you are doing at work and how you might do it better.

By the end of this chapter you should be able to:

1 identify the benefits of reviewing your own work performance
2 identify and use a variety of strategies which enable you to review your performance and experiences at work
3 identify what was effective or ineffective about your performance, attitudes or approaches in work situations
4 seek and use feedback constructively
5 identify what is effective about your performance, attitudes or approaches in the workplace and can be repeated, and what is ineffective and needs to be changed
6 identify your strengths and weaknesses in relation to your work experiences.

See Chapter 1 for the relationship between these learning outcomes and the Key Skills qualifications

1 REFLECTION

. . . .

In this chapter, 'reflection' means looking back on an experience and making sense of it to identify what to do in the future. Reflection helps you repeat what was effective, learn from mistakes, and it can build confidence.

Most of us think about experiences afterwards. We may relive something enjoyable or we may be concerned about something (*'The meeting went well today because ...'*, *'I wish I hadn't said...'*). We may reflect immediately after an experience or later, when something triggers a memory.

2 WHAT DO YOU CURRENTLY DO?

. . . .

2.1 How do you usually respond to experience?

What do you normally do when you have dealt with others, carried out a task, read/seen/heard something? You may tend to reflect in a similar way regardless of the experience, or to think about different sorts of experiences differently.

Way of reflecting	Very rarely	Sometimes	Usually	Always
Avoid reflecting				
Think about it quietly to myself				
Talk about it to somebody else				
Write it down (*e.g. in a diary*)				
Repeat it as it happened (*e.g. replaying conversations*)				
Think about things I feel good about				
Think about things I feel bad about				
Imagine what I wish had happened				
Blame somebody (myself or somebody else)				
Consider how other people involved felt or were affected				
Identify the essentials of what I read/saw/ heard or of what happened				
Identify what aspects are similar to those in other situations				
Identify what I learned and what to do differently				

Which of the above are most likely to encourage change? *E.g. 'blaming' might be more likely to lead to resentment or guilt.*

Taking action as a result of reflection assumes that you are responsible for your learning and that you can do things differently.

2.2 When do you usually reflect?

Your initial reaction and your views may change as you think about something, talk to people, see or read things. Do you tend to:

Have an initial reaction and then forget about it?

Have a reaction some time later?

Find it difficult to let the matter drop?

Think so much about it that it stops you taking action?

Vary what you do depending on the experience?

None of these (when do you reflect?)

Would you like to do what you have ticked above differently? Possibilities include:

◆ set aside time on a regular basis to think things over.
◆ if you can't let a matter drop, give yourself a certain time to think it over and then distract yourself (*e.g. by something enjoyable, or talk out loud to yourself about something different – it's hard to think about one thing and talk about another*).
◆ make a conscious decision to take action after a certain amount of time.
◆ ask friends what they do.

What are the advantages/disadvantages of when I tend to reflect?	What could I do differently?

3 WHY IS REFLECTION SO IMPORTANT?
....

Learning cycle:

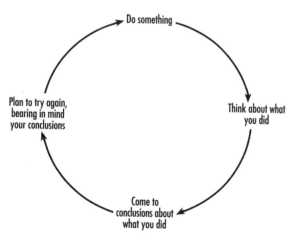

Derived from Kolb (1984).

Some learning theory suggests that we sort information and feelings into categories. When you meet new situations which fit those categories you recall your original thoughts and feelings, *e.g. by associating one thought with another – remembering somebody's name by remembering where you met.*

Thinking about something, reflecting, helps to make sense of it and 'categorise' it, enabling the learning from the experience to be reused. You may not automatically do this, but may just go on doing something, never stopping to consider what works, what doesn't and how to do it differently. You may need to stop and consciously reflect in order to learn from a situation. This is why many forms of personal development, from educational courses to appraisal and CPD, encourage reflection.

Being effective is about weighing up a situation to see what is appropriate. If individuals reflect '**on** action' (make sense of something after an event), they are more likely to be able to work out what to do **in** a situation and think on their feet – reflection '**in** action' (Schon, 1987).

Reflecting helps you understand concepts and principles ('deep learning') as well as knowing facts ('surface learning'), *e.g. reflecting on a work task can help you understand theory* (Gibbs, 1992).

4 IF YOU ARE ASKED BY OTHERS TO REFLECT OR TO REVIEW YOUR EFFECTIVENESS

4.1 When might you be asked to do this?

You may be asked to reflect on how well you have performed at work:

◆ in a staff appraisal scheme (see Chapter 19, Professional Development)
◆ when applying for membership of a professional body (see Chapter 19)
◆ in CPD schemes (see Chapter 19)
◆ if you have to evaluate a project or other task you have been involved in
◆ if you have to evaluate a training course, workshop or conference session which you have run
◆ if you are on a course (*e.g. a postgraduate or professional course*) which asks you to relate your learning on the course to your own experience
◆ casually, every day, by colleagues (*'What did you think of…', 'How did it go?'*).

4.2 What sort of written work might be asked for?

If somebody else, like a professional body, asks for reflective work (*e.g. some ask for a critical review of a project*), they will want to know:

◆ what you did or what happened and what your part in it was
◆ what was good/went well, why, what you achieved
◆ what could have been better, why, how, what you did not achieve, what could have been different
◆ they may want you to point to links between theory and what actually happened (*e.g. postgraduate or professional courses might want this*)
◆ how well you interpreted the situation – identifying what went wrong and what to do differently might be critical to avoid future mistakes
◆ what you learnt and will do in future (an 'action plan') – this may involve how you will go about it and how you will judge your performance.

The following gives examples of work which may be wanted if you have to produce written reviews of your performance.

Work	Points to consider
Reflective log or diary	A diary or log records what happens. A reflective log/diary makes sense of it. It might include what you did well/did less well, what you learned/realised, what you might do differently in future. Some professional bodies require logs or diaries to show professional competence.
Evaluation of work carried out	You may be asked to evaluate your work/that of your team. This means what was good/went well, what could have been improved/be different in future, what was learned or realised. Likely to be required for projects, especially if externally funded.
Portfolio	A portfolio contains evidence of your work, *e.g. written, audio/videotapes, visuals*, making clear what each item demonstrates, *e.g. via a commentary telling the reader/viewer what it demonstrates/how/why.* Artists/designers use them to show work to clients. Some CPD schemes require them.
Report	An evaluative report assesses something and your role in it. Very common at work. See Chapter 4, Report Writing.

5 HOW TO REFLECT
....

How can you improve the way you reflect on your experiences? It will help to have in mind something to reflect on, and to complete the boxes in this chapter in relation to it.

5.1 What to reflect on

The following will help you identify what to reflect on while using this chapter.

1 Are you pleased about something which has happened, interested, curious, enthusiastic?
2 Do you have any uncomfortable or bad feelings about something?
3 Have you become aware that others do things differently in a given situation?
4 Who will see your reflection? What is appropriate for them to see? What is private to you?
5 Can you think of a 'critical incident' which stands out for some reason (*e.g. a turning point, something that demonstrates something, the most crucial aspect of a situation*).

It may help, the first time you go through the process in this chapter, to identify an experience which is not too complicated, *e.g. a small project or a bit of a project, one meeting, one work task.* You can then go through it again in relation to something more complex, like a large project, or a month at work.

What am I going to reflect on while using this chapter? What is my reason for wanting to reflect on this?

5.2 Thinking things through

The following suggest ways to think about your issue. It's worth considering them even if some seem obvious or strange.

TALK TO SOMEBODY
- Explain it to them to get it clear in your own mind.
- Hearing yourself speak can put things into perspective.
- They might have useful questions, similar experiences, new ways of looking at it, give support or reassurance.
- Ask others involved in the same situation what their reactions were or what they thought happened.

WRITE IT DOWN, MAKE A DRAWING
- Write it down, leave it, return to it later to help you see it afresh.
- Actually writing (or wordprocessing) can reduce feelings like anxiety or anger.
- If you can't sleep with something on your mind, get up and write it down.
- Write a letter to somebody (which you may decide to tear up), or write something creative.
- Make lists of pros and cons or likes or dislikes.
- Make a drawing, picture, diagram.

THINK ABOUT IT ON YOUR OWN
- Give yourself time and space – on the bus, while walking, sitting in the bath.

FEEDBACK FROM OTHERS
- Verbal or written feedback from others is very helpful. See Chapter 17, Identifying Strengths and Improving Skills, for advice on how to get useful feedback from others.

NEW WAYS OF LOOKING AT IT

Look at it in new ways. These include:

- replay it as it happened.
- analyse it logically – what went right/wrong, how is it similar to other situations, what could you do in future?
- read – articles, books, newspaper articles etc. to give new insights.
- pictures, films, TV programmes may offer fresh ideas.
- think about what you would like to have happened.
- think of other ways you could have behaved or what you could have done, however unusual or uncharacteristic.
- think about it in the opposite way to how you normally would, *e.g. phrase negatives as positives (such as change 'I didn't like…' to 'I did like…').*
- pretend you are somebody else and describe it as they might. What would they have done?
- identify your feelings about it (what was your gut reaction?).
- ask questions, *e.g. why do I feel angry/upset? Why do others feel in a certain way?*
- question your assumptions (*e.g. were they annoyed with me or were they just having a bad day?*), ask why you feel in a certain way and if you are actually justified.
- identify the main or crucial aspects of the situation, the points which stand out.

TRYING IT OUT

You could try out some of the methods above which are usual for you while considering the next section. For example, you could complete the boxes as if you were another person involved in the situation, or you could complete them and discuss them with a friend. This might help you find new ways of reflecting that work well for you.

6 QUESTIONS TO ASK YOURSELF
....

The following are questions to consider about your issue.

- What happened?
- How did you feel?
- How did others react?
- What was good/did you achieve?
- What needed improvement/did you not achieve?
- What will you do in the future?

If any of the questions don't apply to your issue, pass over them or add others which do matter. Do you need to change the questions, *e.g. if yours is a technical issue do you need to include more specific technical information?*

You don't need to cover the boxes in the order given. What order makes most sense to you? If this process seems too structured, use it to help you think through what would work better for you.

Each box gives an example, of a team project, but it is an example only and is very brief – just to give you an idea. Your own notes will be unique to you. They may be about a completely different sort of issue or experience – individual, group, personal, practical, whatever.

6.1 What happened?

You could describe:

◆ who did/said what.
◆ what you did/read/saw/heard.
◆ the order in which things happened (*e.g. any stages; when; what followed on from what*).
◆ the scale of what happened (*e.g. how much time was taken; costs*).
◆ the circumstances in which it happened, when, where.
◆ what you were responsible for etc.

This is the basic information you need before you start to make meaning out of the experience.

> **Your record**
> *Example. Team project. I had to get information on relevant British Standards for a meeting. Got the information but had a crisis at work and couldn't attend the meeting. Got the information to them as soon as I could.*

6.2 How did you feel?

You could identify your initial gut feelings about the experience. What do they tell you? Relieved, disappointed, happy, afraid – why? What does this say about what was important to you? Did your feelings change? How, why? What does this tell you?

> **Your record**
> *Example. Worried about not delivering. Annoyed when the crisis turned out to be a false alarm. Harassed, trying to get the information to them.*

6.3 How did others react?

Is what other people thought or how they reacted important/relevant? You could consider:

◆ did they react like you or differently – how?
◆ who had which reactions, and what does this tell you?
◆ how did their reactions affect you?

> **Your record**
> *Example. Initially they were annoyed – the information was for a client. When they got the information some were relieved but the chairperson was still grumpy.*

6.4 Identifying the positives

What was positive? You could consider:

◆ what pleased, interested or was important to you.
◆ what went well.
◆ if you succeeded in doing something, what, how, why.
◆ what/who was helpful; what you found out.
◆ what skills/qualities/abilities you used.
◆ what were your positive attitudes.
◆ what approaches worked well.

> **Your record**
> *Example. The information when it finally got to them was fine. I did manage to retrieve the situation by getting the information there. I kept cool when they were annoyed.*

6.5 Identifying negatives, or things that could have gone better

Was there anything which made you unhappy, or didn't work well, or were there difficulties? You could identify:

◆ what you didn't achieve or do.
◆ what or who was unhelpful.
◆ what was the reason for any problems; what needs improvement?
◆ what negative attitudes did you have?
◆ what approaches did you use which didn't work?

Your record
Example. I should have had the information ready earlier. I should have checked whether it was a real crisis.

6.6 What have you learned for the future?

How would you summarise what you have learned from this experience and will do in the future (see your answers in the five boxes above)? You could identify the main points to emerge:

◆ similarities or differences between this and other experiences (why/how/what).
◆ if your feelings were similar to/different from those in other situations, why, how.
◆ what in the future might be the same/different.
◆ what you would do next time.
◆ what attitudes do you think would be helpful in the future? What approaches seem to work?
◆ what does the experience indicate about your strengths and your weaknesses?

Note: the other chapters in this book may help you put some of your actions into practice.

Your record
Example. Plan to complete work before a deadline. Work out what to ask to see if a crisis is real. Remember what I did when I kept cool in the face of their annoyance and do it again!

7 WHAT MIGHT STOP YOU REFLECTING EFFECTIVELY?

. . . .

Could you be doing any of the following? If you tick any, it may help to go back over section 6 and see if you want to alter your replies.

Being defensive
Needing to justify everything I did or thought
Going along with what others think
Trying to please others
Basing my views on an outdated situation (*e.g. what worked in a previous job, in further or higher education*)
Operating from a set of values/own attitudes without questioning them
Seeing things as black/white, right/wrong
Looking at the issue while not feeling very well, or feeling a bit down
Stereotyping
Using language that encourages stereotyping (*e.g. race or gender*)

8 ACTION PLANNING

. . . .

This section is not about the issue or experience you were reflecting on, but about your skills in reflecting. What do you need to do to improve how you reflect and review your effectiveness?

You may want to consider which of the questions in section 6 above you found most difficult. You may want to reconsider some of the suggestions in section 5 and try them out. You may find it helpful to talk over the whole issue of reflection and reviewing effectiveness with somebody else, *e.g. a friend or a mentor* (see Chapter 19, Professional Development).

Action needed	By (date)

9 REFERENCES AND BIBLIOGRAPHY

. . . .

Bannister, D. and Fransella, F. (1971), *Inquiring Man*, Penguin.
Gibbs. G. (1992), *Improving the Quality of Student Learning*, TES Ltd
Kolb, D. A. (1984), *Experiential Learning*, Prentice Hall.
Schon, D. A. (1987), *Educating the Reflective Practitioner*, Jossey Bass.

Acknowledgement: Thanks to Jo Mackett, Combined Studies student at Sheffield Hallam University, who evaluated a draft on which this chapter was based, as part of a final-year independent study unit (1996–7).

Contents
1 Feedback
2 Your current skills and those you need
3 Improving your skills
4 References and bibliography

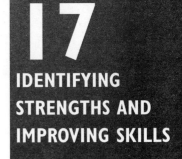

17

IDENTIFYING STRENGTHS AND IMPROVING SKILLS

WHY IS THIS SKILL IMPORTANT?

It is not easy to judge our own performance. Often we prefer to get on with a task rather than think about how we are doing it. However, in professional life, evaluating your own performance is essential.

◆ It enables you to build confidence in what you do well and to improve areas that you do less well.
◆ It is part of your organisation's quality control and assurance.
◆ It is the basis for appraisal and Continuing Professional Development (CPD), and is important in applying for membership of professional bodies (see Chapter 19).
◆ It is crucial in applying for jobs and promotion – employers want to know not only what you have done, but how well, and what you are capable of.

'Leopards can't change their spots. Old dogs can't learn new tricks.' This chapter is based on a different view – that people can and do change. Professional development at work is based on the same view. Increasingly, work organisations expect their staff to take responsibility for their own actions and their own development. Taking stock of your strengths and of the areas you need to improve is the first step.

We suggest you use this chapter:

◆ to diagnose your current skill level – our skill levels change continually
◆ to identify evidence of your abilities (important if you are asked to demonstrate them)
◆ to identify the skills you need for work
◆ to identify how to continuously improve your performance
◆ to identify other chapters in this book which could help you
◆ repeatedly, to help you continually reassess yourself and improve your performance.

By the end of this chapter you should be able to:

1 identify your own strengths and weaknesses, based on appropriate evidence and on a view of what is effective in the workplace
2 identify development needs, set targets for improving skill areas, and review and revise those targets according to changing circumstances
3 actively seek and use feedback constructively and regularly
4 select activities to improve skill performance which are appropriate to your own strengths and weaknesses and to the circumstances
5 acknowledge your own responsibility for skill development, while seeking and using appropriate support
6 evaluate your own effectiveness in improving performance and apply strategies for improvement.

See Chapter 1 for the relationship between these learning outcomes and the Key Skills qualifications.

CONFIDENTIALITY   The notes you make in this chapter may be personal and private to yourself. You could, however, use those notes to form the basis of information you may choose to give to others, *e.g. in appraisal, in relation to professional body membership, for CPD or in job/promotion applications.*

1 FEEDBACK

················

1.1 Seeking feedback

In identifying your skills and areas for development, you will find it helpful to ask others for feedback (you may also need to give feedback to others, see Chapter 14, Putting Your Case: Negotiating and Assertiveness).

Who could give you useful feedback, about what and in what situations? Who would you not want feedback from? Why? If it is because you find them difficult, look at Chapter 14, Putting Your Case: Negotiating and Assertiveness.

Suggestion	My notes
Supervisors/line managers	
Colleagues	
Mentor (see Chapter 19, Professional Development)	
Advisers from professional bodies	
Friends	
Other professionals	
Clients/customers	

When seeking feedback, you need to act in a way which means that you will get helpful feedback and that the person will be encouraged to give it again. It helps to:

◆ ask for feedback as soon after an event as possible (before you and others forget)
◆ ask specific questions. *'How do you think I handled the meeting this morning?'* could elicit useful information (*e.g. 'You kept to time well, but you looked a bit annoyed with J'*). *'Am I OK in meetings?'* is a more general question which may lead to sweeping statements in reply and invites judgemental comments which may be less helpful (*e.g.* 'OK' – this is reassuring but meaningless. *'You're bad tempered'* – you can't act on this as you don't have enough information about when, why, with whom and it will just make you feel bad)
◆ listen without interrupting or defending
◆ check that you have understood (*'Do you mean that…?'*), ask for clarification (*'How do I look bad tempered? When do I get bad tempered?'*)
◆ thank the person for the feedback. If the feedback is positive accept it graciously (*'Good, I'm glad you thought it went well'*, rather than *'Do you think so, I thought it wasn't very good myself'*)
◆ weigh up which aspects of the feedback you agree with and what to take note of (you may think that the other person is wrong or has misunderstood the situation)
◆ it may be helpful to tell the person what you have done about their feedback, to encourage them to give you feedback again.

You may sometimes want to ask for written feedback, *e.g. via an evaluation form if you give a presentation.* In this case, ask questions which will tell you how to improve. Rating scales alone may tell you how much others liked or disliked something, but not what to do about it. *E.g. the following type of evaluation of workshops usually produces valuable information.*

◆ *Please give three things you liked about the presentation.*
◆ *Please give three things you disliked about the presentation.*
◆ *How could the presentation be improved?*

2 YOUR CURRENT SKILLS AND THOSE YOU NEED

....

This chapter assumes that although there are sources of help and support, it is up to you to identify what you wish to improve and to take action. It is important to begin by identifying your current skills. Your skills will change and you will need to revisit the following sections from time to time.

2.1 A starting point

It is easier to identify your current level of a skill if you think about it in relation to a particular activity. *'What are you good at?'* is more difficult to answer than *'What were you good at when working on that project?'* A starting point is to identify the tasks and activities you currently do at work, and to identify the skills you need to carry them out. You may find it helpful to look at other chapters and their contents for an idea of what skills are needed.

The main tasks/activities I do at work	What skills do I need to carry these out?

2.2 Guide to completing the self-audit

The following self-audit sheet (in section 2.3) will help you identify:

◆ which skills you need for your current work
◆ your current level of skill
◆ where you need to improve.

You will find it helpful to use Chapter 16, Reviewing Your Effectiveness, to help you think about your strengths and weaknesses. This takes you through a process which helps you assess how well you use a skill and identify where you need to improve, by reflecting on your effectiveness at work.

In using the self-audit it will help to:

◆ refer to your list of work tasks/activities in section 2.1 and the skills you need to complete those tasks/activities effectively
◆ identify how well you actually used the skill in relation to what was needed.

The following gives guidance and an example to help you complete the self-audit.

Skill area	What level of this skill is needed for my work? High/medium/low?	What is my current level of this skill? High/medium/low?	What evidence do I have for my skill level?	Priority for improvement: high/medium/low?
List all the skills needed for your work (the chapters in this book will help). Add other skills important to your work (e.g. technical skills) which are not covered by this book.	High = expert level needed Medium = competent level needed Low = low level needed The level needed may change as your tasks change. It may help to get others' views, e.g. manager/colleagues/other professionals	High = expert level Medium = competent level Low = low level It may help to get feedback from others, e.g. managers/colleagues/mentors (have you been under- or over-confident?)	How do you know your skill is at this level? What is your evidence? You may find it helps to work through Chapter 16, Reviewing Your Effectiveness.	Is your skill level lower than the one you need? If so, what is its priority for improvement? High priority Medium priority Low priority?
e.g. computing	e.g. medium	e.g. medium	e.g. I can word-process, use email (can't do spreadsheets but don't need to)	e.g. low

2.3 Self-audit

Skill area	What level of this skill is needed for my work? High/medium/low?	What is my current level of this skill? High/medium/low?	What evidence do I have for my skill level?	Priority for improvement: high/medium/low?

2.4 SWOT

As well as getting feedback from others, it may be helpful to look at your skills from other perspectives. A technique often used in business training is the SWOT analysis, which you may find a helpful contribution to a self-audit.

In it you identify items related to your current work situation under four headings.

◆ **Strengths** – what strengths do you bring to this situation?
◆ **Weaknesses** – what are your weaknesses in this situation?
◆ **Opportunities** – what opportunities does the present situation offer? In the context of this book this is opportunities for your own development, but it could also refer to other opportunities, *e.g. to further a work task.*
◆ **Threats** – what are the threats or risks involved in the present situation?

The following example relates to giving a presentation to colleagues about a project.

My strengths	Opportunities for me
Well organised Know a lot about the topic Good at visual aids	To demonstrate what I know To demonstrate my visual skills To find out what the audience thinks
My weaknesses	Threats to me
Soft voice Nervous – tend to fidget	The audience's impression of me Questions I can't answer

The example demonstrates how such an analysis might help you identify actions you need to take. You could carry out a similar exercise for a situation currently facing you using the box below.

My strengths	Opportunities for me
My weaknesses	Threats to me

2.5 Your own attitudes and motivations

Your attitudes and motivations may have a considerable effect on your skills and how you rate them. It might help to consider the following questions.

Which skills do you like/find easy? Why? Identify the positives – i.e. the areas you can build on.

Skill	Why easy/liked?	How I could build on this

Which skills do you find difficult/dislike? Why?

Skill	Why difficult/disliked?	What I could do about this

2.6 Making your self-assessment more accurate

Do you think you are inclined to:

◆ put yourself down?
◆ put your positive side forward?
◆ vary this according to the situation (how?)?

What do you need to guard against in rating yourself on your skills? In making an accurate self-assessment, which of the following could you try?

Ensure you are clear about the criteria, about what makes good or bad performance. You could ask others (*e.g. a professional body, qualified professionals, your manager, colleagues*).	
Rate yourself, leave it for a few days and return to it to see if you want to amend it.	
If you tend to put yourself down, rate yourself at the point higher than you were first inclined to.	

3 IMPROVING YOUR SKILLS

....

3.1 Suggestions for how to improve skills

Ways of doing things differently include:

◆ build on positives to compensate for weaknesses (*e.g. making presentations: if you are good at visual aids emphasise them – the audience will focus on the visual aids rather than on you*)
◆ use an alternative strategy (*e.g. making presentations: show them a video*)
◆ change your attitude (*e.g. making presentations: see the audience as on your side/interested in the topic rather than in you*)
◆ improve the areas in which you feel weak (*e.g. making presentations: prepare well, practise in front of friends or on tape, anticipate questions you might be asked*)
◆ avoid or minimise situations requiring the skill (*e.g. making presentations: avoid jobs that require a great deal of this*)
◆ assess how important it is to you to change – this may provide motivation (*e.g. making presentations: you may need to do this for professional body membership/job or promotion applications, or it may be an essential part of a job you like*).

3.2 Taking action

You need to decide on the action you have to take to improve. You can use the self-audit in section 2.3 above as a starting point. Being as specific as possible about where you need to improve is a first step:

◆ Sometimes identifying what you need to improve makes the solution obvious – *e.g. if you felt stressed because you started work on a project too late, you can plan to begin earlier in future.*
◆ Sometimes you may need to seek advice.
◆ Sometimes you may need more help, *e.g. specialist training.*

We suggest that you complete the action planning sheet in section 3.4 below and (very important) that you review it (possibly with somebody else as part of a CPD scheme, see Chapter 19, Professional Development), say in a month's time, to see what action you have actually taken.

Skill	What I can do	Where I could seek help	I will do this by (give an actual date)
Problem solving	Think about the problem before launching into it Try to identify the main issues first	Chapter 11, Solving Problems and Making Decisions Ask others how they deal with similar problems	Next week In two weeks

One thing which might help is if you imagine that your weaker areas are now your strengths. If they were, what would you be doing differently? What could you do now to move towards that position?

Skill	What I'd be doing differently	How I could get there	By (deadline)

3.3 Where can you find help?

- ◆ **Other chapters in this book**. Look in the Contents list for helpful chapters.
- ◆ **Other books, journals, magazines, trade papers**. Some are listed in the References and Bibliographies at the end of each of our chapters, but there are many more. You could ask professional bodies for advice on which ones to look at, look in bookshops, or use library catalogues
- ◆ **Libraries**. For materials such as books and videos on specific skills.
- ◆ **Feedback from others**. See section 1 above.
- ◆ **Your supervisor/line manager**. May know of other sources of help. Will have helpful expertise and experience, may be able to coach you in the skills you need, may agree to pay for training.
- ◆ **Appraisal scheme**. If your organisation has an appraisal scheme you can use it to ask for support. See Chapter 19, Professional Development.
- ◆ **Mentor**. See Chapter 18, Mentoring, Appraisal and Interviews, for how mentoring works.
- ◆ **Professional bodies**. They provide a range of services for members, many of which are targeted at professional updating.
- ◆ **Continuing Professional Development schemes**. These provide a good vehicle for planning your development, again see Chapter 19.
- ◆ **Colleagues**. They may share the same concerns, know of practice in the organisation, have ideas, be supportive.
- ◆ **Professionals in other functional areas**. May have special expertise to help you (*e.g. finance, personnel or human resources, computer services*).
- ◆ **Friends**. They may have ideas/similar needs/experiences/expertise which could help you, they can give support.
- ◆ **Training courses/conferences/workshops**. If you have a personnel/human resources/training department it can find courses for you, your professional body may advise you, or you could look in relevant trade or professional magazines.
- ◆ **Careers services**. You may find you can still use your university or college careers service even after leaving. You could use a local service, or the service provided by a professional body.
- ◆ **If you have a disability**. You can find out about special support to enable disabled people to work from Disability Employment Advisers at Job Centres.

3.4 Action planning

Skill	What can I do to improve?	Where could I seek help?	I will do this by (give an actual date)

3.5 Reviewing your action plan

If you find, when you reach a deadline set for a particular action, that you haven't met it, it can help to ask why.

- What is preventing you?
- Was your deadline or target unrealistic?
- Do you need a new approach?
- Do you need training or advice?

Changing the way we do things can be difficult. You might need help. You might need to make allowances for yourself. Acknowledge that it's hard and give yourself credit for how far you *have* got.

Unmet target	Why?	Progress that *has* been made	Further action needed

4 REFERENCES AND
BIBLIOGRAPHY
....

Libraries may have materials on this skill. The following gives examples:

AGCAS (1992), *Where Next? Exploring Your Future* (a series of booklets), AGCAS.

Booklet 1   'Taking the plunge'
Booklet 2   'Reflections'
Booklet 3   'Sharpening the image'
Booklet 4   'Choices'

AGCAS (1992), *Discovering Yourself: A Self-Assessment Guide for Older Students*, AGCAS.

Contents

18 MENTORING, APPRAISALS AND INTERVIEWS

WHY IS THIS SKILL IMPORTANT?

A mentor is someone who takes a particular interest in your professional development and supports you at work. Many organisations have appraisal schemes where your performance is reviewed and actions are planned to help you improve. The interview is a more formal way of communicating which can be used in appraisal schemes, to assess ability and potential, *e.g. in job or promotion interviews or for professional body membership.* Handling mentoring and appraisal schemes and performing well in interviews could be very important in your professional development.

We suggest you use this chapter:

◆ to help you use a mentoring scheme or to set one up
◆ when you are about to be appraised – to help you get the most from an appraisal scheme
◆ when you have an interview of any sort coming up.

By the end of this chapter, you should be able to:

1 identify opportunities for mentoring, interview and appraisal
2 identify your own needs, strengths, weaknesses, constraints and values in relation to work and provide appropriate evidence
3 prepare for mentoring/interviews/appraisal procedures to your own best advantage
4 complete relevant documents and provide evidence in the required format
5 communicate effectively in order to meet your aims
6 seek and use feedback and respond constructively
7 agree actions and carry them out using appropriate support
8 evaluate your own effectiveness in dealing with mentoring/interviews/appraisal, identifying areas for improvement, and take action to improve.

See Chapter 1 for the relationship between these learning outcomes and the Key Skills qualifications.

1 HAVING A
MENTOR
....

1.1 What is a mentor and do you need one?

A mentor at work is somebody who takes a particular interest in and supports an individual's professional development. The following is a list of the possible roles of a mentor. What support would you like to have from somebody else in your workplace?

To guide you
To act as a role model for you
To help you recognise your strengths
To encourage you
To teach or coach you
To help you locate/take advantage of opportunities at work
To give you access to management and how it operates
To support you in an unfamiliar environment, *e.g. if you are a woman in an all-male environment (or vice versa), or if you are from an under-represented ethnic group*
Somebody you can confide in
To motivate you
To identify and help improve your weaknesses
To challenge you
To act as devil's advocate
To help you realise your potential (not necessarily promotion, perhaps using your abilities fully)
To help you cope with the formal/informal structure of the organisation/profession
To support you if you have particular needs, *e.g. if you are disabled*

A mentor at work is usually somebody:

◆ with no supervisory or line management responsibility for the individual
◆ more senior to or more experienced than the individual (but where the difference in rank is not such that it creates a gulf between them)
◆ with particular experience or skills which the individual might learn from or need to acquire
◆ from another department or site
◆ with knowledge of the organisation and its practices
◆ who is committed to the idea of mentoring and wants to do it (it is time consuming and may be demanding).

Mentors can have a particular role:

◆ in appraisals
◆ in professional development (see Chapter 19, Professional Development: many schemes for membership of professional bodies use a mentor, although they may be called 'counsellor' or 'adviser')
◆ in Continuing Professional Development (CPD).

There are benefits for mentors as well:

◆ improved job satisfaction/a rewarding experience
◆ developing new skills, *e.g. interpersonal, coaching, counselling etc.*
◆ learning from you, somebody who is recently qualified or has new insights
◆ recognition from others that they have something to offer/gives status
◆ their own career advancement (it will look good to others).

1.2 Who might be your mentor?

If you have a mentor as part of a professional body or CPD scheme, you may find that they are assigned to you. If your workplace has a mentoring scheme, a number of people may have agreed to be mentors and you will be matched with one of them. There may be no existing scheme for you to tap into. If this is the case, but you think it might be useful, you could try to seek out a mentor for yourself.

If you have some choice in who your mentor will be, you need to think carefully about who you would like. A mentorship may last for up to five years, although two to three is more usual, and will depend for its success on how good a relationship you develop. It may not always be a cosy or comfortable relationship, as your mentor will need to challenge your assumptions.

Look at the lists in section 1.1 above of the roles of a mentor and of who mentors usually are. Mentors should also ideally be somebody:

◆ with good communication skills
◆ who is not embroiled in 'corporate politics' (you may get entangled yourself)
◆ who can respond to the changing situations facing you and your developing needs.

Somebody who would be a good mentor for one person might not be good for another, *e.g. some people are motivated by reassurance, others by competition.* What do you need and who might be able to fill the role?

What do I need from a mentor?	Who in my organisation might be appropriate (there may be several?)	Why would they want to do this?

Once you have identified people, you need to go and talk to them in person about the possibility (start with the one you would prefer). They will want to know what is involved and the next section will help with this. You may find it helpful to look at Chapter 14, Putting Your Case: Negotiating and Assertiveness, to help you work out how to approach them.

1.3 Using your mentor

YOUR FIRST MEETING

You need to plan your first meeting in advance. You could use the following to prepare:

Areas to consider	My notes
What do I want out of the relationship?	
What specific objectives do I have for the first meeting and subsequent meetings?	
What limits do I want to put on the relationship (*e.g. things I would prefer not to discuss*)?	
Who will be responsible for what? What is it reasonable of each of us to expect of the other?	
How much time has each of us got available?	
Does anybody else have any expectations of this mentorship, *e.g. a professional body*? What are they? How will they affect what happens?	

It will help get your relationship off to a good start if you can clarify the above items openly with your mentor. The may have different expectations and if so this could cause misunderstandings.

GROUNDRULES

It is a good idea to agree with your mentor some groundrules for how you will operate. The following are examples, and you could agree your own groundrules at your first meeting.

◆ Your discussions are in confidence.
◆ Your mentor will not discuss your private life unless invited by you to do so.
◆ How you will arrange meetings, *e.g. meet regularly (monthly, every three months, every six months) or either of you will arrange a meeting when you see a need.*
◆ That you will not make unreasonable demands on each other's time (you could try to quantify this).
◆ You will not take advantage of your mentor's position in the company without her or his approval.

GETTING WHAT YOU WANT

Given that your mentor is likely to be in a more senior position to yourself, it is possible that you might find it difficult to take the initiative and say what you want or to suggest having groundrules if they do not. Chapter 14, Putting Your Case: Negotiating and Assertiveness, will help you here. You could work through it with your first mentoring meeting in mind.

SUBSEQUENT
MEETINGS

You need to prepare for each meeting with your mentor. Ask yourself questions like:

◆ what do I want from the meeting?
◆ what do I want to focus on/what are my priorities at the moment?
◆ what concerns do I have?
◆ what advice/guidance/help do I need?

In order to make the most of your meetings you could look at:

◆ the section on feedback in Chapter 17, Identifying Strengths and Improving Skills
◆ the whole of Chapter 14, Putting Your Case: Negotiating and Assertiveness
◆ section 2 below on appraisal – there are some similarities between appraisal and mentoring, and your mentor may be involved in your appraisal
◆ Chapter 19, Professional Development, on membership of professional bodies and CPD. Your mentor will have a crucial role in these.

RISKS

There are some risks involved in the mentoring process.

Risk	Suggestions	My own thoughts on this
You do not get on with your mentor. This may make you and the mentor feel bad – as if you have failed in some way.	Use Chapter 14, Putting Your Case: Negotiating and Assertiveness. Identify the problem and what you might be able to do. Discuss it constructively with your mentor. If you are unable to resolve the situation, withdraw from it in a way that does not make the mentor feel bad.	
The relationship has really run its course but still continues.	You may just naturally drift apart. One of you may suggest that there is no longer a need to meet It is important to avoid wasting each other's time and to avoid offence (see Chapter 14, Putting Your Case: Negotiating and Assertiveness).	
Colleagues may resent your relationship, feel jealous of or threatened by it (it may smack of the 'old-boy network' or nepotism).	Ensure that the relationship is open and that others are clear about its purposes. Do not take unfair advantage of the relationship. Take care in what you say to others about it.	
Innuendo among colleagues if the mentoring is between a man and a woman (more likely in organisations with unequal distribution of female/male employees)	Ensure that the relationship is open and that others are clear about its purposes. Take care in what you say to others about it. Do not flirt with your mentor.	

1.4 Action planning

What action do you need to take either if you are about to embark on a mentoring role or wish to establish one?

Action	By (date)	Progress
Setting up the scheme		
Using the scheme		
Developing my own skills to enable me to use the scheme well (*e.g. assertiveness*)		
Dealing with colleagues' or others' attitudes towards the scheme		

2 BEING APPRAISED
....

2.1 What is appraisal?

Most organisations have formal appraisal schemes, through which the performance of individuals is reviewed and an action plan is agreed to help the individual build on and improve their performance.

You may be working for a very small company which does not have a scheme. If this is the case, you may find it helpful to look through this section and then decide if it would be useful for you to sit down with your manager periodically to go through a similar process. If so, you might suggest it to them.

Appraisal schemes usually have the following characteristics.

◆ Appraisal normally takes place once a year.
◆ There are forms for the appraisee (the person being appraised) and the appraiser (the person carrying out the appraisal) to complete in advance, as preparation.
◆ The appraisee's performance over the previous year is reviewed against objectives.
◆ A meeting takes place between appraiser and appraisee, using the preparatory forms as a basis.
◆ Judgements are agreed by the appraiser and appraisee about performance against objectives, and sometimes against statements of competence or standards laid down by the organisation.
◆ Actions are agreed to build on good performance and improve performance.
◆ Objectives are agreed for the next year.

Appraisal is not about agreeing your workload, but about reviewing and identifying how to improve performance. Clearly, in the discussions about action to be taken, workload and work activities will be considered, but this is not the primary aim.

2.2 How to get what you want from appraisal

FIND OUT ABOUT THE SCHEME IN ADVANCE

You can ask:

◆ if there are policy documents in your organisation about appraisal
◆ to see any documents and forms for the scheme (*e.g. they may contain lists of competencies or skills or standards of attainment and these will tell you what the organisation explicitly values*)
◆ what the organisation sees as the main aims and function of the scheme.

For example:

Possible aims and purposes of the scheme	
To improve individual performance	
To motivate	
To identify training needs	
To help individuals prepare for promotion	
To aid human resource planning by ensuring that there will be enough people at appropriate levels with appropriate skills/experience in the future	
Others (please list)	

Who could you ask for information about the scheme? Possibilities include:

◆ your immediate manager
◆ the human resources/personnel/management development/training department – if your organisation has one
◆ colleagues.

Asking colleagues will give you informal information about how the scheme actually works in practice (which may or may not be the same as the intended way). *E.g. are any lists of skills and competencies what the organisation really values or in practice do they value other things?*

WORK OUT HOW TO USE IT TO YOUR ADVANTAGE

Once you know as much as possible about the scheme, you can identify how to use it for your own purposes. The following suggests possible ways and has a space for your notes.

Possible uses	My notes
To ask for training you would like	
To seek advice and guidance about difficulties	
To let the appraiser know what you have done well	
To raise your profile in the organisation	
To let them know if you are interested in promotion	
To find out about realistic promotion opportunities (organisations with flat hierarchies may have more opportunities for sideways than upward moves)	
To discuss any limitations on promotion prospects and identify how to overcome them (*e.g. restrictions on where you can work*)	
To tell the appraiser of any reasons for poor performance or problems of which they may be unaware	
To get things off your chest	
Others (please list)	

You might now ask yourself two questions.

◆ Who will be appraising me?
◆ What are my long-term aims with the organisation?

You could then return to the above table and your notes and ask yourself further questions.

◆ What would the reaction of this particular appraiser be to my using the scheme in that way (*e.g. sympathetic, encouraging, impatient, antagonised etc.*)?
◆ What effect would their reaction have on me (*e.g. day-to-day working relationships, promotion prospects*)?
◆ How would my using the scheme in that way affect my long-term aims (*e.g. to get promotion/move sideways/be happy at work/stay with/leave the organisation*)?

As a result of asking yourself these questions you may want to amend your notes. If there is commitment to the appraisal process on both sides, then being honest about your needs is helpful – but you need to also make sensible judgements about what is in your best interests.

For example, would it be in your best interests to:

◆ pretend you can do something you cannot
◆ accept responsibility for something going wrong when it was not actually your responsibility
◆ blame others
◆ grumble or complain
◆ be defensive or aggressive
◆ insist on training which the organisation cannot afford
◆ say you only want to stay with them for six months
◆ say you want to stay with them for ever?

We are not intending this list to represent items which would not be in your best interests, but rather to suggest that you think about what is. Some of the above items are never a good idea (*being defensive or aggressive*), but for others there may be some situations where it would actually be in your interests to do that.

You could note below what in your particular situation would not be in your best interests to do at appraisal:

2.3 How to prepare for appraisal

Preparation for appraisal is vital if you are to get what you want out of it. You need to complete any forms carefully, making sure you answer the questions asked. If there are no forms, you could make your own preparatory notes and give a copy to the appraiser in advance of a meeting.

You may to be asked to consider and identify:

◆ your work objectives and personal objectives (one scheme advises that you should identify objectives which are important, specific, clear, realistic, controllable, measurable, challenging)
◆ your performance against your or the organisation's last year's objectives, or against specified competencies or standards; there may be rating scales with criteria against which to assess your own performance
◆ your strengths, what you have done well (you will need to back this up with evidence)
◆ your weaknesses, areas of difficulties or for improvement (you will need to back this up with evidence)
◆ your long-term and short-term career plans
◆ your specific training or development needs (*e.g. training courses, secondments, job rotation, coaching and guidance, special assignments or projects, delegation*)
◆ any restrictions you may have (*e.g. in relation to working location, health, disability*).

In order to complete these it will help you to:

◆ work through the chapters in this book on Reviewing Your Effectiveness (Chapter 16) and Identifying Strengths and Improving Skills (Chapter 17)
◆ keep returning to the section above on getting what you want from appraisal
◆ look at your notes in specific chapters of this book which are relevant to your needs (*e.g. if you need to improve on report writing, look at Chapter 4*). All the chapters aim to increase your awareness of what you do, what works and does not work for you in your context, and all can therefore feed into your appraisal.

THE APPRAISAL
MEETING

It may be particularly helpful to look at this from the viewpoint of the appraiser.

The appraiser may feel very nervous about the meeting, particularly about giving you feedback which is critical or negative in some way. Most people genuinely want to help, but giving constructive feedback is hard. They may or may not have received training in appraisal. They will know that it might have a considerable effect on your motivation. In short, they may be as concerned about the meeting as you are, or possibly more so.

What could you do to help them? If you make this easy for them you will go up in their estimation.

Before the interview:

◆ look at Chapter 14, Putting Your Case: Negotiating and Assertiveness, and work through it with the appraisal interview in mind.
◆ look at the section on feedback in Chapter 17, Identifying Strengths and Improving Skills. It offers guidance on how to ask for feedback, how to accept it and how to give it (in the course of the meeting you are likely to need to give feedback to the appraiser, *e.g. on how you have been supported or hindered, on the effectiveness of your training etc.*).
◆ look at section 3 on interviews in this chapter.

2.4 Follow-up action

The appraisal procedure will be wasted if any follow-up action agreed is not taken. You are the one who stands most to gain from it – so it is in your interests to ensure that action is taken.

Providing that you chase action in an appropriate way, you are likely to create a good impression – that you are committed to your own development. You will need to allow enough time before chasing for others to take action to give them a chance to do so and to chase them on points which are significant rather than unimportant.

You could use the following table to ensure that action is taken:

Action agreed	Who will instigate this action?	If I instigate – when? If another instigates, when should I chase them?	Outcomes/progress/ further action needed

2.5 Action planning

The above action plan relates to follow-up action from the appraisal. The one below focuses instead on how you can get more out of your appraisal next time round:

My notes on areas for improvement	Actions I can take	By (date)	Progress
Finding out more about the scheme			
Identifying what I want from it			
Preparation			
The appraisal meeting			
Follow-up action			

3 BEING INTERVIEWED

········

3.1 What sort of interviews?

Some people enjoy interviewing and being interviewed. Some find it very nerve wracking. Some find it mildly uncomfortable. Whatever your reactions to interviews, they may have a significant impact on you. Interviews are usually about your presenting yourself in a good light. You may have:

◆ appraisal interviews or meetings (see section 1 above)
◆ interviews for membership of professional bodies
◆ interviews by clients, customers or funding providers to see if you should get the work
◆ promotion interviews
◆ job interviews
◆ interviews to collect information.

This is an area with a literature all of its own. This section aims to alert you to the main issues. Looking at an interview from the point of view of the interviewer is essential.

3.2 The interviewer's viewpoint

Usually interviews are concerned with making judgements of others in some way. What are these judgements about? What would tell the interviewer if the person met certain criteria?

What will the interviewer want? What will they want to know/find out? Will they have any criteria to meet?	What questions could they ask about this?	What evidence would tell them that I could meet this requirement?

If you were interviewing, what would you find helpful in the interviewee and what would you find difficult? How would you feel if the interviewee just gave one-word answers or talked too much? What could you do to make their life easier?

Experienced interviewers will be pleasant. You get much more and much better information from people if you are.

The interviewer should be aware of ethical issues (see Chapter 10), some of which may be legally binding. *E.g. in job interviews questions should not be discriminatory (are questions asked of women or people from ethnic minorities which would not be asked of men or white people?).*

In panel interviews it is usually decided in advance who will ask the questions, with some leeway built in for probing. Panel interviews may feel more intimidating and the questions may not follow on from each other, since the different panel members may have different lines of questioning in their mind. You need to ask them to clarify questions. You should reply to the questioner but scan the rest of the panel, to include them in your reply.

3.3 Being interviewed

You need to find out as much background information as possible. Possibilities include information about:

◆ the organisation
◆ the structure
◆ opportunities
◆ the products/services
◆ the people involved
◆ the organisation's aims.

You need to work out what the interviewer is looking for and what they will ask. Use section 3.2 above to help you in this. You should prepare answers in advance. It can be very helpful to talk this through with somebody, such as a mentor (see section 1 above) or a colleague or friend. If you think you may have serious difficulties in interviews, you may be able to use the careers service in your old university or college or your local careers service for guidance.

You also need to identify what you want to get over. If the interview is for a job or promotion, appraisal or professional body, it will be very helpful to work through Chapters 17 and 19, Identifying Strengths and Improving Skills and Professional Development.

What do I want them to know about me?	What evidence have I got? (see Chapter 16, Reviewing Your Effectiveness, Chapter 17, Identifying Strengths and Improving Skills, and Chapter 19, Professional Development)

You also need to plan in advance for:

◆ **punctuality**. Make sure you will be there on time.
◆ **clothes**. What will be appropriate? There are no set answers to this, but you need to bear in mind what the interviewers will expect, what impression you want to create and what will make you feel comfortable.

THE INTERVIEW   See Chapter 14, Putting Your Case: Negotiating and Assertiveness, and work through it in relation to the interview.

Some further suggestions:

◆ ensure that you feel comfortable (*e.g. don't accept a drink if handling the cup and saucer will make you nervous, if you have any papers sort them in advance so you don't have to rifle through them*).
◆ sit in a way which might stop you from showing nervous symptoms (*e.g. sit back in a chair, hold your hands*).
◆ if you don't understand the question, ask for clarification.
◆ if you really do not know an answer, admitting that may be better than waffling.
◆ ask for time to think about a question to collect your thoughts.
◆ use notes if they may help, but ask the interviewers if they mind.
◆ make very brief notes (one word) as you go through to keep a track of what you have said, but ask the interviewers if they mind.
◆ think in bullet points. Make big points first and then expand, as opposed to going into detail at once and losing the interviewers.
◆ be professional. Look at Chapter 10, Ethics at Work.
◆ if you haven't had a chance to get in the points you made in the above box about what you want to get over, ask at the end if you can tell them to the interviewers.
◆ thank them at the end and ask any questions (*it is worth planning questions in advance, e.g. if it is a promotion interview, ask questions which make you look very interested in the promotion*).

3.4 Action planning

Whether or not the interview was successful, in whatever terms you might judge that, ask for feedback to help you next time (see the section on seeking feedback in Chapter 17, Identifying Strengths and Improving Skills).

Where do I need to improve?	Which of the suggestions made in this book could I try? What else could I do to improve?	By (deadline)?

4 REFERENCES AND BIBLIOGRAPHY

Clutterbuck, D. (1985), *Everyone Needs a Mentor: How to Foster Talent within the Organisation*, IPM.

Mackay, I. (1989), *35 Checklists for Human Resources Development*, Gower in Association with the Institute of Training and Development.

Contents

19
PROFESSIONAL DEVELOPMENT

WHY IS THIS SKILL IMPORTANT?

There are a range of ways in which employees can develop professionally, *e.g.* professional body membership, *Continuing Professional Development* schemes, or appraisal or mentoring schemes. It is important to make the most of these opportunities.

Your organisation may be too small to have any formal schemes and, if so, you will need to be responsible for your own professional development. This chapter will help here too.

We suggest you use this chapter:

◆ when you face a situation in which you need to be able to handle a particular process (*e.g. appraisal generally*)
◆ to help you in your professional development.

By the end of this chapter you should be able to:

1 identify and access appropriate sources of professional development
2 identify your own strengths and needs for professional development and provide appropriate evidence
3 complete relevant documents and provide evidence in the required format
4 seek out and use feedback and support where appropriate

See Chapter 1 for the relationship between these learning outcomes and the Key Skills qualifications.

1 GAINING MEMBERSHIP OF PROFESSIONAL BODIES

··········

1.1 Why join a professional body?

Increasingly, membership of a relevant professional body is important in career progression. Professionals tend to join together in professional bodies for reasons which can include:

- ◆ adding status to the profession
- ◆ limiting entry to the profession
- ◆ safeguarding the public from unqualified people practising
- ◆ agreeing standards against which to operate as a profession (*e.g. ethical practice* – see Chapter 10, Ethics at Work)
- ◆ representing the profession (*e.g. to government, other professional areas*)
- ◆ forming national or international links
- ◆ providing services to members, such as information or advice, careers services, publications or courses/conferences/seminars for professional updating.

Examples of professional bodies include the Engineering Institutions (*e.g. the Institutions of Civil Engineering, of Electrical Engineering, of Mechanical Engineers*), Accountancy Bodies (*e.g. the Institute of Chartered Accountants*), the Institute of Personnel and Development, the Chartered Institute of Marketing and the British Computer Society. There are also bodies representing particular professions in specialised areas (*e.g. the Institution of Water Officers, the Institute of Hospital Engineering*).

Sometimes membership is essential in order to practise (*e.g. in medical or legal areas*). In other circumstances it is not essential but it enhances your career development (it may show commitment to your profession, give you access to the professional body's facilities, look good on job applications).

1.2 Which professional body?

How can you find out about appropriate professional bodies?

- ◆ You may already know of them if your higher or further education was linked to them.
- ◆ *Associations and Professional Bodies of the United Kingdom*, which you should find in most reference libraries (university, college or public).
- ◆ Ask fellow professionals.
- ◆ Ask a careers service. You may still be entitled to use the service of the university or college you attended, or you could use the local careers service.
- ◆ Look at job advertisements – do the ones you are interested in mention professional bodies?
- ◆ From professional journals.

You could note the ones you have found out about below.

Names of relevant professional bodies, addresses, contact nos	Why would this body be useful to me? What would it give me?	What will it cost to join/become a member?

Will your employer pay your membership fees? If you have to pay yourself you may be able to claim them against income tax.

1.3 Professional body requirements

Professional bodies usually have different grades of membership (*e.g. student members on relevant full-time courses, graduate members with relevant qualifications but no experience, full membership, fellowship – where a member has in some way distinguished her or himself in the profession*).

Membership can be the way you get your professional status (*e.g. it is how you become a Chartered Civil Engineer*). To become a member you may have to meet certain requirements:

Requirement	Further details	How this book might help
A relevant qualification	May be a course approved or accredited by the body May be any degree in any subject May be an alternative qualification The body itself may set exams	Chapter 20, Professional Exams
Evidence of competence in the work area (increasingly common)	May involve: ◆ diaries and log books ◆ self-assessment ◆ critical reflection	Section 1.4 below on competence and evidence Chapter 16, Reviewing Your Effectiveness
Evidence of relevant work experience	May involve keeping diaries or log books	
A particular length of time working in the profession (less common than it used to be)	May specify a minimum time for gaining membership	Section 1.4 below on competence and evidence
Special tasks or hurdles to be passed	These may include: ◆ reports ◆ critical analyses ◆ reflections ◆ oral presentations ◆ interviews	Chapter 4, Report Writing Chapter 5, Making Presentations Chapter 6, Gathering and Using Information Chapter 14, Putting Your Case: Negotiating and Assertiveness Chapter 16, Reviewing Your Effectiveness
Evidence of Continuing Professional Development (CPD) (increasingly common)	May specify minimum number of days' CPD activity in a given time period	See section 2 below on CPD
Supervision and assessment by other professionals (ensures the quality of the process, maintains standards, provides support/guidance/feedback)	Submitted documents may have to be signed by *e.g. the candidate, line manager, adviser/counsellor/ mentor/assessor* May be a formal presentation and interview assessed by professional body members May be regular meetings (*e.g. 3/6 monthly*) to identify objectives/review performance	Similar to appraisal, in some organisations the two functions will be combined See Chapter 18, Mentoring, Appraisals and Interviews

You could list overleaf the requirements of the bodies you are considering.

Name of body	Qualifications/exams needed	Competence or experience needed	Special tasks or hurdles	How long will it take?

You could now consider this table in relation to the one in section 1.2 above which looked at the usefulness of the bodies to you and their costs. Which bodies should you join?

◆ Is the value of membership worth the cost and time involved?
◆ Could you meet the requirements or develop yourself so that you could (if you are going to expend money, time and effort you may need to feel it will all be possible)?

You may find Chapter 11, Solving Problems and Making Decisions, helpful here.

1.4 Competence and evidence

> Example – the Royal Institution of Chartered Surveyors (RICS)
> ◆ A minimum of 24 months' and 400 days' experience to gain membership but no maximum period.
> ◆ Compulsory common competencies of relevance to all types of surveying, core competencies essential to your branch of surveying, optional competencies relevant to your own work situation.
> ◆ Record of Progress – you agree with your employer the competencies to achieve and record progress against them. Reviewed every three months by your supervisor/line manager and every six months by your 'Counsellor' (a surveyor acting as an adviser/mentor).
> ◆ A Diary of daily activities and a Log Book summarising these (the basis for the Record of Progress).
> ◆ An interim submission when you present your Diary, Log Book, Record of Progress, an original piece of work, a critical analysis of a project/projects (identifying key issues, options available, why you chose the option you did, a critical reflection on the experience).
> ◆ A final submission also including these items with a summary of experience since the interim submission, a presentation and panel interview.
> ◆ Those responsible for assessing your submissions include your supervisor/line manager, your Counsellor and a panel of qualified surveyors.

In the past, professional bodies tended to require you to cover specified tasks or experiences at work and for you to have worked in the profession for a given time (two to four years was a common period).

Recently there has been a move towards the view that merely having had particular experiences does not ensure that you are any good at the job, and professional bodies require you to prove that you are competent. In this philosophy what matters is not what content you covered or how long it took you, but whether you can do the job.

Many professional bodies now identify competencies, objectives or skills which must be demonstrated, often with criteria indicating what standard of performance is expected. You may have to assess yourself against these criteria using a given rating scale. You will always have to submit evidence that you have met the criteria.

WHAT IS EVIDENCE?

Evidence is about proving you can do what you say you can do. It has to be checkable, so that you can trace it to its source and find it again. Evidence is concrete.

In the RICS example above, the assessors and supervisors are advised that the candidate's evidence provided must be:

◆ *relevant to the competencies*
◆ *sufficient to demonstrate them*
◆ *current.*

We give an example from the work of a project manager of what might be seen as evidence:

Example competence: be able to communicate	Evidence	Could I prove it?
Orally	Talks/presentations to staff running workshops Meetings, participation in and chairing	Yes – list of talks/presentations/ workshops with dates, topics, summaries of evaluation forms completed by those attending . Yes – list of meetings/types of meeting attended in a given time period, minutes, feedback from others (*e.g. thank-you notes*)
In writing	Reports Emails Letters	Yes – copies of reports, emails, letters selected to demonstrate different aspects of my writing skills
Using visual means	Computer presentations Flow charts and diagrams in reports	Yes – copies of slides, summary of evaluations from those attending presentations Yes – in the copies of my reports

You could practise by completing the table below for yourself in relation to your own experience (virtually all competence-based schemes will ask for evidence of communication skills).

Example competence: be able to communicate	Evidence	Could I prove it?
Orally		
In writing		
Using visual means		

Could any of the following help in providing evidence?

Suggestion	
Have I gained qualifications that demonstrate what I can do?	
Could colleagues provide evidence/make statements about what I have done?	
Could clients provide evidence/make statements about what I have done?	
Could my membership of a professional body, attendance at its meetings or membership of working groups be evidence?	
What effect have I had on my organisation ◆ Are there new systems/products/ways of doing things? ◆ Is money being saved/is there cost efficiency? ◆ Has quality been improved?	
Have I attended any formal events (*e.g. courses, conferences, workshops*)?	
Have I done any private study or structured reading?	
Have I produced any publications or done any presentations?	

In all professional body schemes, other people have to countersign the documents you produce. This is one aspect of evidence provision, as it verifies that what you are writing is correct.

1.5 Rating yourself against competencies, objectives or skills

Example: the Institution of Civil Engineers
You must complete a Chartered Professional Review to become a chartered member. In it you provide evidence of attainment against specified core objectives and other objectives agreed with your employer. There is a rating scale for the level of attainment:

A – appreciate
K – knowledge
E – experience
B – ability.

Each core objective is rated by the Institution for the attainment level required. For example it is sufficient to know about (K) the history, purposes and organisation of the Institution itself, but you must be able to (B) communicate with accuracy and confidence. You agree with your employer for your other objectives what level of attainment is needed. You then meet at regular intervals with the supervisor/line manager to agree an attainment grade (A, K, E, B) against each one with a date of when the assessment was made.

If you need to rate yourself against competence statements, objectives or skills, your judgement needs to be as accurate as possible. Your assessor (likely to be a qualified professional) may downgrade any over-optimistic judgements. It may be more significant if you undervalue yourself – they may believe you!

Do you think you are inclined to:

◆ put yourself down
◆ put your positive side forward
◆ vary this according to the situation (how?)?

What do you need to guard against in self-rating?

In making an accurate self-assessment, which of the following could you try?

Ensuring I am clear about the criteria, what good or poor performance actually is — ask others (*e.g. the Institution, qualified professionals, my line manager, colleagues*)
Use Chapter 16, Reviewing Your Effectiveness
Use Chapter 17, Identifying Strengths and Improving Skills
Getting feedback from others (see Chapter 17, Identifying Strengths and Improving Skills) — show my own rating to others and see if they agree
Rate myself, leave it for a few days and return to it to see if I want to amend it
If I tend to put myself down, rate myself at the point higher than I was inclined to

1.6 Action planning

What action do you need to take to gain membership of a professional body?

Action to be taken	By (date)	Progress

2 CONTINUING PROFESSIONAL DEVELOPMENT

····················

2.1 What is CPD and what are the benefits?

'Continuing Professional Development (CPD) is the planned acquisition of knowledge, experience and skills, and the development of personal qualities for the execution of professional and technical duties throughout an engineer's working life. It encompasses both technical and non-technical matters' (Institution of Electrical Engineers, 1996, p2).

CPD schemes encourage individuals to plan, carry out and record their professional development. A major thrust behind such schemes is that the world of work now changes so rapidly that original professional training may become outdated. There is a growing awareness of the need for continual updating and development throughout a person's working life. The Engineering Council (1994), for example, considers that it is a prime responsibility of all managers to develop their staff, and that staff should be responsible for their own CPD.

Which of the benefits to both the individual and the organisation listed below, usually cited by CPD providers, might apply in your case?

Stated benefits	
Flexible – individuals can plan development activities to meet their own needs	
Gives individuals responsibility for their own development	
Can be implemented using learning that is structured around the job itself	
Can have a European/international dimension	
Encourages individuals to be effective in their work roles	
Encourages individuals to plan for career progression or future job roles and develop the knowledge, skills, expertise needed	
Can save organisations money on training, *e.g. training can be better targeted*	
Can be linked to appraisal schemes (see section 1 above)	

WHO ORGANISES CPD SCHEMES?

Many professional bodies have CPD schemes, some as a membership requirement.

◆ *The Institution of Civil Engineers requires at least 30 days of continuing education. Candidates for membership must keep a Record of CPD.*
◆ *All members of the Institute of Personnel and Development must participate in CPD. It recommends a minimum of 35 hours' CPD a year. Anybody applying to renew or upgrade their membership must give evidence of CPD.*
◆ *The Royal Institution of Chartered Surveyors requires all members to do CPD. It recommends a minimum of 60 hours in any three years. There is a rolling programme of spot checks on members – most of whom are actually doing it.*

Others accredit CPD.

◆ *The Institution of Electrical Engineers gives certificates for 60 or 120 Professional Development Units (calculated for different types of activity or competence demonstrated).*

In some professional areas, conferences and courses which receive approval from the professional body automatically count towards CPD.

In 1995, 31 of the professional bodies belonging to the Engineering Council submitted information about their existing or proposed CPD schemes (Engineering Council, 1995). Only eight professional body members had not replied. This gives an indication of how widespread CPD is.

CPD schemes may be free to professional body members or there may be a charge. Check if your employer will pay.

2.2 What would you have to do in a CPD scheme?

CPD schemes tend to go through a series of stages or processes. The most common ones are given in the following table. Other chapters in this book can help you with these processes. Even if you are unable to work through the chapters at this time, we suggest that you glance at them to see how they connect with the CPD stages.

Stage	Types of activity/areas considered	Sources of help in this book
Identification of needs	Self-audit, identify current skills, knowledge Consider needs of current work role and of changing/future areas of work Identify gaps between what is needed and your skills/knowledge Focus on both technical and 'professional life skills' (e.g. Institution of Electrical Engineers, 1997)	Chapter 16, Reviewing Your Effectiveness Chapter 17, Identifying Strengths and Improving Skills Chapter 18, Mentoring, Appraisal and Interviews
Setting objectives	Setting objectives for a given time period, usually annually Short/long-term development objectives Career aims	Chapter 18, Mentoring, Appraisal and Interviews
Planning action	To meet the objectives by a given date	Chapter 2, Planning and Managing Your Workload Chapter 18, Mentoring, Appraisal and Interviews
Taking action	E.g. learning through the job, projects, formal training courses, distance learning, reading and private study, activities in professional bodies, secondments May become relevant as they are developed at higher levels	Chapter 18, Mentoring, Appraisal and Interviews
Reviewing progress and providing evidence	Against these objectives at regular intervals (e.g. every three or six months) Often they encourage the inclusion of community responsibilities (e.g. organising things for charities/sports etc.)	Chapter 16, Reviewing Your Effectiveness Chapter 17, Identifying Strengths and Improving Skills Section 1.4 above on competence and evidence

They use the following strategies:

Stage	Types of activity/areas considered	Sources of help in this book
Documentation kept by the individual	*E.g. personal development plans, a record, log book, portfolio*	Chapter 16, Reviewing Your Effectiveness Chapter 17, Identifying Strengths and Improving Skills Section 1.4 above on competence and evidence
Support from other professionals	Documents may have to be approved by a supervisor/line manager Discussions with a mentor/supervisor/adviser Coaching by more experienced staff Career counselling – may be formal, *e.g. the support person may have to have training*	Chapter 18, Mentoring, Appraisal and Interviews

This book uses many of these strategies. At the end of each chapter is an action plan. In all chapters we have suggested that you reflect on your current practices, set objectives, plan action, identify support and review progress.

2.3 Involving yourself in CPD

Does your professional body or the organisation you work for have a CPD scheme? If not, how could you become involved?

Suggestion	My notes
Ask at an appraisal meeting (if your organisation has a scheme) if a CPD scheme could be started (see section 1 above)	
Ask relevant professional bodies (see section 2 above) for information about their schemes	
Ask your supervisor/line manager if s/he would support you in a CPD scheme	
Ask your personnel/training/human resource department if they would support such a scheme	
Complete a professional body scheme yourself without support from your workplace	
Find your own informal mentor to help you with such a scheme	
Keep your own portfolio and develop your own scheme based on the information given in this section	

2.4 Action planning

What do you need to do to embark on and carry out a CPD scheme?

What I need to do to get started with a CPD scheme	By (date)

3 REFERENCES AND
BIBLIOGRAPHY
....

PROFESSIONAL BODY
MEMBERSHIP

Institution of Civil Engineers (January 1994), *Grades of Membership*, Institution of Civil Engineers.

Institution of Civil Engineers (1993), *Core Objectives (ICE 180)*, Institution of Civil Engineers.

Royal Institution of Chartered Surveyors (June 1997), *Assessment of Professional Competence (APC): Candidates and Employer Guide*, Royal Institution of Chartered Surveyors.

Royal Institution of Chartered Surveyors (January 1998), *Assessment of Professional Competence (APC): Supervisors and Counsellors Guide*, Royal Institution of Chartered Surveyors.

CPD

British Computer Society (1998), *Continuing Professional Development Scheme*, British Computer Society.

Engineering Council (1994), *CPD: The Practical Guide to Good Practice*, Engineering Council.

Engineering Council (July 1995), *CPD Information Sheets of the Professional Engineering Institutions*, Engineering Council.

Gale Research (1996), *Associations and Professional Bodies of the United Kingdom*, 14th edn.

Institute of Personnel and Development (1995), *CPD for those Seeking Re-admission to IPD Membership*, Institute of Personnel and Development.

Institute of Personnel and Development (undated), *CPD Policy: A Vehicle for Learning*, Institute of Personnel and Development.

Institution of Electrical Engineers (1996), *Continuing Professional Development Scheme: Members Handbook*, Institution of Electrical Engineers.

Royal Institution of Chartered Surveyors (September 1997), *CPD: Guidance Notes and Personal Development Planner*, Royal Institution of Chartered Surveyors.

Contents

20 PROFESSIONAL EXAMS

WHY IS THIS SKILL IMPORTANT?

Gaining professional qualifications may be an important and essential aspect of your career planning and will benefit both you and your organisation.

In order to award membership, professional bodies need to assess certain aspects of your work, *e.g. knowledge, skills, competences and professional attitudes.* They may do this in a variety of ways:

◆ exams, *e.g. multiple choice, essays, problem questions* (see section 1 in this chapter)
◆ interviews one-to-one, by a panel (see Chapter 14, Putting Your Case: Negotiating and Assertiveness)
◆ submission of material, *e.g. designs, reports, essays, problem solving calculations*
◆ practical exercises where your competency is rated
◆ submission of a professional development portfolio.

Some professional bodies may use a combination of the above.

This chapter focuses on how to improve your performance in exams by identifying techniques which work well for you.

We suggest you use this chapter:

◆ when you have an exam coming up, to help you plan the revision for it and then to perform successfully in it.

By the end of this chapter you should be able to:

1 identify the purpose and format of the examination, what the examiners are seeking
2 identify and prioritise which material to revise
3 identify which revision techniques are best suited to yourself, the material and the format of the exam
4 plan actions and the time required for revision, within given time constraints and allowing for strengths and weaknesses
5 monitor progress and review original goals and amend plans
6 identify your own usual reactions and responses to the examination situation and plan strategies to improve performance
7 identify what the question means and analyse what is required
8 identify which questions to answer in an order which will maximise performance
9 plan answers which include appropriate evidence, evaluation and criticism of that evidence
10 review your own revision and examination strategies, identify improved methods for the future and implement
11 identify and use possible sources of support and guidance including feedback.

See chapter 1 for the relationship between these learning outcomes and the Key Skills qualifications.

1 TYPES OF EXAM

AN UNSEEN EXAM

In an unseen exam you do not know what it will contain in advance.

◆ **Essays/problems**. Usually these require you to apply your knowledge to a particular situation, *e.g. to answer a particular problem or to present an argument from a particular standpoint.*
◆ **Short-answer questions**. Here you are given a number of questions which require only a very short answer, often relating to factual knowledge.
◆ **Multiple choice**. Here you have to choose between several given answers.
◆ **Phase tests**. These are short tests of usually no more than an hour. They test that candidates have grasped the essential elements of a specific section of material.

A SEEN EXAM

This is where you are given material or the questions in advance. The focus is less on remembering information and more on what you do with it, *e.g. analysing it, presenting arguments*. In seen exams you will generally be expected to provide accurate information and references.

The following are less common in professional exams, although some Institutes publish a bank of questions each year.

◆ **Open-book exams**. Here you can take material into the exam.
◆ **Take away**. You may be given a question in advance to complete in your own time and return by a given date, or you may be given a question to prepare in advance but answer it under exam conditions (*e.g. in an exam room and within a time limit*). One example is where you are given a case study or data in advance, and in an exam situation you are then asked questions based on the case or the data.

INTERVIEWS

See Chapter 14, Putting Your Case: Negotiating and Assertiveness, and Chapter 18, Professional Development.

2 WHAT EXAMINERS ARE LOOKING FOR

In order to revise and then to perform well in the exam, it helps to identify what the examiner is looking for.

In the following box, tick what you think the examiner will look for in your professional exams:

What will the examiner look for?	
The amount of work you have done	
The amount you can write in a given time	
How you cope with the pressure of the exam	
The factual information you know	
How well you grasp what the exam question is aiming at	
Accuracy, *e.g. dates, calculations, names*	
Your writing style, *e.g. spelling, grammar, how you express yourself and organise the information*	
Ability to apply conventions, *e.g. correct references, ways of presenting graphs or diagrams, use of scientific terms*	
The presentation of your exam paper, *e.g. writing, headings, numbering*	
Being able to apply knowledge to a particular situation	
Showing each step of an argument, calculation or process	

What will the examiner look for?	
The underlying concepts/principles you know	
Being able to argue a particular point of view, backed up by your views, opinions and ideas with referenced evidence	
Being able to analyse information, e.g. what are the implications, underlying issues, correlations?	
Being able to criticise information, e.g. considering questions like why, for whom, what are the alternatives, shortcomings or inaccuracies	
Showing your understanding of the whole field and how a topic fits in with it	
Other(s) (please list)	

If you are unsure how to complete the final column of the above box in relation to your professional exams, you can do the following.

◆ Look at previous exam papers. Ask your manager, mentor (see Chapter 19, Professional Development) or local professional body branch where you could get copies.
◆ What does the format suggest about what they are looking for? *E.g. many short questions may mean that knowledge of factual information is required, or a case study may mean that ability to apply knowledge to a particular situation is being tested.*
◆ What do the type of questions suggest about what they are looking for? *E.g. do the questions ask you to repeat the knowledge you have or to do something with it (to present two sides of an argument, to analyse etc.)?*
◆ Ask your professional body what criteria you are expected to meet.
◆ Read the exam regulations, *e.g. for information about mitigating circumstances, where you are ill or have other difficulties which may influence your exam performance; for information about resitting the exam.*

If you have a disability which may affect your exam performance, speak to your manager and local professional body representative as early as possible about special arrangements.

3 YOUR CURRENT EXPERTISE

Think about the last exam(s) you took.

◆ Did you do as well as you deserved?
◆ What did you do which worked well/less well?

In the following box, focus on how you carried out your revision and how you handled the exam, rather than on how well you dealt with the subject matter.

Revision What I did well *e.g. started to revise early*	What I did less well *e.g. didn't manage to cover all the subjects in the time I allowed*
The exam itself What I did well *e.g. answered all the questions*	What I did less well *e.g. answered my best question last*

◆ What aspects of your revising and exam techniques are effective and can be built on?
◆ What aspects of your revising and exam techniques are not effective and need improvement?

4 PRIORITISING WHAT TO REVISE

How can you choose what to revise? You could ask yourself:

◆ what is likely to come up in the exam? You could look at past papers, talk to other people.
◆ what will maximise your marks? Refer back to section 2 for what the examiners are looking for.

Once you have decided what to revise, you should prioritise by focusing your attention on the important areas. In prioritising, consider the following questions:

How much time is available for revision?
How much material is there to cover?
What is the examiner looking for (see section 2)?

What topics are the crucial ones?
What topics might I do best at?
What topics might I do worst at?
What do I like/dislike doing?
What other demands on my time will there be?
Others (please list)

What can you do if you encounter problems? For example, what happens if a crucial area that is very likely to crop up is the one that you find most difficult? What if you have other demands on your time or other personal difficulties?

What are my problems?
What are my options (generate as many ideas as possible)?
Who can help?

5 WHAT REVISION TECHNIQUES CAN YOU USE?

....

5.1 What helps people remember?

The best revision techniques are active. Just reading through notes is insufficient to make you remember them. Even if you could recite them word for word, it will not be enough. You will not be expected to repeat information in an exam; you must also demonstrate that you can use it in some way.

People are more likely to remember something if:

◆ **it is relevant to them** – how can you make the material more relevant to you? *E.g. see revision technique e below*
◆ **it is associated with something else** (just as we remember a person's name by remembering where we met). *E.g. see revision techniques f, h below*
◆ **they remember things in sequence**, so that one thing triggers the next element (like an actor's/actress's cue). *E.g. see revision technique k below*
◆ **they do something with the information** – all the following suggestions involve actively doing something.

5.2 Suggestions for revision techniques

You could consider which of the following revision techniques are best suited to the subject and form of the exam, as well as to your own way of working. Which could you use?

	Technique	Would this help me?
a	Sorting out your material so that you know how much and what material you have. This will help you plan your revision.	
b	Keeping notes and other materials well organised. Revising is easier if you go through your material each week, making notes clearer, putting in headings and checking on what you don't understand. Use different coloured pens for different topics, highlighter pens or coloured dividers in files. See Chapter 7, Keeping Notes, Records and Minutes.	
c	Identifying the central questions at the heart of each topic and plan how you would answer them.	
d	Testing yourself. Look at some material and jot down what you can recall. Then go back to the original material and see what you remembered. Look at some material and write down some questions on it. Leave it for a few days, then try to answer the questions and 'mark' yourself.	
e	Linking topics together. Produce a card for each topic with notes about other topics it refers to.	
f	Using patterns. Write a theme word on a page and connect it through lines to related topics. This can be more memorable than a list because it has visual impact. You can practise reproducing it from memory and modify it as the connections become clearer in your mind. If, in the exam, a question contains one of the words in the pattern you could reproduce the image in rough as a starting point.	
g	Looking at a section of the material and jotting down a summary of the main points. Keep the summaries to use as a brief reminder.	
h	Using flash cards. Read through your notes, make summaries for each topic and then further reduce them to a few words on a card. As the exam approaches, reading through the flash cards can serve as a quick reminder.	
i	Working with a colleague who is sitting the same exam. Test each other on factual information. Summarise for each other a topic you have just revised. Explain a difficult concept to each other. Discuss what questions might crop up and how you might answer them.	

	Technique	Would this help me?
j	Clarifying your understanding of the material, *e.g. use books, colleagues*.	
k	For science, technology or quantitative subjects, working again through the calculations or problems, to ensure that you understand each stage and can use the techniques. Practising using techniques in advance will make you more aware of which ones to apply to problems presented in exams, and will help you to use them accurately.	
l	Making lists, *e.g. of important sequences, vital points, steps in a process, authors*.	
m	Practising in advance. Think of likely questions and make outlines of how to answer them. Try to answer previous papers in the time allowed; identify likely questions and practise producing answers.	
n	Recording information on tape and listen to it while doing other things, *e.g. driving, cooking*.	
o	Asking colleagues how they revise. They may have useful suggestions.	
p	Understanding your own capacities for concentration. How long can you concentrate for? Build in breaks. The above techniques should help you concentrate, as they involve doing something.	
q	Not being tired or hungry. If you are distracted by a thought (*what to have for tea, somebody you need to phone*), write it down, put it to one side and look at it later. If your mind wanders you may need to stop for a while. Revising different topics on the same day might add variety.	
r	Creating the right environment for you, *e.g. quiet? With or without music? Warm? Cold? Alone? With others? Where could you work?*	
s	Giving yourself treats. Revising is hard work.	

6 PLANNING YOUR REVISION
....

6.1 How much time have you got to revise?

Many people put off revising and panic when they realise that time is running out. Panic can mean you think less clearly and it interferes with memory. You will need to fit in your revising around your work and social life. Identify what you could do to manage all the demands on you in advance. See Chapter 15, Dealing with Pressure, and Chapter 2, Planning and Managing Your Workload.

Will your organisation allow you some time off to revise for professional exams? Ask your manager, mentor or personnel or human resources department.

The following is an example only:

Two months in advance	Sort out notes, ensuring that they are understandable
One month in advance	Make summaries of notes
One week in advance	Test yourself
One day in advance	Use flash cards

6.2 Coping with pressure

You need a balance between revision and the rest of your life. You need breaks, exercise, variety, and to maintain your family and social life.

You are more likely to cope with pressure if you are physically fit and keep things in perspective. See Chapter 15, Dealing with Pressure.

What other demands on your time exist? Could you plan ahead to create some space near to the exams? If you produce a day-by-day revision timetable, you can build in breaks and make sure that you take them.

6.3 Make a plan

A plan might include what you are going to revise, how and when. It can:

◆ indicate if you are spending too much time on one subject
◆ alert you to what still needs to be done
◆ serve as a psychological boost by showing what you have already done.

You might find it helpful to make a few photocopies of this blank plan. Review it at regular intervals, by asking yourself the following questions, then draw up a new plan using one of the blank sheets.

◆ Are your priorities still the same?
◆ Is your timescale realistic? Have any unforeseen demands arisen?
◆ Are your revision techniques working?

What to revise in priority order	By when? (deadlines)	What techniques will I use to revise?	Progress notes and further action needed

7 THE EXAM ITSELF
·······················

7.1 What do you usually do in exams?

What do you usually do? Does it work? Is there anything you used to do in exams which no longer works? How do you feel in exams? What do they do to you? What do you need to do differently?

What works well?	What doesn't work well?	Improvement needed

In considering how to improve, you could identify sources of help:

◆ share ideas with friends.
◆ seek colleagues' advice.
◆ look in libraries for materials.
◆ look for courses on study skills, *e.g. local college*.
◆ consider for yourself what would help you. Sometimes identifying a problem makes the solution obvious.

7.2 Coping with nerves

Exams are stressful – but stress is not necessarily negative. You can be more mentally alert under stress, which is why you can produce so much in the short space of an exam. Research indicates that you will perform better if you view stress as positive and exams as a chance to demonstrate your abilities, rather than as a way of tripping you up.

If you feel that your nervousness may hamper rather than improve your performance, you could consider past situations. What effect did nerves have? What might have made it better?

Although solutions will vary from person to person, possibilities include:

BEFORE THE EXAM

◆ **good preparation**: *e.g. learning your topic well in advance.*
◆ **finding out in advance what the exam conditions will be**: *e.g. date, time, room, what the 'rules' are (about going to the toilet/leaving early), what equipment you can take in.* Going into an exam without being fully informed about its operation may increase anxiety.
◆ **knowing the criteria against which the exam will be assessed**: *e.g. do all the exam questions carry equal marks? What percentage of the overall mark does it represent? What happens if you are ill or if you fail?*
◆ **taking care what you do before an exam**: try to avoid drinking alcohol (exams and hangovers don't mix); being overtired (is it really worth staying up late to cram in extras?); take some exercise (walk to the exam).

◆ **avoiding last-minute revision**: anxiety created by last-minute 'surface learning' (i.e. memorising facts) may block out 'deep learning' (i.e. understanding of principles and concepts), which will be very important in professional exams.
◆ **making yourself as comfortable as possible for the exam**: *e.g. have enough handkerchiefs, wear comfortable clothes (how hot/cold will it be?).*
◆ **arriving on time**: so you don't panic. Will it help you to talk to others or will that make you more nervous? If so, avoid conversation.
◆ **having all your equipment ready**: *e.g. pens, ruler, calculator.*

ON THE DAY

Work out in advance what you will do if you panic. Options include the following:

◆ stop, close your eyes and breathe in to a count of six and out to a count of six, 10 times.
◆ stop, reread the question and jot down in pencil any ideas you have, then sort them into some sort of order.
◆ stop, and move on to another question, returning to the question later with which you are having difficulty.
◆ stop, and do a question you *can* answer to get a 'success' under your belt.

Whichever option you try, all involve **stopping what you are doing** and then deciding what to do next.

7.3 Exam techniques

A range of exam techniques are described below.

SELECTING
QUESTIONS

◆ Spend five minutes reading the exam paper, deciding which questions to answer. Clarify the instructions, so that you answer the correct number of questions. If you only answer three instead of four, for example, you automatically lose 25 per cent.
◆ What do the questions mean? Underline the key words in each question to identify exactly what is being asked. You will get no credit for an answer which is irrelevant even if it is excellent. It is easy to misread things if you are nervous, and it can help to paraphrase the question in your own words and to keep referring back to it while answering it.
◆ Try to avoid questions which contain a word or phrase that you don't understand. If you guess wrongly you may get few marks.

PLANNING AND TIME
KEEPING

◆ Decide how long you will allocate to each question, then monitor your timekeeping. Allow 10 minutes at the end for checking.
◆ Spend a few minutes planning your answers. You can jot down notes and then cross them out, so the examiner knows not to assess them. You may get better marks for coherent and logical arguments than a list of ideas on a topic.
◆ You could plan your answers to the second, third, fourth etc. questions after you have finished your first answer. At this stage you are over the initial tension of the exam, but you still have time for planning – time which you may run out of as the exam progresses.
◆ Would it be best to answer those questions where you feel you will get high marks first, or to dispose of the more difficult ones? If you chose the latter option, make sure you leave enough time to do yourself justice on your best topics.

ORGANISING
MATERIAL/ORDERING
YOUR ANSWER

◆ Do you operate best if you draft a brief outline answer before writing or if you write an answer straight off? If it is the latter, you will need to allow time for checking.
◆ The first 50 per cent of marks for a question is the easiest to obtain. The next 25 per cent is harder. The last 25 per cent is very difficult to achieve. Two half answers may be worth more than one whole.
◆ If you do overrun the time you have allocated for a question, jot down rough notes of the main points you still need to include while they are fresh in your mind and move on to the next question. If you have time you can return to it later.
◆ Quantity will not gain marks. It is more important to make relevant points than to include irrelevancies or padding. Padding takes valuable time to produce without improving your grade.

◆ Write clearly! A model answer will gain no marks if the examiner cannot read it. Examiners are influenced by how well work is presented (imagine marking 100 exam scripts).

◆ Avoid unsupported opinions and include evidence to demonstrate your points.

◆ For exams taken under normal exam conditions, how much can you cover in the time allowed for the question? How much can you physically write, say, in the 30–45 minutes you have? 500 words? If the average paragraph is 100 words, and if you make one main point per paragraph, you can make five main points. Which of the points you could make are the most important?

◆ You need to organise your answer in an effective way, *e.g. for essay-type answers*:
  – a clear opening paragraph explaining what you intend to cover or what stance you are adopting; making your points clearly and in a clear order; having a final paragraph drawing conclusions and summarising
  – a step-by-step procedure, where a sequence or stages are important
  – a main initial point to make an impact which you then develop
  – a series of points leading to a conclusion which has impact
  – different sides of an argument
  – theories or concepts grouped together by a theme.

FINAL CHECKS

If you leave 10 minutes at the end of the exam to check your work, how can you best use that time? You might:

◆ check a weak spot, *e.g. a particular answer or something running through all answers (poor spelling, handwriting, ensuring that all the steps have been shown in a calculation)*

◆ check on the layout, *e.g. underlining headings, subheadings, numbering*

◆ finish off a question

◆ check details, *e.g. that figures, references, names, dates, tables and graphs are labelled*

8 IMPROVING YOUR PERFORMANCE

You may need to take further exams. How could you improve your performance?

Revision Positives to build on	Action	By (deadline)
Areas to improve	Action	By (deadline)
Exams Positives to build on	Action	By (deadline)
Areas to improve	Action	By (deadline)

9 REFERENCES AND BIBLIOGRAPHY
....

Libraries may have materials on this skill. The following gives examples:

BOOKS AND WRITTEN MATERIAL

Acres, D. (1992), *How to Pass Exams Without Anxiety*, How To Books.

Buzan, T. (1973), *Use Your Head*, BBC Publications.

Coles, M. and White, C. (1992), *How to Study and Pass Exams*, Collins.

Gibb, G. (1981), *Teaching Students to Learn*, Open University Press.

Habeshaw, S., Habeshaw, J. and Gibbs, G. (1987), *53 Interesting Ways of Helping Your Students to Study*, Technical and Educational Services Limited.

Jacques, D. (1990), *Studying at the Polytechnic*, Education Methods Unit, Oxford Polytechnic.

National Extension College (1994), *Learning Skills*, Units 42–50, National Extension College.

Northedge, A. (1990), *The Good Study Guide*, Open University Press.

VIDEO

Secrets of Study (interactive video), Mast Learning Systems, 1989.

Association of Accounting Technicians (AAT)
154 Clerkenwell Road
London EC1R 5AD
Tel: 0171 837 8600

Award Scheme Development and Accreditation Network
   (ASDAN)
University of the West of England
ATC Unit
6 Iddesleigh Road
Bristol BS6 67J

British Horseracing Training Board
Suite 16, Unit 8
Kings Court
Willie Snaith Road
Newmarket
Suffolk CB8 7SG

City and Guilds of London Institute (C&G – now part of AQA – Assessment and
   Qualifications Alliance)★
1 Giltspur Street
London
EC1A 9DD
Tel: 0171 294 2468

Council for Awards in Children's Care and Education (CACHE)
8 Chequer Street
St Albans
Herts AL1 3XZ

Education for Excellence
EDEXEL (includes what was formerly BTEC)★
Central House
Upper Woburn Place
London WC1H 0HH

Engineering Construction Industry Training Board
(ECITB)
Blue Court
Church Lane
Kings Langley
Herts WD4 8JP
Tel: 01322 555322

Engineering & Marine Training Authority (EMTA)
Vector House
41 Clarendon Road
Watford
Herts WD1 1HS
Tel: 01923 238441

Engineering Training Council for Northern Ireland (ETCNI)
Interpoint
20–24 York St
Belfast BT15 1AQ
Northern Ireland
Tel: 01232 329878

Hospitality Awarding Body (HAB)
International House
High Street
Ealing
London W5 5DB
Tel: 0181 579 2400

The Institute of the Motor Industry (IMI)
Fanshaws
Brickendon
Hertford
Herts SG13 8PQ
Tel: 01992 511521

Local Government Management Board (LGMB)
Layden House
76–86 Turnmill Street
London EC1M 5QU
Tel: 0171 296 6600

London Chamber of Commerce and Industry Examinations Board (LCCI)
Marlowe House
Station Road
Sidcup
Kent DA15 7BJ
Tel: 0181 302 0261

Management Verification Consortium (MVC)
Management House
Cottingham Road
Corby
Northants NN17 1TT
Tel: 01536 403831

Meat Training Council (MTC)
P.O. Box 141
Winterhill House
Snowdon Drive
Milton Keynes MK8 1YY

The Open University Validation Services (OUVS)
344–354 Gray's Inn Road
London WC1X 8BP
Tel: 0171 278 4411

Pitman Qualifications
1 Giltspur Street
London EC1A 9DD
Tel: 0541 561061

Qualifications for Industry Ltd (QFI)
80 Richardshaw Lane
Pudsey
Leeds LS28 6BN
Tel: 0113 227 3300

RSA Examinations Board (RSA – now part of OCR – Oxford, Cambridge and
   RSA)★
Westwood Way
Coventry CV4 8HS

Steel Industry Qualifications Board (SIQB)
5 & 6 Meadowcourt
Amos Road
Sheffield S9 1BX
Tel: 0114 244 6833

Vocational Training Charitable Trust (VTCT)
46 Aldwick Road
Bognor Regis
West Sussex PO21 2PN

★These are the main, general awarding bodies for Key Skills.

Provided by the Qualifications and Curriculum Authority, July 1998